HELLO MY NAME IS SHARKBAIT

A 2,000-MILE ADVENTURE ON THE APPALACHIAN TRAIL

MICHAEL NEIMAN

HN PUBLISHING

First Edition.

HELLO MY NAME IS SHARKBAIT
A 2,000-Mile Adventure on the Appalachian Trail

HN Publishing books

ISBN Ebook: 979-8-9939363-2-1

ISBN Paperback: 979-8-9939363-0-7

ISBN Hardcover: 979-8-9939363-1-4

Photos by Michael Neiman.

Cover design and illustrations by Emily Abel, ELA Design.

Interior formatting by Michael Davie, Grim House Publishing.

For additional information, contact michael@helloneiman.com.

*To Dana, who may have pointed out all the reasons
I shouldn't do it, but never once said I couldn't.
And of course, to Dad, whose infectious passion for
mountains inspired me to climb before I could walk.*

It's my life
It's now or never
I ain't gonna live forever
I just want to live while I'm alive

JON BON JOVI

PREFACE

I stood under a stone archway at the base of Springer Mountain, pack strapped tight, staring down the approach trail. My friends were by my side, but I was deeply alone in my thoughts. I was hesitant to take the first step, knowing how much more weight it held than the pounds on my back.

Five months and five million footsteps stretched before me, an idea that had defined my life for nearly twenty years. I wasn't just starting another backpacking trip. I was stepping into the dreamscape of a long-sought world, where each day would be stripped down to the simplest of questions: Where is the next water source? How far can I go before dark? Do I have enough food?

This hike was not just part of my bucket list... it was the list. I had longed to know what it felt like to live by the rhythm of my feet, to wake up with nothing more than the trail ahead and the sky (or more often, trees) above. To feel every mile of the Appalachian Trail under my legs. But I also wanted to share it. Each night, no matter how tired or sore I was, I pulled out my phone and tapped out an online journal entry from my bed, chronicling the blisters, the sights, the storms, and the strangers-turned-friends. By morning, people across the country were reading and commenting along, following the shadow of my footsteps and providing the motivation I needed to push onward. I was doing it for me, but I was doing it with them.

It was 2018, when Snapchat, Instagram, and TikTok were emerging as the content platforms of choice. Where fifteen-second videos and five-second attention spans were quickly overtaking long-form writing and in-depth video blogging. Facebook was still king, though, where Groups modernized online forums that previously brought people of common interest together.

The journal was raw and unedited, published on a resurrected WordPress blog site. It was a simple trail diary written in real time and shared with email subscribers, social media followers, and other curiosity seekers who found their way to it. This book grew out of those entries, but it isn't just a republishing of those entries. I've shaped those daily reports into a story, one that tells not only my journey but the spirit of the Appalachian Trail itself. And without the use of generative AI tools, so often shortcutting the gift of writing in today's world.

Along the way you'll meet my family and friends, as well as a few characters who represent the countless hikers, trail angels, and odd encounters that can't all be included individually. Those characters are sometimes composites, drawn from real people and experiences, crafted to capture the essence of trail life while remaining faithful to the thru-hike I experienced.

This isn't a book about self-discovery so much as it is about passion, about perseverance, about loving the simple act of walking. It's about family and friends who cheered from home or laced up their boots to join, and about hundreds of others whose kindness made every step possible.

I invite you to come with me, from Springer to Katahdin. To hopscotch rivers, climb veiled peaks, feel the relentless drum of rain as I walk across America. It is a story about walking, anchored by real waypoints and actual mileage, so you, the reader, can metaphorically walk alongside.

With the aid of an Appalachian Trail guidebook, you may even find it a helpful roadmap to your own journey someday. Maybe you'll finish this book with the same longing I once had all those years ago, to shoulder a pack and accomplish something awesome. To see what adventure lies beyond the next white blaze.

CONTENTS

PROLOGUE

"Holy sh—!" I shot up in bed with a rush of adrenaline, clutching the book I'd been reading like my heart had just been jump-started with a thousand volts. Clamping a hand over my mouth, I glanced at my roommate, Max. Arm flung off the side of the bed and mouth hanging open, he remained blissfully unaware of my outburst as he slept off last night's expensive bar tab.

I placed the book on my bedside table and lay facing it, staring at the spine. A narrow glimpse of trees, sky, and trail hinted at the contents within. I was 21 and in my senior year of college. You know, the year when unlimited possibilities lie ahead of you, and everyone, including the drive-through lady, is asking for your plans after graduation. So far, I'd avoided exposing my uncertainty with the general line, "I'm just taking classes I enjoy." I knew there was too much life to experience before jumping into a career, and although I'd always been organized, I wasn't sure yet what that path looked like.

I had, in fact, been pondering this very question as I sat down for lunch with my mom the day before. I stopped by, as I usually did on weekends, for a free meal and load of laundry. As we sat discussing my latest term-paper woes over lunch, she suddenly tilted her head at me. "You okay, honey? You seem a bit distracted."

Maybe I wasn't giving fresh cold cuts the attention a starving college kid should, or perhaps I couldn't fake interest in my Irish history thesis as well as I thought. But a mom never misses a chance to call out when her kid isn't paying attention.

"I'm fine, Mom." I adjusted quickly, then swallowed another bite. "I guess I'm just thinking about the trip again. Hard to focus on anything else these days. I still can't believe Dad is letting me go backcountry this year."

All my life, I had watched my dad obsess over his annual backpacking trip to Glacier National Park in Montana. Leading these recreational trips out of Minneapolis, where months of teaching ended with two weeks of hiking in the Rocky Mountains, was a high point of his career. These trips had long been woven into the fabric of our home, with framed mountain backdrop photos lining the walls, folk songbooks scattered around his guitar, and endless stories hanging in the air whenever guests came to visit. Backpacking in the mountains was something special to him—to many, it defined him. So imagine how that invitation came across to a young boy who worshiped his father.

It was like entry to the Garden of Eden. We'd visited Montana a few times as a family, taking the train out to meet him after the work trips ended. But, for all the majesty I saw, I had never been allowed on the group backcountry trip he led. I yearned to trek through the wilderness with him for days on end, with nothing but the items on my back for survival. Our family trips were always day hikes. No sleeping in tents, no cooking on tiny stoves, and no digging a hole to crap in the woods. So, for all it meant to my dad, backpacking in the mountains was still the forbidden fruit that I was too young, inexperienced, and naïve to taste.

Until now, that is. After months of discussion, I finally convinced him I was mature enough to handle traversing Montana, and he agreed I was old enough to join the official trip. I'd even invited my roommate to join, who had enthusiastically accepted.

"What's that you've got there?" I gestured to the small plastic bag my mom had set on the table between us.

"Oh, this?" She asked as she pushed it to me. "It's for you. A gift from work."

My mom worked at the public library. She was one of those wonderful people who embodied the spirit of librarians. She loved introducing people to new authors who might spark curiosity or adventure, and handing that gift to those who would truly appreciate it.

I glanced down at the title of the book I'd pulled from the bag— *A Walk in the Woods* by Bill Bryson. I looked up to see a sly smirk stretch across her face, her way of saying that she already knew what was on my mind. Intrigued, I opened the first page to see a map with a line crossing fourteen states. I turned the page to Chapter One and read, "Running more than 2,100 miles along America's eastern seaboard, through the serene and beckoning Appalachian Mountains, the AT is the granddaddy of long hikes."

With those words, the seed of an idea was planted. I couldn't quite see what it was yet, but I knew I needed to find where it would lead. Neither of us knew it then, but my mom had just handed me the book that would lead to one of the biggest treasures of my life. I could hardly wait to head back to campus and devour the rest of Bryson's journey on the Appalachian Trail.

As I sat in bed later that night, mental wheels spinning uncontrollably, I stared at the spine, which was noticeably more creased and worn than when my mom handed it to me. That seed was already a sapling, growing into a strong oak tree of a promise to myself. Maybe after I proved myself on this summer's Montana trip, the Appalachian Trail could be next. *What if the longest continuous hiking path on the eastern seaboard could be my Glacier National Park?* The thought thrilled me with the shiny newness of its possibilities. Plus, I'd finally have something to tell

Helen at McDonald's the next time she asked about my plans for life.

"What were you dreaming about last night, Neiman?" Max asked in the morning, as we readied ourselves for a full day of classes.

"Huh?" I glanced at my roommate, brow furrowed.

"I woke up at some point and saw your legs thrashing around while you slept. If you were upright, you probably would have walked right across campus in your boxers."

Had I been sleep-backpacking the Appalachian Trail, the granddaddy of hiking trails? I laughed before replying, "Probably. I don't remember dreaming anything, but that reminds me, my dad sent a packing list for the Montana trip. I don't want to be caught unprepared, but it's... well, you could probably call it hefty."

I scratched the morning stubble on my face as I read the paper titled *Glacier Park Backpacking Equipment List*. A short disclaimer at the top read:

The following list of items is a guide for what you could anticipate bringing for hiking or backpacking. This is not a required list etched in stone. You should modify it as necessary to accommodate your plans. Some similar items are duplicates to choose between; others can be shared among people in your group.

I had read the pages several times already, and it looked like all the items listed would be necessary for our trip.

Max strode over and plucked the list from my hands just as I was making my way through the towel section. He scanned it from bottom to top and handed it back to me seconds later with a shrug. "I think I'll just wing it. You know, pack what feels right."

I stared at him incredulously as he turned back to his morning ministrations. Wing it? On a multi-day backpacking trip? And who works through a list from bottom to top? I narrowed my eyes. Was I going to survive in the backcountry with this guy? *Just to be safe*, I thought, *I better bring a spare box of granola bars.*

I placed the list carefully back on my bedside table, secured safely under *A Walk in the Woods*. There was no way I was winging anything. This would be my first backpacking trip, but it wasn't just that. All my previous hiking adventures had been leading up to this one, and now I would get the chance to show Dad that his faith in me this year was justified. But I also knew I needed to spill the beans on this idea about the Appalachian Trail, even if premature. For as long as I could remember, he had been my barometer for decision-making, and this one was no different.

Thirty minutes and four rings later, Dad picked up the phone.

"Helloooo?" he said in his usual cheery way. I always loved the way he greeted every caller as if it were his duty to make their day brighter.

"Hi, Dad. It's me."

"Pride!" he belted out heartily. And while I rolled my eyes at the nickname, I couldn't keep a grin from breaking out.

"Yes, Dad, the pride of the Neiman household, at your service."

"Always! What's going on?"

"So, I've got a plan after graduation," I said slowly. Dad, always an avid storyteller, appreciated the art of a dramatic buildup.

"Uh-huh. I'm listening."

"I think you're really going to like it."

"Okay..."

And with the appropriate amount of flair, I announced, "I'm going to thru-hike the Appalachian Trail."

Silence.

"Dad?"

"Yep, still here. I was just checking my Chinese dictionary for the translation because I could have sworn you just spoke Mandarin."

I let out a deep, quiet sigh as I shook my head.

"You've heard of the Appalachian Mountains." This was delivered as a statement because I knew for a fact that Dad, who had countless geology books and rock samples lining his bookshelves, had most certainly heard of this very large, very well-known topographical landmark.

"I've heard some call them mountains."

I groaned inwardly, knowing where this conversation was headed in three, two, one...

"Of course, that's probably because they haven't seen the Rockies." He sighed wistfully. "Now, those are mountains!"

Dad's love of mountains and backpacking was singular in its passion for the Rockies. He had never wavered since first discovering them as a young adult, and the recurring work trips to Montana had only strengthened that admiration.

"Don't you want to try out Glacier first?" he added.

"I was thinking this would be after. It would have to be planned out. It's expensive. Plus, it takes a pretty long time."

That captured Dad's interest. "How long?"

"From what I've read, most people take bout about six months."

"Six months?! What do they eat? Squirrels?" I could hear the concern in his voice, even while he joked.

"I think the idea is to restock supplies along the way. It's more than 2,000 miles long, but it walks through many towns." I spoke gently, responding to the fatherly concern I could still feel radiating from the other end of the phone.

There was another long pause. "So, the plan is to hike 2,000 miles over six months, relying on gas stations in Virginia to carry freeze-dried meals?"

"Yes. I think." I had to admit, I didn't know, but somehow that excited me more. "So that's the plan. I'm going to do it."

Another long pause.

"Michael, if anyone can achieve what they set their mind to, it's you. But have you really thought this through?"

I did stop to think for a moment. Mom had just given me the book, but I had consumed it in just one day and felt certain I needed to hike the trail. So, I replied with confidence, "Yeah, Dad, I have. By this time next year, I'll be hiking the Appalachian Trail."

Oh, those famous last words.

My overstuffed pack in 2002 at Glacier National Park, MT

PART 1

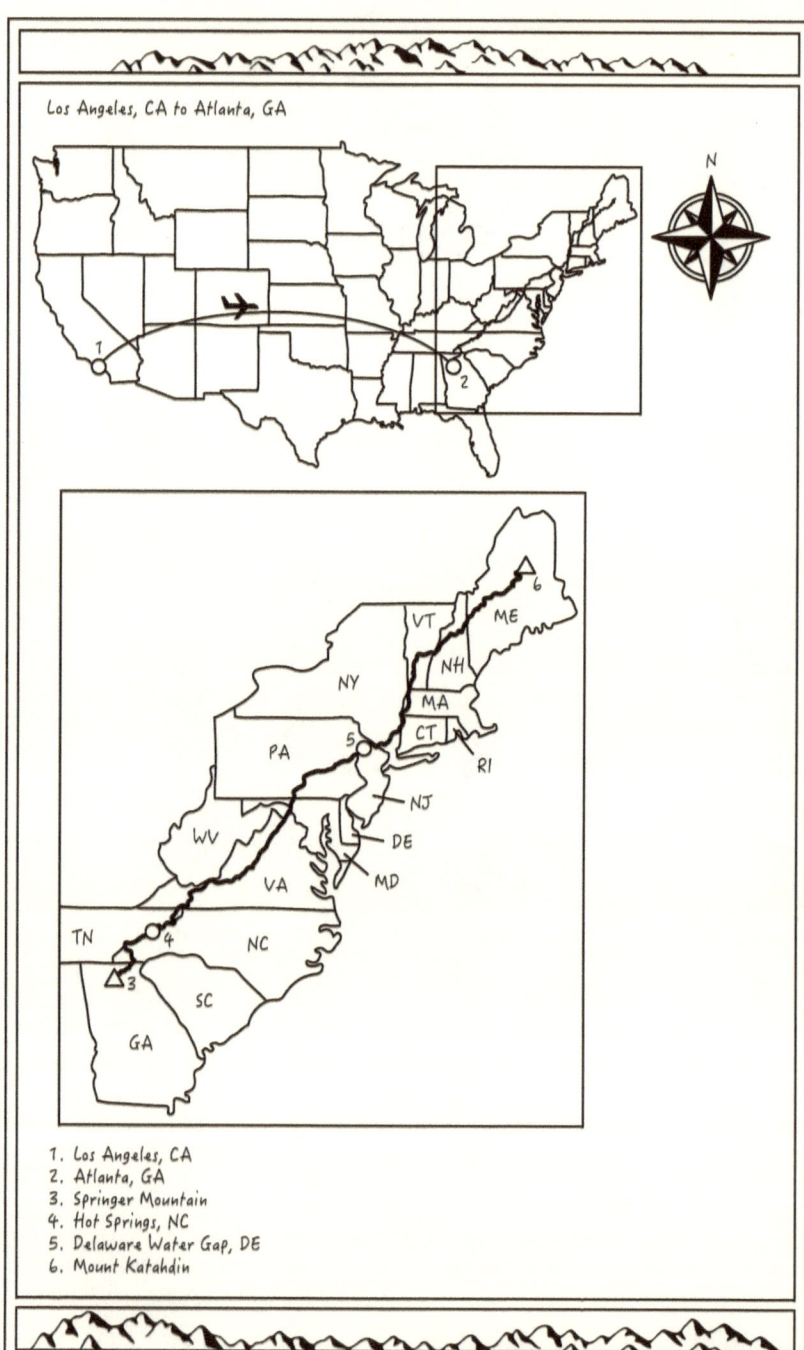

Los Angeles, CA to Atlanta, GA

1. Los Angeles, CA
2. Atlanta, GA
3. Springer Mountain
4. Hot Springs, NC
5. Delaware Water Gap, DE
6. Mount Katahdin

1

IT'S NOW OR NEVER

When I read Bill Bryson's book in 2002, I never doubted I'd hike the AT the year after graduation. Some people backpack through Europe; I was backpacking the Appalachians. After successfully navigating Montana (more on that later), it was my only real dream.

But big deal—we all have dreams. I tend to be a bit dramatic in life, so a dream is a very big deal. To me, dreams aren't just floating ideas passing through the night; they give life its purpose. An idea is just a temporary thought, but a purpose is a North Star driving everything about ourselves toward.

Fulfilling this dream would be achieving one of my greatest goals. I wanted to hike the AT because I believe life's measurement is counted by how many times one says, "That was difficult, but I had the fortitude to overcome it."

I was so sure of my plan, but then right after graduation I received an unexpected job offer. Now I was torn between two paths —the AT that had become an obsessive passion, or the first step to my career dangled tantalizingly before me. At the time, it seemed simple enough. Take the job now, save up money, and in a couple years I'd be ready to make the AT dream happen.

So I did. But that job led to another and another, and there never seemed to be time for a six-month break from life's routine. I kept backpacking with friends, kept reading others' AT journeys, kept updating gear, never quite finding the right moment to make it out on that elusive Appalachian Trail.

Now, in the summer of 2017, nearly fifteen years later, the moment might actually be here. I paused in our Los Angeles apartment doorway, watching my wife's head bent over her computer, filling medical records with one hand while scanning the day's handwritten notes with her other. She was in the final months of her veterinary residency, and her schedule was relentless. I'd always been amazed at her ability to shut the world out while working, and tonight was no exception. But I needed her attention, so I dove in, clearing my throat.

"Dana?"

"Hmm?" she responded, not turning or pausing from typing.

"I think it's time."

"You do?" she muttered faintly.

Clearly, I hadn't gained full attention yet. I couldn't just enter into a conversation about something as monumental as the Appalachian Trail. This required delicate perseverance—which, incidentally, is an excellent trait for thru-hiking.

"Dana, can you pause?"

She glanced up, noting the earnest expression on my face. Lowering her laptop, she swiveled around. "Sure. What's wrong?"

"Nothing's wrong," I began, pausing to prepare her for the full weight of my next words. "I think it's time to hike the Appalachian Trail."

Silence. This response to my AT plans had become a theme.

She sat slowly back, crossing her arms as if reviewing MRI results for a particularly interesting labradoodle she needed to diagnose.

After a lengthy examination that could've cured canine cancer, she said, "Today?"

"Oh," I hiccupped a laugh. "No, not today. I was thinking next spring."

Her eyes took on a faraway look, thinking through the timing of my proposed six-month absence. Finally, she zeroed in again. "That's when I'll be studying for board exams."

"Yes," I said slowly. "That's one of my threefold reasons for thinking it's good timing."

"Threefold?" She arched an eyebrow, amusement tugging at the corners of her mouth. "Really, I couldn't expect anything less from you, Mr. Neiman." I grinned. She knew my detail-oriented ways well enough to lace her sarcasm with formality. "I'd love to hear your reasons. Go ahead."

"Well, number one is we already know we're moving back east after you finish residency next summer. Number two is that I was already planning to quit my job then, so I can just move the timeline up by a few months. And number three is, as you've just identified, you'll be studying for board exams, and I know how focused you'll be." So focused we'd barely see each other anyway, but I thought I'd omit that part. No need to poke the proverbial bear. "You'll probably want the peace and quiet."

She narrowed her eyes, opening her mouth to speak, only to be interrupted by our dog, Pippa, barreling into the room. She did that lovable thing terriers do—running circles at full speed for no discernible reason and exhausting themselves moments later. After accomplishing this, Pippa collapsed belly-up, begging for her one-thousandth meaningful touch of the day.

Dana laughed. "I don't think there'll be much peace and quiet." After doling out affection to Pippa and watching her wander back to the couch, she continued. "I don't love the timing, and your threefold reasons aren't completely wrong, but I'm not sure I can handle you being gone. I mean, who's going to cook and clean while I'm studying to become the greatest veterinarian in the world?"

She followed this with a grin, waiting for the amused reaction she knew she'd get.

"But," she finished, "you need to do it. It's been the only item on your bucket list since before I met you, and I guess we'll just have to figure out how to make it work."

The smile I gave her would've lit up all of LA. I had the green light. The Appalachian Trail was finally happening.

2

TIME FOR ME TO FLY

"I've found the section we can hike together," I announced to Dad over the phone several weeks later.

"Oh, yeah?" he asked, with more than a touch of laughter. "Does it have mountain peaks sculpted by millennia of ice, crystal-blue glacial waters, and a profusion of wildflowers painted in delicate harmony?"

Dad had just successfully described everything the Appalachian Trail was not. And he knew it. But despite teasing, I also knew he was now as invested in this trip as I was. Somewhere over the years, we'd transitioned roles in our backpacking relationship. I had become more the explorer, paving visits to new National Parks and backpacking trails that excited him with visions of grandeur. So when I announced over the summer that I planned to hike the AT the following year, he was skeptical of the merits but also very curious about the adventure. When I asked him to join me for a section, because I couldn't imagine doing it without him, his excitement took off.

"Dad, you're going to love it. I'll probably have my trail legs by then, but I'll still let you lead." I was alluding to the ever-present parental urge to take charge, but I also knew the phrase "trail legs" would remind him that by then, I'd be able to hike ten miles without breaking a sweat.

I really couldn't imagine anyone not loving the AT by this point. The more books I read and the more YouTube channels I watched, the more convinced I was that this was an excellent idea for everyone in my life. And truthfully, I'd done all this research gleefully. As a corporate consultant, I appreciated project management and planning—defining a strategy, aligning stakeholders, managing budgets, these were fun tasks to get a job done right. So although many AT thru-hikers prefer to get out there and not overthink it, I'd embraced the planning obsessively and wholeheartedly. And I knew Dad shared that appreciation.

Laughter filled my ear as he chuckled along. I couldn't imagine doing this without him.

"Have you got anyone else joining you?" he asked.

"Not yet, but I promised Dana I'd try to get people out with me as much as possible."

My mind flashed back to the conversation with Dana a few weeks before. Words like bear, anaphylaxis, hypothermia, and Lyme disease were being thrown around. When she got to the dangers of *Deliverance*, I threw my hands up in surrender.

"Okay, I hear you," I told her. "I'm going to resurrect the old blog to share about my hike and promise to put a call out for people to join me."

Dana's heavy-browed sideways glance told me this might not be enough.

"Okay, three call outs. And I'll share on Facebook that I'm looking for company. Sound good?"

She agreed, but I could tell the image of Ned Beatty being told to squeal like a pig was still at the forefront of her mind.

In truth, I was happy to oblige, but I wasn't worried. Since I planned the start of the hike to coincide with the most popular route and time—walking north from the southern terminus of Georgia's

Springer Mountain on March 1—there would be plenty of people to befriend and hike with. I was really excited for new friendships to come, but I didn't mind sharing it with old friends too.

"Well, Dad," I said, returning to the phone conversation, "I'm going to start blogging my preparations and see if I can inspire any innocent souls to join me in the wilderness for six months."

And that's what I did. What had started years ago as an online diary of random thoughts from a millennial would now become an online record of my experience leading up to and on the trail. Like many hikers before me, I was going to publicly share all my planning and preparations, from decisions on gear and approach to resupply to research on must-see landmarks. Then once I set out, I'd use it to complete a daily log of miles and adventures on my way to the northern terminus at Mount Katahdin in Maine. Hopefully, some people reading along would think it was a good idea to take a small hiatus from life and experience this epic journey with me. Little did I know then, the ripples of significance that dropping this blog into the sea of online content would have on my journey.

The first hint came through a Facebook group for 2018 AT thru-hikers. Facebook had become a hot spot for potential hikers and curiosity seekers to discuss planning, share advice, and ask for guidance in the months leading up to their hikes. Each year, these groups were strong support networks, with membership often in the tens of thousands.

I started posting my thoughts and comments there often, along with blog links, in case it would encourage interested followers or interesting advice. Then one morning, I opened my email to see a comment on my latest entry. Some guy named Edie had written, "*You seem to have a lot in common with my 18-year-old son. That incredible excitement about attempting a thru-hike, uber planning, and an early start. I'm sure you'll cross paths!*"

I felt a buzz of excitement. My first personal connection to someone I'd be on the trail with! If I met Edie's son, would we become what's known as a tramily (a trail family), that I'd read so much about? The concept of a tramily excited me. Previous thru-hikers talked about joining forces with people who start around the same time and hike in a similar style. You form a sort of familial coalition—ending at the same shelters, taking meal breaks, making hike decisions in partnership so you can traverse the physical and mental obstacles together.

After Edie, I soon began corresponding with more would-be hikers, sharing details of our lives and hopes for the journey. It felt so natural, so real. I got to tell Dana I was already building a community on the trail that would help me fend off any wilderness dangers, and it felt good to see the beginnings of relationships this thru-hike could bring. Things were moving along nicely.

3

THE FINAL COUNTDOWN

The fall months sped along, as did my obsessive-compulsive brain. One late October night, I lay in bed wide awake, unable to shut down the parade of questions marching through my thoughts. Should I wear hiking boots or trail-running shoes? Is it safe to drink the water unfiltered? Does freeze-dried or dehydrated food weigh less? I reached for my phone and pulled it under the covers, not wanting to disturb Dana sleeping peacefully beside me. It had been another long day at the hospital, and the last thing she needed was my screen's bright glow disturbing her beauty rest. But I needed to contact the one other person who'd appreciate my dilemma. I opened my messages app and clicked Max's name. I typed:

> *Could you eat trail mix every day for five months?*

He'd still be awake. He was always awake. Maybe it was the three screaming kids, maybe the three pots of coffee he drank daily, but he never seemed to fully shut down at night. Seconds later, his reply appeared.

> As in, only? Not sure, but if it's that caramel cashew mix we brought to Yosemite, I could definitely outlast you.

This is what I loved about Max. He never failed to spice things up with a challenge, even if hypothetical. But this wasn't hypothetical, and I had a feeling he already knew what was coming next.

Got any plans for March 1?

Why beat around the bush? We'd talked about this for years and always assumed he'd join for some part of it. Might as well jump right in.

> As in next year?

It's October, so unless you've figured out how to turn a DeLorean into a time machine, yeah, next year.

> I'm still working on it. Can't find flux capacitor specs online.

So, are you free?

> Let me check... yeah. Strangely enough, I'm wide open four months from now.

I suppressed a laugh into the pillow, trying not to shake the bed.

Want to hike the AT with me?

I really didn't need to wait for his response. That first backpacking trip after college had solidified our hiking partnership. We returned to Glacier a few years later and kept going. Max had moved to Chicago after school, slowly making a name for himself in the steel industry, while I'd been touring the country with Dana through the various stages of a medical professional's training. Internship here, residency there... but even though we were rarely in the same time zone, we still made annual backpacking trips a priority. These trips weren't just to scratch the adventurous itch of climbing mountains, but also a chance to maintain friendship's strength as life marched on. Last year in Alaska's Denali National Park, we'd spent significant hours discussing parts of the Appalachian Trail together.

Obviously!

His predicted response appeared, but I could see he was still writing.

Are you going to pack ultralight this time?
I'm not sure you'll make it to Maine
with your usual packing list.

I shook my head at the mocking reference to the first Glacier trip. He'd never let me forget that I took the "suggested" packing list and brought it all. Stainless steel pots, two kinds of flashlights, spare tent poles, jeans for town, a bath towel, a hand towel, and a face towel. I learned an important lesson that summer: if you pack your fears with the mindset that you *might* need something "just in case," you'll end up carrying nearly seventy-five excruciatingly heavy pounds in your pack. I typed back:

I don't remember you turning down those extra granola bars I packed for you.

> *I never turn down free food.*
> *Did Ad commit yet?*

Max was referring to our friend Adam, who I'd met at work a few years ago in Minneapolis. We quickly discovered a shared love of outdoor pursuits, so an invitation to join our annual trips was a natural progression. Max and I had invited other friends over the years, but few seemed interested in repeat adventures. I never took it personally—our route planning can get a little unorthodox, and not everyone enjoys wandering off trail through thorn bushes and vertical scree scrambles just for a rare summit view. Adam wasn't fazed, though, joining multiple times and quickly turning into a regular. Our group dynamic worked well... I led the well-planned charge, Max brought a fearless can-do attitude, and Adam lent a voice of reason to make sure no one died.

Adding him now...

A couple quick taps later and Adam's name appeared in the group.

Hey, man. Were you serious about wanting to hike the AT with Max and me next spring?

I kept the message thread open while waiting to see if Adam was still awake. It was late in Minnesota, and he wasn't the same kind of night owl. A few seconds later, Max's name popped up with what can only be described as a "helpful" reply.

> *Neiman's bringing a portable generator*
> *so we can charge our phones.*

Before I could think of a response fully conveying the depths of my momentary dislike for him, Adam's reply flashed onto the screen.

The AT is a definite go? That's awesome!
Pretty sure I can hang a bit. Get you started.

After several more minutes of back-and-forth ideas and jokes at my expense, we had it worked out. Max and Adam would meet me in Atlanta and hike the first four days, and we agreed to look at planning a second round when I was further down the trail. They both had responsibilities that couldn't be left for half a year, but we were all excited to at least start together. I laid my phone down and finally closed my eyes, excitement overtaking the questions of what was to come.

There's something about that first caffeine intake of the day that just hits differently than all the others, I mused as I took my first sip of flawlessly brewed perfection. My laptop sat open in front of me, and I flexed my fingers in anticipation of the hardcore productivity about to go down.

Immediately following Dana's green light, I'd begun the first of many spreadsheets laying out my thru-hike plan in all its detailed glory. Over the years, I had amassed a small library of guidebooks, journals, and memoirs breaking down what to expect and how to prepare. Turns out, Bill Bryson wasn't the only author with insights on tackling the AT; the internet was flush with materials to help would-be travelers like me. My favorite go-to resources were David "AWOL" Miller's A.T. Guide, a handbook of every detail found along each mile, and WhiteBlaze.net, an online forum named for the AT trail markers that had already answered every random thru-hiker question imaginable.

These kept me company as I started inputting data into cells whose size didn't convey the magnitude of achievements they contained. I knew from previous hiking trips how far my legs could take me each day, and AWOL and WhiteBlaze turned out to be excellent resources for campsites, water sources, and small towns I could expect to find along those stopping points. Each day of my planned hike now received an entry for my ambitious progress. Each and every day. For five long months.

But I wasn't satisfied to stop there. During my research, I'd seen former thru-hikers describe their hiking costs for the entire trip. The advice was simple, expect to spend about $1,000 a month. This estimate was based on rudimentary costs of $20 a day for food, $100 per town stop, and an extra $1,000 for replacing shoes and miscellaneous broken gear. Adding it all up, my five-month hike with approximately one town stop per week would cost me roughly $6,200.

"Damn. That seems pretty high," I muttered at the numbers blazoned across my laptop. "I should be able to do way better than that."

The competition had been set, and I was now fully caffeinated and ready for the challenge. So there I sat, building data models, plugging formulas into Excel spreadsheets, and refining numbers to prove that a delicately planned budget could deliver extraordinary cost-saving results.

The sun shifted across the room as hours passed. Pippa slept, stretched, and slept again in various positions around me in the kind of committed moral support only canines can offer. At some point, Dana, recognizing my zoned-out focus, slid a bowl of candy in front of me. I grunted thanks toward her, dipping my fingers in while never removing my eyes from the screen.

"You're welcome," she called out as she exited the work zone.

As light shifted toward that golden-hour glow, I filled in the last rows, summarizing the final days to Baxter State Park and Mount Katahdin at the AT's end. I leaned back, exhilarated by the feeling I'd just done a virtual hike of all fourteen states and every heroic milestone. With all theoretical miles hiked, meals eaten, and hostel beds slept in, my valiant efforts produced a much more detailed and accurate estimate of $5,066. I added the $1,000 for anticipated gear replacements, bringing the grand total to...

"$6,066," I groaned.

"Did you say something?" Dana trilled from the other room.

"I just spent all day figuring out how to shave $134 off the thru-hike budget," I called out to her.

"Oh, that's, um, good?" she said hesitantly, appearing in the doorway with an assessing look in her brown eyes to accompany the questioning tone in her voice.

I stared at the screen before bursting out laughing. One of those bordering-on-hysterical outbursts that come from nowhere.

I felt Dana's hand on my shoulder, and I looked up to see concern clearly etched on her face. Wanting to reassure her of my sanity, I gasped out, "It was a complete waste of time, but I have to admit, it was kind of fun."

A grin broke out on her face as she shook her head at my absurdity. "You do love spreadsheets."

"Even have a novelty mug to prove it," I confirmed, lifting the coffee cup beside me with its green and white pun, *Excel-ent at my job.* Feeling like an errant child, a few more small chuckles escaped.

As Dana returned to her reality TV show droning on in the living room, I navigated over to the 2018 AT Facebook page. I'd posted the day before, asking if anyone had gear recommendations they thought were unique and interesting. In the spirit of giving back, I'd shared I was planning to use a Wiffle ball to massage my feet at night, a trick I read about on the WhiteBlaze forums. It was a small investment I was told would pay dividends after too many miles hiked.

I saw now that I had notifications of several comments on my post. With anticipation of the gratitude I was sure to receive for my advice, I clicked over.

"*Have you ever actually used a Wiffle ball?*" the first commenter asked. Without waiting for a response, he replied to his own comment, "*It's going to flatten under the weight of your foot.*"

"Huh," I uttered, completely nonplussed. I retrieved the recently purchased Wiffle ball from the spare room that had quickly become AT supply headquarters. Sitting with it, I pushed it against my foot. Sure enough, the flimsy plastic bent, giving me no pressure to massage.

"*What do you recommend?*" I typed back. Burst pride aside, this is why I loved having a community. No one hiker had all the answers. I kept reading.

The next person to comment responded to my gear question with one word: "*Poles.*"

The comment under it read, "*YES, I second poles.*"

The comment under that said, "*I third poles.*"

And the final comment went even further: "*I COULD NOT backpack without poles. Literal lifesavers.*"

Poles?! I scoffed internally. Who were all these people? Max and I had debated and concluded our opinion on hiking poles long ago. While using all four limbs to scramble up a mud-caked canyon wall in Teddy Roosevelt National Park, the subject had come up.

"There's just no way we could do this with poles, Neiman," Max grunted as he used his right foot's toes to push his whole body up to the next muddy handhold.

"Yeah, man. I'm with you," I groaned back, my own body starfished near vertically against the rock face as I assessed my next move. "How the hell am I supposed to hold a pole when I need all four limbs to avoid falling to my death? I guess maybe it could be nice when we're hiking on groomed trails that don't require climbing ropes and harnesses?" I laughed hesitantly, knowing we had neither.

He peered up at me. "How are we supposed to eat while we hike?"

My mouth opened as I considered his question, then closed again as I gave a single shake of my head. "So, poles are out."

"Poles are definitely out," he huffed back.

"Definitely," I confirmed, pulling myself up over the final ledge and taking in the unending panorama of rolling prairies and distant herds of bison that were my reward for this full-body exertion.

Maybe these Facebook commenters were less experienced? More used to gentler suburban trails. I set the thought aside and scrolled back up, revisiting the Wiffle ball discussion. My question about a replacement had already been answered by someone else.

"*Pickleballs are where it's at. Same concept but much stronger polymer. I had to buy a 3-pack, so I have extras. Message me your address and I'll send you one.*"

I immediately Googled pickleballs. After getting through numerous images for sour pickle balls, a candy that looks like it's been masticated by a cow, I read up on some newly trending paddle sport in Sun Belt retirement communities looking for a low-impact court game. The commenter was right. This looked exactly like what I needed. It was slightly heavier than a Wiffle ball but was made of harder plastic that would give the necessary pressure to ease out the lactic acid causing aching feet. I messaged the guy my address, expressing gratitude for his suggestion, and rubbed my screen-weary eyes.

"Dana," I called out. "Do you want to join me for a Ramen bomb?"

She appeared in the doorway again, a slight tinge of panic in her face.

I plowed forward. "It's a combination of ramen noodles and instant potatoes that packs over 800 calories. I want to try it out. You know what Dad always said, never try a meal for the first time in the backcountry... you have no choice but to eat it."

"Oh, I, uh... I think we still have leftovers from last night. Don't want them to go bad, you go ahead."

"Okay, but you're missing out."

"Yeah, I'm missing out on something, alright," she answered.

I side-eyed her at the sarcasm dripping in her voice. Dana loved hiking but wasn't so keen on the camping experience, including the minimalist approach to backpack cooking. As I laid out all the ingredients, I felt a small wave of adrenaline at the realization I'd be eating solely trail food like this in just a few short months. Sighing happily, I started a whistling rendition of Bobby McFerrin's "Don't Worry, Be Happy" as I boiled water and got to work.

4
_____

THE ROOM WHERE IT HAPPENS

With winter holidays now receding, anticipation for my March 1 departure was building. Over the past months, I'd been busy with preparations. Daily miles, meal plans, cost breakdowns, town stops, and sleeping locations were all meticulously planned on spreadsheets and blog posts.

I started spending more time in the spare room, going through gear, organizing, and economizing in fine detail. For more than a decade, I'd been collecting, testing, and upgrading gear I thought I'd eventually want for a thru-hike. At this point, I easily owned everything I would need three times over. That was the problem with dreaming about the AT for so long. As my interest and knowledge deepened, so did my awareness of new gear on the market that could shave a few extra ounces or improve design flaws. The backpacking industry had become incredibly innovative, with numerous mom and pop shops called "cottage vendors" designing and selling products from home-based online stores. Literally anyone with a sewing machine could do it, and the quantity of options could easily overwhelm.

For years, I'd been caught in an unending tug-of-war between well-worn gear I loved and flashy, new, expensive gear that offered something different. Thankfully, though, the resale market among enthusiasts was also quite reliable. So I sold and upgraded, sold and upgraded, and sold and upgraded. And now, with the hike mere weeks away, I was happy with the gear I'd chosen. In fact, stealing a page from Dad's Glacier prep classes, I made sure of it. Living in Los Angeles, I was able to take advantage of the beautiful winter weather and get out to do a couple prep hikes in nearby mountains to field-test my gear and routine.

These hikes were great for trying out gear, sampling meals, and checking my physical readiness. After a couple field tests, I realized more adjustments were needed to make this a lifestyle I could live with for months on end. And it was these adjustments I was researching in our spare room when I heard the unmistakable sound of a FaceTime video call.

"Hey, Dad," I said as half his face appeared on the screen. He was your typical Baby Boomer who loved the younger generation's technology but didn't fully understand how to use it. He always wanted to video chat but would still hold the phone face up to his mouth, so the receiving end got a great close-up visual of his nose and forehead. It made me cringe every time, but I had to admit, I loved the quirk.

"Hey, Pride!" he sang out. "Checking in on your last prep hike. How was San Bernardino?"

"It was great, Dad. I learned a ton about winter camping. I'm just researching hammock quilts online. My sleeping bag didn't quite solve that cold-butt syndrome from being suspended midair. All the stuffing just gets compressed and doesn't insulate at all. Do you know a company in Minnesota called Enlightened Equipment? I'm checking out their Revolt underquilt. It attaches below and keeps you warm from blowing wind down to 20 degrees. Looks to be popular."

"Oh, yeah? Still insisting on a hammock then?"

Dad was an avid tent camper and a creature of habit. He'd hiked with the same daypack, boots, and khaki shorts for the last thirty years. The great debate of hammock versus tent, the one that divides thru-hikers as effectively as political party lines, had already gone several rounds in our conversations.

"If you would just try it, Dad, I promise you won't go back to sleeping on the hard ground. It's lighter. And you don't have to carry fragile tent poles! The Appalachian Trail is called 'the green tunnel' for a reason—it's a canopy of thick oak, pine, and fir trees all the way to Maine. And there's something about a gentle breeze that rocks you like a baby into the best sleep you've ever had."

"I think I'll keep my butt toasty in my tent, thank you." Dad chuckled, knowing the debate was heading toward two well-beaten but diverging paths. We were two stubborn mules on this topic, both determined to pull the other down. "Alright, son. What else have you got for today?"

"Not too much, probably just fine-tune supplies for my stove. I've found some dinner options I'm excited about and can be prepared with just a couple tablespoons of alcohol, if I can figure out how to contain the heat better."

Dad's laugh at this could only be described as raucous, but I knew it was coming. When I started experimenting with homemade stoves several years ago, my first attempt at boiling water ended in a small, somewhat-contained fire in my kitchen that had given Dad a year's worth of material for alcohol-stove-related jokes. It didn't deter me in my zeal for the DIY option though. Instead, I continued to tinker with designs and accessories that would make it a success on the trail. My latest version was a tiny Fancy Feast cat food can, emptied and lined with a ring of hole punches just below the rim. It was incredibly lightweight, required no setup, and cost virtually nothing to replace. I knew I'd found the future, I was just waiting for everyone else to catch up.

"Are you also bringing a fire extinguisher in case you start burning down the campsite?"

"Yeah, yeah," I shook my head, even as a smile spread across my face. There was nothing a Neiman enjoyed more than a good inside joke. "That was one time, but this will work. Trust me."

"Alright, son," he said again, a smile also unmistakably visible across the half of his face I could see.

"So, I'm thinking I'll go with the ol' external frame backpack when I join you. You know, stick with the familiar. What are you packing your gear in?"

I propped my phone against a box of Milky Way bars waiting to be packed into resupply boxes and shuffled backward to grab my trusty Osprey Talon backpack.

"The same one I used in Denali and Yosemite." I held it up to the camera and watched Dad's right eyebrow raise. Presumably the left one raised along with it, but that remained stubbornly off-camera.

"For the thru-hike? You're going to carry everything you need for five months in that tiny thing? It's just a daypack!"

"Sure am. It holds forty-four liters. More than enough to carry everything I need."

"Where are you going to hang your drinking cup?"

I grinned widely. Dad just opened an opportunity for me to prove the superiority of my ultralight cooking system.

"Won't need a cup. I'll just use my stove pot after I boil the water," I triumphantly declared.

It was Dad's turn to shake his head, and he did it in what I have to assume was pure wonder. "You seem to have it all planned out; I'll give you that."

I felt the deep tug of joy that receiving praise from a parent elicits in a child, even a fully grown one. Our choices may be different, but we both appreciated the pleasure of well-planned gear.

I sensed movement behind me and turned to see Dana surveying the spare room chaos.

"Hey, Tom." Dana waved, smiling at Dad's half-face before returning her gaze to the room's contents. I could see from the tense look that now flooded her face that something was on her mind.

"Is that Dana? Hey, love," Dad called from the phone, never adjusting to look at the screen and answer his own question.

"I'm going to go, Dad. Those quilts won't purchase themselves."

Ending the call, I turned to Dana. "What's on your mind?"

After a seemingly much too long scan of the room's contents, she turned back to me. "This is a lot," she admitted.

I mirrored her gaze and swept the room where gear lay in numerous, amorphous piles. Scattered between were Ziploc bags, junk food, and packages of dry goods. And in the spaces between them sat shipping boxes. Some filled and some in various semi-filled states. There were maybe three square feet of total visible floor, with the rest looking like an understaffed Amazon warehouse on Black Friday.

It all represented my resupply strategy. A popular approach among thru-hikers for mailing pre-purchased food in bulk to yourself along the trail, where good options aren't easily found. It was also a great way to ensure you stick to a specific meal plan—like the one I'd already detailed at length in yet another spreadsheet, and which was now proudly published on my blog. By preparing distinct weekly meal plans, packaging up all the ingredients before I left, and having Dana ship them to me each week, I could keep costs down and avoid the rut of poor roadside convenience-store dietary options.

"It looks like a lot, but I promise it'll all be straightened out before I leave," I said.

Dana shook her head. "That's fine. I'm just overwhelmed. How am I supposed to help mail all of this?"

I jumped up. "It's easy!" Not sure if it was more for her or me, but I couldn't resist a chance to explain the MasterClass-level resupply system I'd perfected the past few weeks.

I headed to the nearest food stockpile and picked up a Costco box of Nature Valley granola bars. "Once these and everything else for a week's meals are packed into individual boxes, I'll close them up and stack them against the wall. Then, a few days before I need it, I'll create a label on the USPS app from my phone, email it to you, and then you'll just have to print and attach it."

That would've been enough, but I kept going, clearly reveling in the presentation. I pulled the laptop over and showed her my blog, which had lately been serving as the web browser's permanent home page.

"The boxes correspond to the town stops I've worked out here." I clicked a tab at the top, navigating to a new page titled "Hiking Plan." A quick scroll down revealed a table that broke down my entire hike into daily details. Pointing out the orange highlighted rows signifying town stops, I added, "I'll put numbers on each box too, so you'll know which order they go out in. Then you just put them on the doorstep for pickup."

"Alright, I understand. These boxes need to get shipped to you in the correct order to the correct address. But how will I know if you get it?"

That's when I realized what she was saying behind what she was saying. Dana was worried I'd disappear into the wilderness. I set the laptop down and pulled her into a hug. "I'll have cell service almost everywhere, and I'll call or text you every day. You'll know when I get it."

I felt her shoulders relax at my words.

"Although," I added, "if you don't hear from me, you can always check my blog."

Her shoulders stiffened again, and she pulled back.

"Joking! Completely joking," I said quickly, seeing the wide-eyed look on her face.

"It's just... it's such a long time," she whispered.

"Yes, it is," I admitted quietly. "But then I'll be back, and even though the days will feel like weeks, the weeks will feel like days. And before you know it, the whole thing will be over and we'll be together again."

She nodded, casting her eyes around the room once more. "A phone call or text every day?"

"Every day," I reassured her.

And things continued just like that for the next few weeks. More meticulous plans in Excel, more blog posts detailing preparations, and more reassurances to family and friends that this wasn't so crazy an idea if you were prepared. Before I knew it, February 27th flew swiftly toward us... the day before departure day. My backpack was packed, my resupply boxes were neatly stacked, and we could see the spare room floor again. I was ready to thru-hike.

PART 2

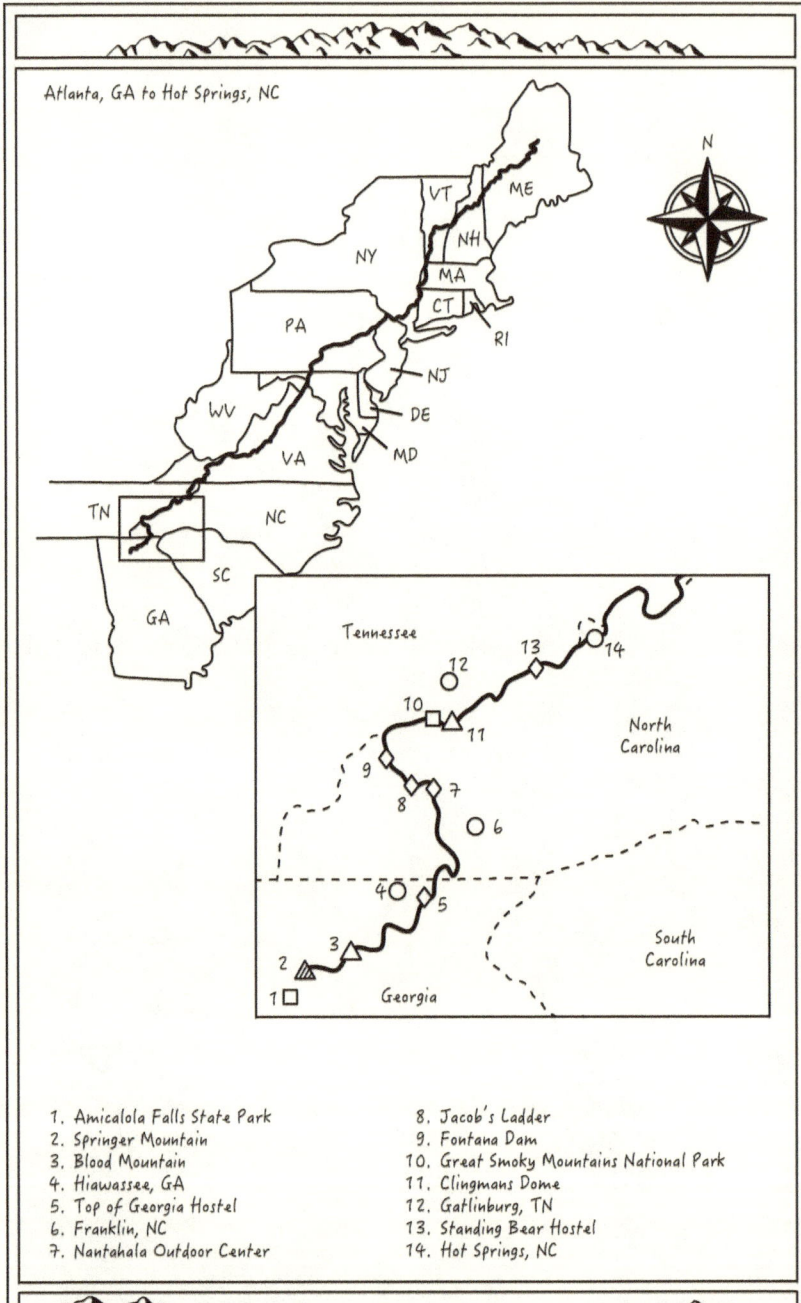

Atlanta, GA to Hot Springs, NC

1. Amicalola Falls State Park
2. Springer Mountain
3. Blood Mountain
4. Hiawassee, GA
5. Top of Georgia Hostel
6. Franklin, NC
7. Nantahala Outdoor Center

8. Jacob's Ladder
9. Fontana Dam
10. Great Smoky Mountains National Park
11. Clingmans Dome
12. Gatlinburg, TN
13. Standing Bear Hostel
14. Hot Springs, NC

HURRY UP, CAN'T WASTE TIME

The day of departure finally arrived. With my bag in the back seat next to Pippa, Dana drove me to LAX, the rising sun in pursuit through the rearview mirror. And after a goodbye that was a little too long but also not long enough, I headed to the ticketing counters.

During the spreadsheet planning, I'd mapped out almost 150 days of thru-hiking, and this preliminary travel day to the trailhead at Amicalola Falls State Park was no different. I'd found the perfect flight that would traverse the continent and drop me in Atlanta by 2 p.m., where I'd meet Max and Adam, arriving at the same time. Then a prescheduled shuttle driver would take us 70 miles north to Amicalola Falls Lodge in time to grab dinner and one final night in a bed before setting out the next morning. Unbridled excitement coursed through my veins as the evening played out in my mind.

I almost couldn't believe it. After years of prep, this idea I'd spent half my life crazed over was really happening. I could barely keep from running through the terminal as I realized how close I was to those first steps with Max and Adam at my side. Then I thought of the look on Dad's face when he'd join up and spot his first white blaze painted on a nearby tree. And of everyone else back home reading and cheering me on through the blog—I was finally doing it.

In no time, I was through security and onto my plane. It felt a bit odd having all my worldly belongings sitting in the luggage bay, but also exhilarating that my only worries from here on out were to follow trail markers, ration supplies, and find the best place to rest my head at night.

Dutifully clipping my seatbelt into place, I waited for the announcement to close the doors and prepare for departure. Fifteen minutes later, I was still waiting. Thirty minutes later and I could feel ripples of agitation begin to roll down the rows of passengers.

"Good morning, ladies and gentlemen," the captain's voice rang out confidently. *"We are experiencing a slight delay. The ground crew is working on their final checks, and we should be heading out soon. I'll update the new arrival time to Atlanta just as soon as we get cleared for takeoff."*

That sounded positive, I thought. Grumbling swelled around me, but I'd just hit play on a new playlist created for the thru-hike. Nothing passes time better than humming along to classic rock hits. So with Simon & Garfunkel's upbeat tones ringing through my headphones, I maintained a sense of calm, determined not to let a delay's inconvenience ruin my journey's first day.

Ninety minutes later, that resolve started to shred. The captain's voice rang out again. *"Ladies and gentlemen, unfortunately, we're going to have to disembark the aircraft. We've experienced some mechanical issues that are going to need further attention. Thank you for your patience. If you will please exit back into the airport, staff members will assist you."*

Groans reverberated around me, with mine joining the chorus. My day's itinerary was perfectly planned down to the hour, and this wasn't part of it.

Time crawled past as I sat in mutual frustration with 200 other passengers waiting for the airline staff to tell us our options. Finally, I was rebooked on an afternoon flight, landing in Atlanta at 9 p.m. I could kiss dinner and meeting other hikers at the Lodge goodbye.

Stress and anxiety mixed with the frustration I already felt, swirling a very unpleasant mixture in my gut. I'd mentally prepared for the "change of plans" mindset that would accompany a trip of this size. I also knew not every day would be a picturesque utopia; sometimes, I'd need to "embrace the suck", as other thru-hikers often said, and take whatever misery the trail sent me. But I didn't expect to need these mantras quite so early. I pumped up the volume of tunes now blasting through my headphones, adding The Beach Boys to try and trick my brain into happy thoughts. I'm not going to lie, the battle raged as the hours dragged by.

Eventually, after spending eight more hours in LAX and four more in the air, we touched down in Atlanta. By this time, Adam had been waiting in the airport all day, and we'd missed the pre-booked shuttle. Max's flight was also delayed, so Adam made the executive decision to rent a car and drive us out to Amicalola Falls Lodge instead.

"Day one didn't go quite as planned, huh?" Max noted with humor I couldn't quite meet about the situation. I wasn't going to correct him that tomorrow was technically day one from a hiking perspective, but the truth was that I felt robbed of my start to the adventure. I'd spent years anticipating all the elements of the thru-hike and had already been forced to miss out on some preliminary excitement-building experiences. We were on our way now, but I was still salty about the late arrival and missed opportunities.

"Not exactly," I replied, watching the back-and-forth swish of windshield wipers clearing rain that accompanied our drive to Amicalola Falls. Adam drove us along the winding mountain road, a route I knew should've welcomed us with breathtaking first views of the mountains we'd be hiking but instead was just dark and bleary with rain.

A few minutes later, we pulled up to the Lodge, and I felt my irritation fade at the sight of warm orange lights glowing invitingly through glass that stretched from the ground to the pointed top of the hotel's lobby.

The inside was just as impressive. It managed to combine a log-cabin feel with a mountain ski-resort atmosphere. Its floor-to-ceiling stone chimney was still ablaze with a roaring fire, while exposed beams crisscrossed above simple hotel furniture meant to be functional rather than fashionable. The rooms were basic but clean, and the warm bed and hot shower went a long way to lifting my spirits. I loved everything about the Lodge's combined simplicity and grandeur.

"Tomorrow is a new day," I told my steam-fogged reflection. "Today was the first test but tomorrow is when the challenge really starts."

The next day dawned gray. Fog lay stranded in thick threads along the mountain range, and I didn't need to step outside to know frigid air would be waiting for me. But I whistled as I walked to breakfast beside Adam and Max. Weather wouldn't put a damper on my buoyant mood. Today I was finally going to start my thru-hike. My feet would take me up the 8.8-mile approach trail to Springer Mountain; then I'd take my first steps on the Appalachian Trail. And I'd experience it alongside two great friends. What could be better than that?

At breakfast, Max had an answer... butter biscuits. Amicalola Falls Lodge certainly knew how to keep its guests happy, and after the rough day and short night, nothing felt better than those fluffy, delicious, homemade butter biscuits. Max joked he was willing to set up camp in the dining room and call it a day if it meant three square meals of those heaven-baked wonders, and I'll admit I was tempted to delay my hike to see it. But eventually the room emptied of hikers as quickly as it had filled, and we agreed it was time to make things official.

We retrieved our packs and headed to the Amicalola Falls Visitor Center to officially register as a thru-hiker. I was the 436th person already for 2018, and even though most hikers heading north don't even make it to Virginia, I was surprised to see how many people were ahead of me.

A park ranger finished recording my info, then wrote my number on a bright orange triangular keychain. On the other side was the trail's iconic logo, the crosshair of an A vertically sharing the top of a T. As I clipped it on my pack, I couldn't help but beam at what felt like a badge of honor.

"Gonna break records this year. We don't usually hit 300 by March," he said, shaking me from my heroic thoughts.

Break records? I did some quick mental math. I knew roughly 2,000 hikers typically register each year. If it was already a third more hikers, did that mean we'd pass 3,000? I wasn't sure whether the thought excited me for how much more social it would be... or concerned me for how crowded it would be...

Next, we weighed our packs on the giant hook and scale outside the Visitor Center. Years of gear researching and trading had paid off well. With four days of food and two liters of water, my pack came in at thirty-three pounds. I estimated that meant my base weight without provisions was around nineteen.

"Not bad!" Max announced, capturing the ritualistic photo on his phone.

"I guess, though I was hoping to be a bit lighter," I responded. Although not official, most backpacker purists say a base weight under fifteen pounds is required to be considered ultralight—a valuable strategy for long-distance hiking. An ultralight pack was always my goal to ensure the most daily mileage, but with still so many unique items I felt needed to last five months in the woods, I was already learning the challenge of adjusting as you go.

"It's not seventy-five," Max pointed out.

I rolled my eyes at him as I loaded the pack on my back, making some final adjustments to account for the extra helping of butter biscuits I had consumed for breakfast. Turning to greet the iconic stone arch that designated the approach trail to Springer Mountain, I felt a renewed thrill of anticipation for the adventure ahead. A wooden sign to the left announced it was 2,190.9 miles to Mount Katahdin, Maine.

"So, not too many." Adam gestured at the sign as he stepped through the arch onto the trail.

Max followed, chuckling. "You'll be there in no time, Neiman."

I grinned before taking my own ceremonial first step through the arch, planting my foot in the first of many steps I'd take on the way to a similar wooden sign welcoming finishers at Katahdin's final summit. I was here. A deep gratitude rose within me for the opportunity I'd finally been given the chance to take. The trail before me was well-worn and muddy. The trees arching over it were beginning to unfurl new leaves. It seemed appropriate—the battered path beaten down by so many feet before me yet covered by the unfurling newness of my own steps upon it.

I felt a hand clap me on the shoulder, and I turned my head to see Adam gripping it as he smiled knowingly at the goofy grin covering my face.

"Are you planning to take any more steps today?"

Laughing, we headed away from the arch and into our first day on the trail. And as if to symbolize the difficulty of the months to come, within an hour, the rain started. A cold, sideways-blowing rain that stung as it pelted me in the face. I grabbed my raincoat, strategically kept in an outside pocket of my pack for moments just like this.

Zipping up the thin material, I pulled the hood up in a futile attempt to protect more bare skin from the freezing rain. The lack of vision on either side of my face and the sound of rain hauling itself against the waterproof fabric gave me a cozy, inside-a-tent feeling. But in the back of my mind, a wary concern began to grow as I recalled something I'd read on WhiteBlaze about this particular jacket. Adored for its lightweight fabric and durability, the Outdoor Research Helium II was a popular choice for thru-hikers, but it had one fatal flaw—no pit zips. Those extra few ounces for zippers under the armpit seemed like an easy sacrifice in pursuit of ultralight perfection. But that concern grew with each step as I realized I'd never actually field-tested this jacket, and warnings of this flaw were quickly materializing. Without pit zips, there was nowhere for my body's condensation to go, making the Helium II just as successful at keeping moisture in as keeping it out. I pushed the thought aside, confident it couldn't really be that big an issue.

We caught up on each other's lives as the first few miles of the approach trail fell behind us, exchanging updates about careers, wives, and all the small details in between. I'd known them both for most of my adult life, so conversation flowed easily between us. But beneath the casual banter, there was also a collective determination to push through the rain and the constant uphill climb to quickly reach the shelter atop Springer Mountain, where we planned to spend the night. Keeping our heads down, we attempted to avoid pellets of icy water that continued to mount a frozen assault.

"So, have you thought of our trail names yet?" Max was referring to another special AT custom, the common practice of taking on a new moniker that uniquely fits your thru-hiker persona. He and Adam were enthusiastically on board after reading one of my blog posts on trail culture, quickly assigning me the role of trail name designator.

"Actually, I have been thinking about that." I looked over my left shoulder at faces filled with eager expectation, only to regret it when I received a face full of freezing rain pellets. I lowered my head back to the trail and raised my voice in compensation.

"Adam, because of the passion for Minnesota breweries you've taught me to appreciate, and your unique skill to somehow convince us to end trips early in exchange for a night of drinking with the locals, your trail name is... Keg."

I paused to fully absorb the burst of laughter breaking out from both Max and Adam at this reference to Adam's subtle pressure to always quit a day or two early and find a bar for drinking shenanigans.

"And Max, you've always been our leader for adventure on the trail." I paused before adding, "But really, because of how you always snuck into college parties with a 1.75-liter handle of Captain Morgan attached to the back of your pants, you'll now be known as... The Captain."

Another burst of laughter and another satisfied trail name customer. I risked a glance up at the trail ahead to see a small clearing, fog, rain, and what looked distinctly like a flash of white paint on the ground a few yards in front of us.

"Is that a white blaze?" I yelled out to the others, pointing in its direction.

We'd already seen the distinctive blue rectangles painted intermittently on trees during the morning's hike signifying side trails to towns, water, shelters, etc., but the AT doesn't officially start until Springer Mountain's summit, so if this was the first white blaze, that meant we'd finally arrived.

I pulled out my phone and clicked on Guthook Guides, an app I'd downloaded a couple weeks earlier tracing the entire AT, documenting all the waypoints of interest with descriptions, photos, and geolocation accuracy. It found our current position and confirmed we were indeed officially at mile 0.0 and the southern terminus of the Appalachian Trail. Next to the first white blaze was a small bronze plaque picturing a man with a backpack that read: "*A footpath for those who seek fellowship with the Wilderness.*"

"It is! We're now officially walking the AT!" I yelled, though neither stopped at either the question or exclamation. It was a big moment, but the dense fog and freezing-cold rain made any attempt to stop and look around both insufferable and pointless.

I snapped a quick picture with the plaque for the blog, then rushed to catch up. Almost immediately, a blue blaze appeared ahead, marking the side trail leading to the Springer Mountain shelter we were aiming for. We reached it and turned right onto a much narrower track. I took the lead for the couple hundred yards to the shelter and campground area, my completely drenched torso ready to be unburdened and my feet ready to be released from their hiking duties.

The shelter appeared like a ghost in the distance, through a haze of fog and trees. It was a spartan wooden box enclosed on three sides, covered with a sloping roof, and standing slightly up off the ground on concrete pillars. At 10 by 10 feet, it would've fit no more than six people comfortably—nine if you wanted to be really friendly with the people sleeping next to you.

It was also gloriously dry, and as we all traipsed up onto its covered front porch, we were glad to unload wet bags and free our bodies from their waterproofed enclosures. But we quickly realized we weren't alone. A series of creaks emanated from within the small space. We stood hidden from view by a partial front wall and exchanged quick, wide-eyed looks. The creaking grew louder as floorboards closer to our location shifted under whatever weight was already occupying the shelter. Suddenly, a tousled brown head of hair appeared, followed by the very unmistakable form of a human.

"Hey!" he greeted us, a giant grin breaking out across a face still bridging the gap between boy and man.

"Hey," we all chorused in response.

"Did you get caught in the rain?" The Captain asked, gesturing to the sopping-wet T-shirt, which dripped streams of water onto equally wet running shorts and black tights.

"Oh," our new friend said, looking down at himself like he was previously unaware he was standing in a pool of water. "Yeah, I guess I did." He scratched the back of his head before looking back at us with a wry smile and slight shrug of his shoulders.

"Doesn't look like your rain gear held up very well. What are you using?" I asked.

"Um, well, I think I forgot it."

"You don't have a rain jacket?" I didn't mean for it to sound accusatory, but I wasn't sure he fully understood the risk of being constantly exposed to the elements.

"Nope."

"What about a hat? Got anything to cover your head with?" The Captain asked.

"Nope."

We all exchanged another look, this time of disbelief. What was this kid doing out here? Maybe he was a day-hiker? But as we all shuffled into the one main room of the tiny shelter, it became apparent he was here for the long haul. His backpack sat in the corner with its own pool spreading around it, while gear spilled out onto the floor like some REI-sponsored yard sale. We'd clearly interrupted him in the middle of some sort of shakedown. It at least looked like he'd thrown some things into stuff sacks, as not everything littering the shelter was soddened.

"You're doing a thru-hike then?" The Captain posed the question with the same uncertainty we all felt toward his ability to make it through one more day, let alone multiple months.

"I am!" he replied enthusiastically. "You guys too?"

"Just this guy," The Captain responded, aiming his thumb toward me. "We're just here to provide distraction for any rabid bears or deranged locals that try to chase him."

I smiled at the laughter this elicited and offered out my hand. "I'm Michael, but my friends just call me Neiman."

"Kyle," he replied, shaking my hand with a firm and very damp grip.

"This is Keg and The Captain."

"Oh, cool! You guys already got trail names? I can't wait for mine." His excitement was as endearing as his current condition was alarming. I could see the purpling of his lips and shivers starting to overtake his body.

"Hey, why don't we all get out of these wet clothes? Get some dry stuff on and have some lunch," I suggested. "Have you eaten yet, Kyle?"

"Not yet. Was waiting to first juice up my phone, but this solar charger isn't doing much good today."

I muffled a laugh, knowing a solar charger was just a five-pound paperweight on this trail that rarely sees open sky. I didn't want to offend him, and he was going to learn for himself soon enough.

So there we sat eating lunch together and getting to know our new friend Kyle, his interesting selection of gear, and his motivation for completing a thru-hike. And where Kyle lacked experience, he made up for it in boyish wonder.

Growing up in Dalton, Massachusetts, one of many trail towns the AT literally walks down the middle of, he'd seen the white blazes his whole life. He was raised a few blocks off Main Street, so every summer, Kyle would see thru-hikers pass through town. But he'd never hiked any of the trail himself, at least not beyond Dalton. He was still young, not quite eighteen, and a high school dropout. The only plan for his future was to try and play video games competitively.

But in the last year, life had taken an unexpected turn. His childhood babysitter had turned into a romantic relationship, and he was head over heels in love. He bought a ring from a nearby department store and proposed to her, but she'd turned him down and instead ended the relationship.

"She said I wasn't old enough for that kind of commitment." He pulled on a chain I hadn't noticed before, revealing a small diamond ring looped through it. "She broke my heart, but I made a decision right then and there. I was going to hike the AT. Prove that I'm not a child."

We nodded along, not sure what to say to this pretty remarkable story, and not sure if the proof was meant for her or himself. Every hiker has their own reason for being out there, and being raised with Dad's love of storytelling, the thought of talking to them and learning their stories like this excited me. But Kyle's story was slightly disconcerting. It was still being written, just beginning, in fact, and the results he hoped to achieve were still very much in question.

By this point, lunch was complete, and wind was starting to whip through the shelter's opening. The rain was lighter but much more horizontal.

"I don't think much of this shelter for warmth," Keg quietly noted.

I pulled up the Guthook app again and could see another shelter 2.8 miles down the trail on the other side of the mountain. It had been a late lunch, but it was still early afternoon, and there should be enough daylight to make it before dark.

Reviewing the shelter details and photos, I added, "The next shelter is in a valley, so it's going to be a lot more protected from the wind, and it's not too far. Want to pack up and head that way?" I asked.

"Let's do it," The Captain responded, while Keg nodded his agreement.

"Kyle? Want to join us?" I added, so he knew it was unanimous.

Kyle looked out at the rain and then at his still-dripping clothes, now hanging from the shelter walls. "I think I might stay here actually. Wait out the rain. Hopefully, I'll catch up with you again."

The Captain, who'd been rifling around in his backpack, straightened and threw a wool beanie at Kyle.

"Keep it. You lose forty percent of your body heat through your head," he advised.

"Really? Wow, cool. Thanks." Kyle stuck it straight on his head and sighed contentedly.

We said our goodbyes, waterproofed up, and headed back to the main trail.

"Think we'll ever see him again?" Keg asked us.

The Captain snorted in response. "Not a chance."

I kept quiet, my mind running through Kyle's gear, his story, and the youthful inexperience mixed with clear exuberance. Part of me related, finding familiarity in how innocent and naïve my approach to backpacking was at first. If I'd taken off for the AT right after college, would I have been so different? Now, more than fifteen years later, my heart told me there was little chance this kid could complete a strenuous thru-hike all the way to Maine. But my gut told me not to discount him quite yet either.

Standing at the southern terminus on March 1, 2018.

6

TOMORROW IS ANOTHER DAY

"Ahh, the infamous cat food stove," Keg laughed as he pulled out his Jetboil for dinner that night, the canister-style gas stove just about every other thru-hiker used. "Shall I move a few feet away?"

We'd made it to Stover Creek shelter, which turned out to be a much nicer campsite with a picnic table under the awning. Following a quick pitching of tent and hammock, we were now getting ready for dinner. The rain finally let up as we arrived, and though it was still cold, I'd been right that it was more sheltered from wind.

"You may laugh now, but just wait until I patent this baby. It's the only stove a backpacker will ever want," I replied, setting my homemade aluminum foil wind screen around the tiny stove.

I measured the alcohol in a tiny medicine cup, dropped it in the stove, lit it, and watched as blue flames licked up the side of the titanium pot holding my water. On tonight's menu, Pesto Chicken Ramen—another one-pot meal I'd unsuccessfully recruited Dana to test with me. I pulled out my phone and opened the messages app while I kicked back and waited for the water to boil. I texted Dana a quick update on progress so far and some pictures from earlier on the trail.

That complete, I looked up to see Keg and The Captain diving into their instant mashed potatoes with enthusiasm. I checked my water. Not boiling yet, but I was content in my innovation. Modern gas canister stoves were fast, but also heavy and expensive, and I had nothing but time out here. This was all about being present and enjoying the process.

Two more minutes passed; then three more. Keg and The Captain were starting to rinse out their pots, and I was only just getting small bubbles on the bottom of mine.

"Screw it," I muttered and threw in the ramen noodles. It wasn't like it really *needed* boiling water.

After a couple minutes of stirring, I added in the freeze-dried chicken, pine nuts, dried basil, and garlic powder packed in a tiny Ziploc bag, and dove in ravenously with my spork... discovering that apparently ramen noodles do need boiling water. I completed my now-renamed Crunchy Pesto Chicken Ramen and returned my rinsed-out pot to my food bag hanging from the shelter rafters. Keg and The Captain were already in their tent, but I had something I needed to do before I could snuggle into the depths of my hammock.

Back before blogs, texting, and GPS, a basic yet powerful mechanism was used along the Appalachian Trail to communicate among hikers. Each shelter would be equipped with a simple notebook, where hikers could pass notes to those behind them, preview what was ahead from those going the opposite direction or simply sign their name with the day's random thoughts. These logbooks were a tradition of the AT experience, even after their existence became more about nostalgia, and I still had use for them.

Locating the logbook inside the shelter, I scanned through the entries that had come before mine. It was exciting to see the names of thru-hikers already ahead of me. Meeting Kyle today had given me another glimpse of the community waiting out here. I flipped past a few pages of scribbles and signatures to the first empty one and laid the book down on the shelter floor.

Digging into my pack, I retrieved a stash of miniature "Hello My Name Is" stickers I made up before the trip. There was nothing fancy about them, except the unique orange color, the faded AT logo in the background, and a small URL to my blog printed at the bottom. It was a small luxury item Dana would replenish in resupply boxes, allowing me to leave a calling card of sorts for others to follow. I wrote "Neiman" in the blank white space and stuck it to the page.

"*Tough hike today uphill in the rain, but we ended up doing more miles than planned,*" I wrote underneath the sticker. "*Kyle, hope to see you tomorrow. Keep moving forward!*" I added a tease for would-be readers to see more of my story at the blog address, then stepped away satisfied with my first logbook entry.

"My legs are screaming profanities at me," Keg called out.

"Yep, mine don't feel so hot either," I replied, packing away the stickers and getting out my pickleball. My own feet felt like a strange mix of shooting pain and limp Jell-O, and I let out a small grunt as I pulled off my boots. Time to try this bad boy out.

I sat on the shelter's edge and started massaging the arches of my feet, trying not to moan with ecstasy at the heavenly feeling of pressure on my aching muscles. I really pushed down hard, impressed with the plastic's resilience. That guy on Facebook had been right to recommend this after all.

"Today's increased miles have presented us with a dilemma. The next shelters are five or fifteen miles away," I advised my friends.

"And how much did we end up doing today?" The Captain asked.

"About ten," I rounded.

The Captain huffed a short laugh in acknowledgment of my well-known tendency to exaggerate miles on a hike. The truth is, calculating distance accurately on the fly isn't one of my strengths. Add that to my glass-half-full outlook on life, and you have a perfect setup for slightly longer distances than expected. Both Keg and The Captain had hiked with me enough by now to know they needed to add extra miles on top of any number I announced.

"It was 11.6." The Captain, as if expecting it, was ready with the stats.

"Well, what's a couple extra miles between friends?" I joked. "Anyway, back to tomorrow. Any thoughts one way or the other?"

Keg groaned as he shifted in his sleeping bag. "Even the thought of putting those wet boots back on my feet makes them ache."

"Maybe we can see in the morning? You know, once we've hopefully slept off the pain?" The Captain added, always hinting toward a challenge.

My excitement for the trail urged me to push further, but I didn't want my friends tortured because of a decision I made on the group's behalf. I agreed to wait until morning to see how we were all feeling. After saying my goodnights, I headed to my own bed.

As I walked up, I could see the hammock gently swaying as the wind passed through the trees, and I had to admit, I was pumped to spend my first night on the trail in my new camp setup. After years of research, I really felt I had the perfect combination of gear to rock me into a deep, gentle slumber.

The DutchWare Chameleon hammock was the center of it all, stretching up to 30 feet between trees and covered on top with a mesh bug net, which meant there was a good chance I'd be able to spend most nights comfortably suspended in the air. Surrounding the hammock was a rain fly explicitly designed for the AT's rough weather conditions. The Winterdream tarp by UGQ was made of lightweight silnylon material that pitched low and included doors that snapped shut at the front and back, making it a fortress against heavy wind and rain from any direction. Adding in the 20-degree underquilt and matching top quilt that I'd discussed with Dad earlier that year, I felt ready for anything this trail decided to throw at me. Plus, all the items were orange and black, beckoning me at night with my favorite colors.

I climbed into the cozy nest of bedding, bringing my phone with me. I knew before I could close my eyes for the night, I needed to record the day's events while still fresh in my mind. Opening the WordPress app, I scrolled down through comments from yesterday's post detailing the journey from Los Angeles to Atlanta until I came to one attributed to Tom Neiman, who'd helpfully added "aka Dad" behind his name in the author line. Just in case I'd had a sudden onset of amnesia since landing in Georgia. I smiled as I read, "*No surprises... a little rain, a little pain, but a positive attitude makes all the difference. Wish I was there too. Keep heading NORTH.*"

"*Thanks, Dad, I learned from the best,*" I typed before hitting reply. Then I started to compose my first post from the trail: "*Day 1. Today was a good day. It was a very cold, wet, and painful day, but it was a good day nonetheless...*"

Winter camping is rough. All that planning to create a perfect hammock setup of components from expertly chosen cottage vendors, yet I'd spent the night alternately sweating out the previous day's water intake in the warmth of the quilts and shivering to every gust of wind that blew through them. It was a balancing act all night, but was slightly tipped in my favor, and I managed to get some decent sleep. I vaguely heard Keg and The Captain moving around as dawn suffused the campsite with its light, but no part of me wanted to set foot outside the cozy warmth of my hammock, so I let sleep drag me under again for another couple hours.

When I finally emerged, a quick and much-needed cup of instant coffee rendered me able to discuss new thoughts for the day. Five miles or fifteen? Keg and The Captain were optimistic, so with the unanimous decision to push on for our second day of extended hiking, we broke down camp and loaded up our gear.

Excited to begin, I bounded down the side trail back to the AT, swift of foot and full of springy confidence that a whole day of successful hiking had instilled.

"Come on, guys!" I called over my shoulder. "More trail adventures this way!"

Nothing would stop me today. Sure, it had been 30 degrees last night, and yes, the fog, freezing temperatures, and rain had made yesterday's hike a gruesome start. But today's glow of sun was already beginning to warm the air, and we were still in its radiant glow.

About thirty feet past the shelter, I recognized a small stream from yesterday's approach. Before I fully connected the dots, Keg and The Captain noticed as well.

"Isn't this the southbound route? Are we going the right way?" jabbed Keg, fully knowing the answer.

"Uh, right, I knew that. Just making sure you were both paying attention." The weak attempt at humor did little to shroud my mistake.

"Try not to make that a pattern; it's going to really slow down your progress," The Captain joked in response.

"Okay, okay. More adventure THIS way," I said, fully emphasizing "this" as I turned around.

"Only 2,188 miles to go!" I shouted. Then, as if triggering an itch needing a scratch, I began to sing, "... but I would walk 500 miles, and I would walk 500 more. Just to be the man who walks 2,190.9 miles to Katahdin's front door!"

I heard dual groans behind me and turned to see Keg and The Captain shaking their heads in disbelief and what appeared to be pain.

"You sure do like to sing," Keg said, emphasizing his discontent by mockingly clutching his hands to his ears.

I grinned. It was true. I'd always loved a good tune, especially if it allowed ad-libbing a few Neiman-original lyrics. The Proclaimers' hit song from the '90s may not check the first box, but it certainly did the second.

Our chatter joined that of the birds as they exultantly greeted the sky. The morning heated up fast and so did our hiking pace. I'm not sure if it was the warmth of the sun or the way its shafts of light broke through trees to light the trail before us, but we approached the first of the day's shelters with plenty of time and morale to push on.

The next few miles, however, involved summiting Sassafras Mountain with an incredulous 1,000-foot elevation gain and loss in less than two miles. We knew going into the hike that this one would be a challenge, but the trail gods, in a display of defiance to our positive attitudes, decided that a bitter frontal attack wind would be a good addition.

Our pace slowed to a crawl, and we trudged forward up the side of the mountain, experiencing a thigh workout that felt like it could rival the intensity of Olympic rowing time trials.

"This wind is insane!" The Captain needlessly pointed out.

The wind was successfully whipping away all the moisture from every one of my exposed orifices by this point, so with my mouth too dry to allow my tongue the movement it required to form words, I let silence emphasize my response. A few more minutes and a few dozen steps later, Keg asked the question no hiker wants to hear.

"Anyone got any water? I'm out."

I checked my water bottles to find I was also out, just as I heard The Captain confirm he was in the same predicament. The realization hit me that we'd forgotten to check our water levels before walking up the mountain, knowing most sources lie in the valleys between. I stopped and turned my back to the wind, facing the path we'd just hiked up. It was surprisingly motivating to see the progress we'd already made, rather than focusing on progress yet to be accomplished. But what was not motivating was the information my Guthook app provided me.

"Damn it," I cursed, seeing the little blue raindrop icon that indicated the closest water source was very unhelpfully down the other side of the mountain we were still climbing up.

Keg and The Captain crowded around my phone, drawn in by the obvious distress in my voice.

"That doesn't look too close," The Captain pointed out.

"It's three miles away," I growled, frustration taking over control of my tone.

We stood in silence for a minute, each of us absorbing this sobering piece of information and its meaning. We were going to have to hike the next three miles in a full-blown gale, up a mountain and back down again, and with no water.

7

SEND ME AN ANGEL

Our arid trek over Sassafras Mountain's exposed pinnacle continued as we fought with the wind at each step. The descent back down into the protection of the woods shielded us from wind but also made it very clear that dehydration was becoming more of a pressing reality the longer we went without water. So when I looked up and saw what appeared to be a circus big top on the trail ahead, I thought maybe I was already hallucinating from extreme thirst. The flapping baby-blue sheet also seemed to be moving forward along the trail, which only increased my concern that I was indeed experiencing a vision brought on by dehydration.

Then, suddenly, I noticed I was gaining on it and realized the structure had set up camp on the side of the trail. As the distance between us lessened, the truth came into focus. It wasn't in fact a billowing circus tent, but a person wearing a billowing blanket of a rain poncho. It completely covered the man's body, head, and backpack, flowing out from all sides, and a moment later, I saw why he'd halted. A woman who looked in her mid-fifties stood next to him, clad in athletic gear, her short brown hair wrapped in a flowery bandana, and her hands holding onto what looked suspiciously like bottles of water.

"Hey, y'all," she drawled in that Southern accent that sweetens the air as it takes its time to reach your ears.

My tongue still stuck to the roof of my mouth, I gratefully took the bottle she held out and chugged half of the best-tasting liquid I'd ever had the fortune of swallowing. It was just water, but it was also the elixir of life in that moment.

"Hi," I now managed, glancing over at Keg and The Captain to see their faces lit in the same well-watered ecstasy I felt.

"I'm Flower, nice to meet ya." Her smile was warm and open, inviting further conversation.

"Trail name?" The Captain more announced than asked.

"Sure is, hon," Flower beamed at him, her bright blue eyes crinkling at the edges. "I'm hiking the AT in sections, so I had my husband drop me at Cooper Gap parking lot to do a day hike today. When I saw the weather forecast, I thought early thru-hikers may need some trail magic up here."

"Trail magic, you say?" The Captain slapped a hand on my arm, gripping it in his excitement. "Neiman, our friend Flower here is our first trail angel!"

I grinned at him, sharing the joy at this first encounter with a defining element of thru-hiking culture. Trail angels had come up often in my research, and for good reason. They were kind, generous people on whom the AT had left an indelible mark. Whether they themselves had done a previous thru-hike, enjoyed hiking sections, or lived near it, these kind souls were drawn to give back to future hikers as they walked out their own stories along its vast length.

"I'm Michael," I pointed at myself. "And these are my friends, Keg and The Captain."

I looked over at the blue-covered man beside us. Up to now, he'd been quietly sipping the water Flower had handed him, watching our interaction play out. But when he saw my gaze land on him, he offered me his hand.

"What's up, fellas," he smiled widely. "Are you thru-hiking?"

I nodded before adding, "I am. These guys are hanging with me until we summit Blood Mountain in a couple days."

"Awesome." He surveyed Keg and The Captain for a moment and then pulled off his poncho in one fluid movement. The muscle-tight athletic shirt tucked neatly into his black shorts and trail-running shoes showed this guy was no stranger to long-distance traveling. He was some sort of endurance runner, and he was shredded. His shaven head and strong jawline completed the look. There was a military feel to him, and I pictured this being what Hasbro would market as a new G.I. Joe model for a man in his upper forties.

Dropping his pack to the ground, he got down on his haunches and neatly folded his poncho onto the top of it. I realized I'd now been staring for what was becoming an uncomfortable length of time. I took another swig of water and asked the age-old question to break the silence, even though his clear accent gave it away. "So, where are you from?"

"Boston. Townie born and raised." He stood up and stretched his arms above his head, eliciting the kind of cracks that chiropractors dream of. "I retired from the army a while back and just needed something to do. I'm not very good at sitting still. You know?"

He gave a wry smile that spoke of the awareness he held for the military veteran stereotype he'd just confirmed.

Returning his smile, I nodded. "I know the feeling well. Are you doing a thru?"

"Sure am. I like to do trail running to keep in shape, so I thought hiking the AT might not be too different."

He swung his pack back onto his shoulders, and I could see in the easy arc that it made through the air that it was a lot lighter than mine.

"Looks like you did some strategic packing there," I commented, hearing the admiration in my tone.

"Oh, yeah." He puffed out his chest in what was either naturally perfect posture or pride at his packing achievement. "It's still twenty pounds or so, but I've been whittling it down with lightweight gear I make myself. Definitely helps to shave off some weight."

"Which gear did you make?" I asked, having visions of us sharing our camping stove innovations.

"All of it. Just figured, as I couldn't find stuff how I wanted it, I'd go ahead and make it. Much easier that way, you know?"

I nodded slowly as if I did know, but the eyebrows that were now somewhere near my hairline probably gave away my complete awe-filled amazement at this distance running, ex-military, DIY-gear-carrying sculpture of a man.

"Well," he exclaimed. "Onward to Maine." And when it came from his mouth, it really did sound as simple as that. The mountains might just very well bow out of the way when they saw his mighty form striding up.

He started cruising forward, and a sudden idea came to me.

"Hey," I called out, realizing I'd never gotten his name. He turned around. "Got a trail name yet?"

"Nope," he called back.

"How about Poncho Villa? That awesome rain cover alone is worth the namesake, but your military background and revolutionary spirit to do things your way... it just feels perfect."

He paused for a few seconds before a wide smile appeared. "Poncho Villa," he repeated inquisitively, trying it on for size. "I like it. Thanks, brother."

And with that, he was gone. I hoisted my own pack from where I'd laid it down on the side of the trail, trying not to groan at the thirtyish pounds that for some reason now felt a lot heavier.

"Well," I said to Keg and The Captain as we also waved goodbye to Flower (after showering her with profuse thanks), "I don't think we'll be seeing that guy again. He'll probably summit Katahdin before I make it to West Virginia."

The next morning, I woke to the gentle sounds of the still mostly bare branches tapping against each other in the wind. We'd finally hobbled into Gooch Mountain Shelter the night before, each of us in various degrees of foot and knee pain. The last three miles navigating the ups and downs of the trail had been excruciating.

We were exhausted, and it was freezing once the sun went down. Too cold and tired to enjoy much of the shelter's amenities, we quickly set up camp, hastily ate dinner, and fluffed up the security of our quilts for a much-needed night of rest. I'd hoisted our food bags high up into a tree to deter any nearby bears and then crawled into the awaiting comfort of my hammock, knowing the next day's nine miles to Lance Creek Campground would come too quickly.

And it did. I was still shaking off the morning's stupor in my hammock, ignoring the need to prepare my thoughts for the day, when I heard decidedly human noises from within our tent area. Peeking my head out, I expected to greet Keg and The Captain, but instead was met by an unfamiliar bespectacled face.

"Oh," I managed.

The man before me laughed. "Sorry, didn't mean to surprise you. I'm MacGyver."

My initial surprise wearing off, I swung out of my hammock and into my hiking shoes, trying not to physically show the stinging pain that quickly rushed up my toes to my waist.

"Hey, MacGyver." I coughed to cover the sound of my winced pain. "I'm Michael."

"Are you thru-hiking?" he asked, a question I was beginning to see would be a common one over the next few months. I've found this an interesting element of the human psyche—categorizing others into easily understood boxes so we can work out their relationship to our surroundings and our relationship to them.

"I sure am. My two buddies are probably still asleep. They're hiking this first part with me, too."

"Not asleep," mumbled a groggy Keg from the tent next to us.

"Well, if y'all would like some hot breakfast sandwiches, I set up a grill about a mile away at the Highway 42 crossing."

Did I want hot breakfast? On a morning that was starting well below freezing, and with the alternative plan being a couple granola bars and instant coffee? That was like asking Pippa to walk to the park. The answer was, of course, an emphatic, "Yes!" But with much less tail wagging.

It's amazing how quickly three people can get dressed, break down camp, and hike out of a campsite when the promise of hot breakfast awaits. That one-mile hike on an empty stomach was more than worth it, though, for the incredible spread that awaited us. Even the lingering knee pain couldn't hold me back. MacGyver, we learned, was an Atlanta native and a thru-hiker who'd completed the trail several years before. Each season since then, he'd pack up his truck with fresh ingredients, a huge double-burner propane stove and friendly demeanor, and head back to the trail for one day to provide trail magic to other thru-hikers. We'd just gotten lucky on it coinciding with our itinerary.

I loaded up my plate with a toasted bagel that was overstuffed with fried eggs, cheese, and turkey sausage. Then, adding a banana and soda, I sat in neatly laid-out folding chairs and listened to an impassioned telling of his thru-hiking journey.

"... I remember how early mountains like Sassafras beat me up, and then I just knew I wanted to give back to others the way so many had given back to me," he concluded.

I grunted through a mouthful of sandwich. It was the same feeling so many other trail angels described, and it was the same feeling that I'd had when I first came across them in Bill Bryson's book.

"Damn, that's inspiring. I'm definitely coming back next year to be a trail angel."

"I'll join you," The Captain said.

"I'm in," Keg added.

That was the thing I was learning about the AT... it could grab you by the feelings and take you for a joy ride along the experience of a lifetime, only increasing your desire for more.

Fueled up and ready for the remaining eight miles of our day, we rejoined the trail, spirits high as the sun traveled farther into the sky and the temperature rose right along with it.

While the previous couple days had seen us walking along sections that were brown and sparsely vegetated, this part of trail was very densely wooded. The trees grew close to the side of the trail, and their waving branches in the gentle breeze brought out a feeling we were the parade they came to cheer on. Leading Keg and The Captain through the winding trail, my spirits soared, and it just felt appropriate to sing a modified rendition of my favorite Bon Jovi song.

"Whoa, we're halfway there. Whoa oh, livin' on a prayer. Take my hand, we'll make it to Lance Creek. Whooooa oh, livin' on a prayer!" I sang, adding in expertly rendered electric guitar noises to ensure my captive audience of two got the full concert effect.

Keg and The Captain groaned, yelling for me to stop, but this plea was suddenly moot when they became my backup vocalists.

We made our merry way along the trail, navigating the frequent switchbacks, until we reached Big Cedar Mountain. I knew this would be a tough one, especially with the current state of our knees, which picked up where they left off last night in reminding us that our bodies were closer to fifty than twenty. But as we began the climb, I realized it was a gentle giant. And the view at the top made the hike up completely worth the effort.

"Wow," I exclaimed as we crested the peak known as Preacher's Rock. An appropriate name for the giant flat rock that overlooked a vista and could turn the shyest public speaker into an outstanding orator.

"Wow," agreed Keg in response.

The rock summit was crowded with people. Some wearing larger backpacks like ours and some with small daypacks. We waited for our turn at the front and released our shoulders from our packs before sitting down. I pulled out my intended lunch for the day—a mixture of cheese sandwich crackers, beef jerky sticks, and dried fruit I affectionally called trail charcuterie—but I just wasn't hungry after MacGyver's breakfast feast. In fact, I hadn't really been all that hungry since the hike started. Spare food was piling up in my bag, but I couldn't bring myself to eat more than what I was already consuming. And given how many calories we were burning, I really thought I'd be desperate for more.

Placing my trail charcuterie back into my pack, I pulled out a peach-flavored Bobo's granola bar instead. At 360 calories, it would at least give me the quick shot of energy needed to make it to tonight's campsite.

Next to me, Keg sighed languorously as he laid back in the warm sun, using his pack as a pillow. "This is the life, gents. A sun-warmed rock, some snacks, and an incredible view."

I looked out over the mountains layered before us, my gaze lingering on row upon row of giant guardians. The brown of the trees on closer ranges gave way to the hazy blue of the distant goliaths. These mountains were mere shadows compared to their Rocky Mountain brothers of the west, but with their gentler rolls and less austere rock faces, they presented a quiet, peaceful contentment I felt resonating in my chest. Keg was right, this really was the life.

8

WE DIDN'T START THE FIRE

Our nine miles for the day stretched behind us by 2 p.m. as we leisurely strolled into Lance Creek Campsite. It had been a much shorter day, but a needed one as we were all feeling the pain from the last two long treks. And tomorrow would bring the grueling death march over Georgia's vicious Blood Mountain to Neel Gap. This was also a strategic camping decision, and one I'd planned for. This was the last official camping area before entering a zone that required bulky bear canisters for overnight food storage—even though we'd yet to see a four-legged native of the area, which didn't mean they weren't around. We didn't have bear canisters, and I knew my knees weren't going to make it eight more miles out of the bear zone, so this remote Lance Creek Campground was the only choice.

It was also a great choice. The campsite was heavenly. I set up my hammock in a clearing and got my gear organized for later that night. Then, realizing the sun was hitting my bed perfectly through an impeccably placed gap in the tree canopy, I decided to pack my rain tarp away and expose my bed to the gentle breeze and bright blue sky. And, with everything prepped to my satisfaction, I laid my head down and stretched my body out into the pool of light for a perfectly set mid-afternoon nap.

Thirty minutes later, I woke refreshed and warmed by the sun. Too content to get up, I scrolled through my phone, reading a text from Dana detailing a hilarious incident with one of her well-known clients who insisted a nurse sleep in the kennel with a new puppy that had to stay overnight at the hospital.

Chuckling, I responded, "*Celebrity pet owners. We won't miss that about LA.*"

Below it was a text from my sister. She'd worked out vacation schedules for the spring and wanted to confirm plans to join me in Virginia for a couple days' hiking with her family.

"*Still on track? Looks like we can meet you in Lexington, VA in a month,*" she'd typed.

"*Sounds like a plan! As long as the Smoky Mountains behave,*" I replied.

A sudden clanking of metal, I recognized immediately as the sound of stove cookware crashing together, made me look up from my phone. I got up, following the sound to another section of this small campsite area. A young man and woman were kneeling next to another small clearing that looked to be a communal kitchen area.

"Gently, gently," came a frustration-tinged exclamation from the guy aimed at the girl.

"I was just laying it down," she exclaimed back, gesturing at the discarded pack on the ground between them. The pack that was adorned with multiple hanging pots and cups.

The man grumbled a response, rummaging in his own bag for something. "Let's get a fire going."

He then held up a tiny flint rod and a Swiss Army knife, like an overzealous Cub Scout leader would use to educate the troop on extreme wilderness survival tactics. The girl's face collapsed into laughter as she crossed her arms over her chest. "Now, this I've gotta see. You think we're going to start a fire with that?!"

"Oh, yeah." He tilted his face up at her from where he now crouched next to a pile of tiny twigs and grass clippings.

She pursed her lips, considering the opportunity to take advantage of the situation, before pushing her glasses back up her nose. "I'll cook dinner for the next week if you can do it."

"Easy money, bet taken. You may as well start prepping tonight's meal now." The man responded without even looking up this time, deep in concentration as he prepared the pile of tinder.

As I sat on a rock, watching in amusement, the girl cleared their packs from the area as the guy gathered tinder and kindling into the tiny teepee structure that all good fires start with. Sticks crunched behind me as Keg and The Captain joined, apparently woken from their own naps by the unfolding scene before us.

"Am I seeing this right? Just some flint and steel to get a campfire started out here?" The Captain whispered before sitting down to join me in pretending to fiddle with our cookware, so as not to appear eavesdropping.

"That's what the guy thinks." I nodded in his direction. "But what I presume is his girlfriend doesn't seem so sure. Even put a sizable wager on it."

"Good thing I brought snacks to the show then," The Captain laughed, pulling some trail mix from his pants pocket. He offered it around to us, and we all sat crunching our way through our dinner appetizer while the determined fellow in front of us attempted to harness the power of fire. Five minutes later, the trail mix had been washed down with some ice-cold spring water, and the teepee was no closer to being ablaze.

The guy's frustration was evidently mounting while the girl's delight was barely being restrained. She sensed victory was imminent. Dusk was starting to draw in by this point, and they hadn't even begun to set up their tent for the incoming night.

"Well, I've seen enough. I think my assistance may be required here," The Captain said, standing and making his way to our food bags. Taking out my tiny bottle of cooking alcohol, he waggled it at us with a wicked grin. Sauntering over to the couple, he stopped a foot short of their stone-cold makeshift fire pit.

"Howdy," he said. "I'm The Captain. You guys seem to be having a little trouble with that fire. Care for some help?"

The guy took his floppy-brimmed sunhat off his head and scratched at the close-cut black hair beneath it. "I watched a dozen videos of this at home. Looked easy enough... seems to work fine for everyone else."

"Looks like you've got the technique down. Maybe you just need some behind-the-scenes prep before filming." The Captain declared and promptly poured out a few glugs of clear liquid onto the sticks. "Try it now."

The guy huffed a short laugh and bent back down low, striking his knife against the flint rod once more. A second later, blue-hued flames licked across the wood, soaring a foot into the air.

"Whoa," the guy shouted, leaping back before he lost some of the magnificent beard that adorned his face.

We all laughed, enjoying the campsite camaraderie being built. But the girlfriend, watching closely, interrupted with a quick laugh of her own. "Ha, looks like I won."

"What?" the guy announced. "No, you didn't. I won."

"How do you figure that?"

"I started the fire, just like I said I would."

"You did not. That guy had to pour lighter fluid on it first."

"Our bet didn't say it had to be *just* the flint and steel."

Her face started to turn red, and I didn't think it was just from the heat of the impressive flames my alcohol had produced. So I thought it might be wise to intervene.

"Hey," I called out, making my way closer to the fire. "Bet or not, that's the start of a great campfire for all of us tonight. What do you say we boil up some water... since I'm now low on stove fuel, thanks to my buddy here."

They both turned from The Captain to me, the dull hiss of

building flames the only sound for an uncomfortably long stretch of time.

"Also," I stumbled in the intensity of their silence, "Have you guys been given trail names yet? I was thinking that Flint—" I pointed to the guy, "and Steel—" I pointed to the girl, "might be a fun way to tell this story in the future. That way, you both win."

The wager results put aside, their faces relaxed, and they smiled at each other.

"Yeah, I like that," Flint said.

"Me, too," Steel added.

"Alright, then, that decides it," I proclaimed with finality, glad the awkward silence was behind us.

We all shook hands, exchanging names like new friends do. Then, suddenly, an excited voice sounded from the semi-darkness outside the circle of light the fire created.

"Guys! Guys!" the voice bellowed. I squinted into the distance to see the source and discovered a familiar face beaming with joy.

"Kyle?!" I jumped up, striding over to him, grabbing his hand, and pulling him in for a hug.

Keg and The Captain joined us, giving their own hugs and excited greetings.

Introductions were made all around again, and we caught up on Kyle's last couple days. He'd found some friends his age to hike with after we left him and had been enjoying their company and trail life since.

"In fact, they're supposed to be camping here tonight. I got a bit ahead of them, but we planned to meet up and spend the night together. Want to keep a lookout for them with me?"

"Sure," Keg, The Captain, and I readily agreed as we followed Kyle back up toward the trailhead. I noticed he was still wearing the same beanie The Captain had thrown at him after our first meeting, and I smiled at this sign of trail generosity. Then it grew bigger as I realized The Captain didn't even know he, not Flower, had actually performed our first act of trail magic.

A couple minutes later, we heard the loud chatter of twenty-somethings as they rounded the corner. They were scavenging the ground for dry firewood and almost missed the side trail to our campsite, finally looking up when Kyle called out.

We all walked back to the fire together, arms laden with extra firewood and dinner supplies, and joined Flint and Steel, who'd finally managed to get their tent up.

"Huevos," one of the girls in the new group yelled out, and Kyle swiveled his head toward her. "Want to share water?"

"Huevos?" I asked Kyle.

He gave us the same wry smile we'd seen at the first meeting. A smile that seemed to speak, *you got me.*

"Yeah, my trail name," he explained. "I was making some hard-boiled eggs the other day, and these guys were impressed how much I loved them, so the name kind of stuck. I love it."

I clapped him on the back, not sure whether to ask where the fresh eggs came from, why it was the Spanish translation, or what he did with the eggshells afterward.

"I love it, too," I said, deciding not to ask anything that would tarnish his joy in the new name.

The night continued in easy conversation as we all huddled around the glowing fire and got to know each other. Steve, a former member of the Australian Royal Navy, and Julia and Rachel, the Vermont college girls, were welcome additions to our campsite. As darkness fell over the clear black sky, Rachel amazed us all with an astronomy lesson, pointing out constellations, naming specific stars, and offering astral navigation instructions as if sailing at sea.

"Here's a fun fact," she said with eager zeal. "Most people think the North Star is the only way to know which direction you're facing at night. But you can actually use any star if you track its movement in the sky over time. If it goes up, you're facing east. If it goes down, west. Cool, right?"

"I've been staring up at the stars from campsites most my life, and I never knew that," I commented, seriously impressed with her knowledge for someone so young. "So, what brought you out on the trail?"

"Julia and I just wanted a break from school. We both felt like we were missing out on life a bit and wanted to live it more physically before going back to books and lectures."

I nodded, understanding the need to experience life outside a classroom. There was only so much that could be taught by observing. Sometimes, one needed to see things for themself.

After more socializing and joking around a much-appreciated campfire, we eventually called it a night. Leaving the circle of campfire heat sent shivers through my body. It didn't take long for me to brush my teeth, change into long underwear, and curl up snugly with a headlamp in the confines of my quilts.

Pulling my phone out, I brought up the WordPress app for my nightly update. The excitement of the day ran along each word I typed. I couldn't wait to share my experiences with those following along. Daily entry completed, I noticed several new comments were waiting for me on previous posts, including one from Edie, the father of the teenager who was supposedly out here at the same time as me: "*Hello Neiman, great start. If you need a shuttle around Neel Gap, look up Brett, my son booked a ride with him.*"

I smiled at this evidence of my community being built, not only in the new group I'd found on the trail, but also in the extended group following me and offering guidance online. I sent a quick response thanking him for the advice. Then, turning my phone off, I listened to the sounds of the campsite settling around me before drifting into a deep, dreamless sleep.

9

AIN'T NO MOUNTAIN HIGH ENOUGH

"Hoarfrost," Rachel declared, holding out her hand to display something that looked like a miniature albino porcupine.

"Hoar what?" I asked, moving closer to see the needle-shaped icicles glistening in the early spring sunshine.

Rachel laughed, something I'd realized since spending the last day with her that she did frequently and easily. "Fun fact... though it looks like quartz, it's actually a crystalline deposit of frozen water vapor that forms on cold mornings. Here, take it."

I held out my hand and Rachel gently dropped it onto my palm. The tiny glasslike sculpture was cold and fragile. I hadn't seen anything like it before.

"That's really cool," I exclaimed, looking back at Rachel, who'd resumed packing her food bag near yesterday's fire ring. "You know... last night's constellation lesson, this morning's hoarfrost knowledge... you really know a lot of fun facts. So I think I have a trail name for you."

"Oh yeah? Let's hear it." The excitement in her voice was hard to hide, so I paused for a little dramatic effect.

"Fun Facts."

Laughter filled the woods, and I knew I had a winner. Julia, overhearing from the nearby clearing where she packed her tent, yelled agreement, "It's perfect! You really are a walking encyclopedia."

"I love it. Thanks."

"Ready to head out?" Steve asked, surveying our group from last night's campsite. We'd decided to hike together today and were almost all packed up. "We've got seven long miles before reaching Neel Gap," he added, pulling his hat over curly black hair. The sun was warming up but still held a chill in the air.

"Yeah, and those miles include all 4,500 feet of Blood Mountain," Steel added.

Fun Facts grinned at me as she strode over. "I'm actually looking forward to it," she admitted, a faint smile curling at her lips' edge. "Perfect day for what I've heard are incredible views."

Even in the short time since meeting Fun Facts, she was already impressing me with her attitude and maturity for someone so young. On paper, Blood Mountain looked painful, and I'd heard many hikers call it quits at Neel Gap because of how unexpectedly tough they'd found it. Fun Facts, though, was looking at elevation gain and seeing the reward it would bring—and from what I knew of her, she wasn't speaking naively.

I decided to fold my attitude in with hers, embracing whatever Blood Mountain would bring. I jumped up from where I sat on the ground... only to feel the now familiar sharp pain from tendons behind my right knee.

A protracted grunt escaped as I hopped onto my left leg.

Fun Facts immediately stretched her hand as balance, and I gratefully took it.

"You okay?" she asked, full of motherly concern.

"Yep," I winced and gingerly placed my right foot down. It was still tender, but the pain was tolerable enough to keep hiking.

"When we get to Neel Gap, you should look for something to support that knee," Fun Facts advised.

"Yeah, it's an old sports injury. Tore my ACL in my more youthful days. I planned on packing a knee brace but cut it last minute. Was hoping to rely on willpower to manage any pain and avoid carrying a heavy neoprene sleeve," I replied, noting I was walking with a slight limp.

"They make these thin ones that go under the kneecap and hold your patellar tendon in place. You'd be surprised how much support it gives."

"Might have to try that." I zipped up my Patagonia sweatshirt, pulling the hood up for extra warmth before following the group back onto the main trail toward Blood Mountain.

"Well, that wasn't so bad," The Captain announced as we crested Blood Mountain's top a couple hours later.

And it actually hadn't been. Perhaps because it was all we had today, or because the view from the top was so stunning you forgot everything before, but the hike had been enjoyable rather than something to endure. The uninterrupted blue of sunlit sky topped a magnificent view of mountain ridgelines. In the distance we could even make out downtown Atlanta's skyscrapers, which from this 60-mile distance could have been mistaken for a mirage—both from its faded gray haze and how out of place concrete buildings now felt from trail life.

"I've got to call my parents," I told The Captain. "It's their anniversary, and Dad won't want to miss this."

"Hey, Pride," Dad's familiar greeting rang out as he answered the video call.

"Hey, Dad. Is Mom with you?"

"Reading upstairs, I think. Hang on."

Dad disappeared from the screen, and I happily surveyed the view in the couple of minutes it took to find her.

"Happy anniversary!" I announced when both faces returned.

"Oh, Michael. You remembered." My mom's face was suffused with joy.

"Of course, and I wanted to tell you in style. Check this out." I spun the phone around until the screen filled with mountains and sky.

"Wow," I heard chorused.

"Where are you, son?" Dad asked.

"Still in Georgia, it's called Blood Mountain. We're heading down to Neel Gap after this, then I booked a nearby cabin for tonight." I turned the phone again so they could see my face. "Think I might need something to aid my knee. It's been bothering me again."

"Happens to the best of us, Pride. You're no spring chicken!" Dad chortled at his joke while my mom swatted him.

"He's not that old, Tom."

I laughed. "Dad's right, Mom. Time to compromise on some gear for this old rooster. I've got a long way to go."

"Speaking of which, I've been thinking about my gear..."

"When are you not thinking about gear, Dad?" I interrupted, mouth turning up mischievously.

"Ok, you got me there, Pride," Dad chuckled before continuing. "My REI rebate just came in, and I was thinking about that titanium kettle I've had my eye on. What do you think about hot tea with breakfast when I join you?"

I thought back to the morning's instant coffee and handful of almonds. It was all the energy I could muster in the frigid 30-degree air. I couldn't imagine waiting for a teapot to boil, let alone a teabag to steep. But then again, by the time Dad joined, early morning temperatures should be more agreeable for sitting and waiting.

Bringing myself back, I said, "If it brings you joy, Dad, put it on the packing list."

I said goodbye and hung up, heading back to the others, who were all capturing evidence of our Blood Mountain summit on their phone cameras. Downhill was welcome after so much up, being easier on the lungs, but my knee protested under my pack's weight at each step. I was ready to take the literal load off.

A few miles later, Neel Gap was a welcome sight. It was the first road crossing after Blood Mountain and was appreciated in the thru-hiker community for its expansive but expensive outfitter, Mountain Crossings. The gear was typically high quality, and with the offer to perform free pack shakedowns to help shed weight, replace items, and spend future children's college funds, many hikers were drawn into its illuminated aisles. And a refrigerator stocked with cold sodas and frozen pizzas, both worthy rewards after days of hard hiking, didn't hurt sales either.

"Poles," the sales assistant said, one hand holding a Mueller's knee brace, the other gesturing toward a small selection of hiking poles around the corner. "The knee strap will definitely help with pain you're already in, but poles are going to stop you doing more damage to those overworked ligaments."

I sighed. There was that word again, the one I'd scoffingly dismissed when every hiker and their mother recommended them. But after three days of increasingly unbearable knee pain, I was willing to eat some humble pie if it helped me stay in the game and on the trail. I handed over my credit card in exchange for the knee brace and a pair of LEKI hiking poles. $150 lighter, I headed out where Keg and The Captain sat waiting. Their time hiking the AT ended here, not needing Mountain Crossings' shiny offerings, so opted to sit barefoot in the sun while I dipped into my savings.

"What are those?" The Captain asked, pointing at the black-and-white sticks that really couldn't be mistaken for anything but what they were. "Are they...?"

"Yes," I confirmed, handing them over for inspection as I propped my leg up on a rock wall. I rolled my pant leg up and positioned the thin knee strap under my kneecap, exactly where Fun Facts had indicated and modeling in the shop. I tried a few steps, sighing happily at the immediate difference I felt.

"I thought you said..." The Captain began, eyes wide with shock, and readying what I could only assume was a joke at my expense.

"Yep," I repeated, shaking my head at his predicted reaction.

"I guess he changed his mind?" Keg asked, always the calm negotiator in our trio.

"I guess he changed his mind." The Captain replied.

"I think my knee changed my mind for me," I clarified. "I've got a lot more days, miles, and brutal terrains to conquer, and I don't want to be forced home because my knees have twice the wear and tear of everyone else I'm hiking with."

"Fair enough," The Captain conceded, handing back the poles. "Just never thought I'd see the day."

"If it makes you feel better, they're women's poles," I said with a hint of joy in my voice. "They weigh an ounce less and pack shorter for hands-free scrambling."

"Good thing no one else heard you say that with so much excitement." The Captain gave a short laugh. "Or Women's Poles might be your new trail name, whether you like it or not!"

Before I could think of a suitable retort, Keg groaned, stretching his arms over his head. "Well, I don't know about you, but I'm ready for a real bed tonight," he started, then paused and sniffed, nose crinkling at the smell. Moving closer to his left armpit, he quickly pulled back, dropping his arms, "And a shower. Jesus, I stink."

Laughter filled the air. We all knew too well the familiar foe of backpacker B.O. But then a thought hit me. I did a surreptitious sniff of my own pits. Nope, nothing. After three days of hiking, I really didn't smell anything bad.

"You know, I think I smell pretty good, all things considered. This new Merino wool really works wonders," I informed them.

In planning, I'd debated the splurge for this popular but expensive hiking shirt material, originally thinking a polyester T-shirt would do just fine instead. But the sheer mountain of positive reviews for its odor-resistant feature swayed me. I caved when I saw one in orange. And now I was glad because walking around not reeking of stink was a different feeling, and simply amazing.

"You guys ready to head to our cabin? A friend gave me the name of a nearby shuttle driver we can call." I made a mental note to thank Edie for yesterday's tip in tonight's blog.

"Sure am," The Captain confirmed.

While waiting for our ride, the rest of the group emerged from Mountain Crossings, carrying packages of their own. Huevos brought up the rear, a huge grin across his face as he smoothed down a bright green rain jacket.

I whistled appreciatively as he joined us. "Huevos," I exclaimed, walking a full circle around him. "That's a sweet jacket."

"Thanks, man! I got the full shakedown in there." Then his voice sank before adding, "They threw out my solar charger."

"Oh yeah?" I responded.

Huevos's face shadowed as he stroked the fuzz lightly covering his unshaven upper lip. "They said it was an unnecessary weight. I guess they're right... but it was cool, right?" He looked up, eyes filled with hope I'd affirm his decision to include the extra weight on a fun but useless item.

I clapped his shoulder, gripping it firmly. "It's hard letting go of things we love, but you made the right decision today."

"I do feel lighter," he said, a complete smile returning.

I smiled back before turning to the other. "The Captain, Keg, and I are heading to a place called Misty Mountain Inn for their last night. You guys still planning on staying in the bunkhouse here?"

Steve, taking charge, answered, "That's still the plan. Want to meet back here in the morning and hike together?"

With nods of approval all around, our plans were set, and we said goodbye for the night. I was content missing out on sleeping with the rest of the group in the cheap bunkhouse attached to Mountain Crossings. I knew extra comfort was waiting for us at the private lodging I'd already booked just a short drive up the road.

I wanted to celebrate Keg and The Captain's final night in style, and Misty Mountain Inn certainly achieved that. It was a picturesque mountain B&B with a main lodge and several small cabins. They did our laundry and drove us to town for food and beer —both consumed heavily. It felt amazing stretching out on a real mattress in a wonderfully warm cabin, and for the first night on the AT, none of us uttered a single complaint.

After our shuttle back to Neel Gap the next morning, it was time for The Captain and Keg to return to the real world. Hugs and heartfelt goodbyes complete, I rejoined the crew from yesterday now waiting for me. Steve, Julia, Fun Facts, and Huevos were quickly becoming the tramily I'd envisioned in early planning stages. I was excited to continue our AT adventures together, ready for this next section of the trail that would bring some big firsts, welcomed highs, and some unexpected lows.

10

A CHANGE WILL DO YOU GOOD

As we wound our way through the trees that day, I caught glimpses of windswept clouds chasing each other across the sky.

Fun Facts, who had joined me on a wider section of trail, noticed my gaze and pointed up through the canopy. "Clouds like that mean the weather is changing."

Huevos turned, having heard us, and offered his phone. "Check this out."

It was open to the radar on his weather app, revealing a thick band of dark green that signaled a significant amount of rain heading our way. The tops of the storm were tinged with the blue of snow, and I was suddenly grateful that I'd decided to wear my long underwear that morning.

I eyed Huevos's new rain jacket, relieved that his pack shakedown meant he was now better prepared for the freezing rain this storm would bring.

"Looks like it's supposed to hit later tonight, so if we stay on pace, we should reach Low Gap Shelter before it begins," I noted, handing back his phone and retrieving my own from my hip belt pocket. "I think it might be time to ramp up the motivational tunes."

I hit play on a Disney playlist, shuffling to feel-good songs that immediately had everyone singing along. Julia, who earlier in the day had received her trail name of Jukebox, dropped back to join Fun Facts, Huevos, and me. Glowing with delight, she immediately joined in singing the familiar *Frozen* and *Lion King* lyrics, proving how fitting her new name was.

As the day's 11 miles accumulated behind us, I was amazed at the difference I felt almost immediately. Where knee pain had been a constant concern, it was now just a slight ache of strengthening muscles. The knee strap was doing precisely what Fun Facts had said, perfectly supporting my ligaments and kneecap. But I was ready to admit the real heroes were the hiking poles. Why had I resisted them for so long? They were a game-changer in distributing the thirty pounds on my back, handling work that my knees had been doing. By the time we reached Low Gap Shelter, I felt like a new man.

After sharing a campfire-popped bucket of popcorn Huevos had bought at Mountain Crossings, we all happily dove into the warm comfort of our sleeping arrangements. Most of the group opted for the shelter as rain was already lightly covering the ground. Not eager to sleep on the ground, I'd set up my hammock under my rain tarp, and sleep rolled in easily as I listened to the gentle patter of raindrops on nylon above me.

As the night wore on, that gentle patter turned into heavy battering. By morning, everything outside my hammock was drenched. We packed up in the rain, sparing little thought for anything else like breakfast or small talk. The temperature hovered around 40 degrees, which made progress slow as I worked with various ties and zips with stiff fingers. We hiked out of camp in a foggy downpour, everything swaddled in rain gear.

The reduced circle of vision my rain jacket allowed, along with the thick fog and rain, made conversation difficult. I found my thoughts drifting introspectively. It had been almost a week since I'd seen Dana, and I felt a pang of sadness not knowing the daily details of her life. I let myself fall behind the group as I called her, hoping to catch her on the drive to work.

"Hey, stranger," I joked when she picked up.

"Hey, hon. Where are you? You sound muffled," she responded.

"On the trail, but it's pouring and I've got my hood pulled up over the phone."

"Rain again?" she exclaimed incredulously. Then tentatively, "So, how's it going?"

I launched into tales of the new friends I'd made and the tension the onslaught of rain was laying on my shoulders. Then she caught me up on her hectic schedule with demanding clients and late-night studies.

Hanging up after our brief check-in, I studied the phone in my hand. The conversation between us had been such a contrast. We were both dealing with new stress in our lives, but Dana's was mental and human-centric, while mine was physical and nature-induced. It was tough to relate to, and difficult to provide any real comfort to each other where needed.

I stashed my phone away from the incessant rain, ready to refocus on the trail ahead. And then I realized there was no one and nothing in sight. Just cold, wet fog as far as I could see—which was about 20 feet. I scanned through the trees, hoping for a glimpse of bright colors from the tramily's bouncing backpacks. Nothing but brown greeted me. For the first time, I was alone on the trail. The irony of it happening while talking to the one person most concerned about me being alone wasn't lost on me. But there was nothing to do except move forward. Planting my feet and poles firmly, I quickened my pace, hoping to catch the others.

Three and a half hours later, I pulled up to Blue Mountain shelter, shucking off sodden gloves that turned out were not as waterproof as advertised. The plan had been 15 miles to Tray

Mountain Shelter, but with my partially frozen appendages, I was already rethinking anything closer.

"Neiman!" a familiar voice called out. I looked up from my sore red fingers to see Steve waving from the shelter's porch. The others framed him, faces hazy through billowing steam emitting from the metal cups they each held.

"You have no idea how happy I am to see you guys!" I said, walking over to the porch. "I thought I'd have to hike alone in this crap all day."

"Want some hot Gatorade?" Fun Facts asked as I loped up the shelter steps.

She offered her cup, which was indeed filled with the piping-hot blue sports drink. I sipped tentatively, then groaned at the pleasure this curious and steamy drink brought to my frigid lips.

"Good, right?" Steve laughed, seeing my face.

"This is the *best* Gatorade I've ever had," I confirmed, only lifting my mouth long enough to speak.

Fun Facts's smile spread wide as she reached for the cup. "Yeah, it's the ultimate cold-weather hydration technique. We used this trick at cross-country races in high school."

My fingers and innards finally warmed as I drained the last sips, and I suddenly felt just how wet I truly was. And it wasn't all from rain. My suspicions from earlier that week were confirmed when I unzipped my rain jacket—yes, it was just as good at keeping sweat in as rainwater out.

While I ruminated on my nonventilated jacket, Steve was forming a coalition. I tuned in to the conversation when I faintly heard the words "beer" and "burger."

"I think staying on the trail tonight could be bad, like hypothermia bad," Steve finished.

Hypothermia was a very real concern for thru-hikers, and the toll this weather had taken on our bodies in just one morning foreshadowed what three days in freezing rain could do next. But, with the Gatorade warming my insides, I felt a resurgent energy to go for the initial 15-mile goal. And stopping now would mean a much longer hike to the Top of Georgia Hostel, which I needed to reach tomorrow night if I was going to keep my prebooked reservation. In fact, that hike would be the longest day so far, and with my knee's recent turnaround still fresh, I wanted a pace my body could handle.

"I think we can make it," I added, every head turning to face me. "Sure it's miserable, but we only have about five or six more miles to Tray Mountain Shelter."

"Just five or six?" Fun Facts asked, echoing my thoughts, "With another cup of Gatorade, I think I could handle that."

"It's eight miles," Steve amended, jabbing a thumb toward the wall of rain and fog. "And that's going to quickly wipe out any warmth this rest stop has given you." He turned to the group. "Let's vote. Eight more miles to Tray Mountain Shelter, or two miles to Unicoi Gap and a motel for the night?"

Fun Facts and I lifted our hands for Tray Mountain Shelter, but Huevos, Jukebox, and Steve decided getting off trail was a better plan. And with the combination of wet gear and low spirits, I couldn't argue further.

Unicoi Gap was a common shuttle pickup spot, given the large trail town of Hiawassee nearby with motels, restaurants, and convenience stores. It would let us dry out and refuel in comfort before hitting the trail for tomorrow's long day.

While Fun Facts called around for reservations and Steve booked a shuttle van, I took the opportunity to mentally switch away from today's goal and review tomorrow's now-longer agenda. I wanted what was best for the group, which was taking it slow—but I couldn't let prioritizing comfort get too far in the way of my itinerary.

"Last night was awesome," Huevos noted, pulling the beanie down over his mop of brown hair. It was a disheveled style I now realized was a permanent feature. We stood back at Unicoi Gap, at the beginning of our 17-mile hike, about two hours later than originally planned.

The night before, we'd pulled into Hiawassee's Budget Inn dripping wet and frozen to the core, only to be greeted by a large gathering of thru-hikers who'd shared our same thoughts on more hiking. It didn't take long to exchange wet clothes for warm blankets and enter animated discussions on various equipment wins and woes.

Several hours and a few adult beverages later, we had embraced the camaraderie and all thoughts of getting to the trail for an early start evaporated.

I opened my mouth to respond, but a spectacular face-stretching yawn appeared instead. We were all bleary-eyed and low on energy, but anticipation of our last full day before reaching North Carolina got our feet moving. And what a day it was.

We hiked in cold but bright sunshine, surrounded by the silent watch-folk of the woods. Sometimes, our conversation and singing rang out through branches that each day unveiled a little more green. At other times, only the crunch of leaves and the swish of water-repellent nylon accompanied each step.

After the first few miles, we encountered another trail angel offering coffee and hot cocoa on the side of a road. It was hard not to feel spoiled by Georgia's southern hospitality. As we made more miles, I began to hear a rushing sound of water to the left. Curious, I waved the others on to investigate. A strategy I'd come to appreciate when hiking with a group was to hike together but in your own way —each taking breaks when needed, knowing that eventually the day would close at the same endpoint.

A few steps into the foliage of some rhododendron bushes, I spotted the source and almost burst out laughing. A small creek had met a rock outcropping's edge and was falling about two feet onto the rocks below. Georgia's smallest waterfall. To add to the experience, some creative soul had erected a tiny sign on a stick beside it. Carved into a piece of wood were the words "Carnes Cascade." I supposed that naming the creek's downward trajectory made it official. A miniature bench, just 6-by-12 inches, sat nearby, allowing me to sit and experience what living in a hobbit's world might feel like.

After enjoying the peaceful solitude for a few minutes, I hit the trail to catch up with the tramily. Soon I saw Jukebox's green backpack bobbing ahead. As I joined her and Huevos, trees began to stretch over our heads, forming a tunnel of the canopy. I looked up, captivated by the twisted, weaving boughs, and felt a sharp pain shoot from my right foot's arch up my leg.

"Ow," I muttered quietly, not wanting to alarm the others.

I wondered if my brace had somehow displaced knee pain to a new location, but that was quickly disproved when my left foot planted to the same feeling.

"Oof," I muttered again. I had never experienced this type of pain before and wanted to figure out what was going on before bringing anyone else in. Maybe it would ease up with more walking. We were reaching the day's last couple miles, so I knew my feet were tired. The pain, like shooting pins and needles, continued through the sixteenth mile into our seventeenth. Then suddenly, it disappeared, replaced by complete numbness. Willpower had pushed me through the pain, but to what effect? Each step became sloppy as I lost my dexterity and feeling.

Concern growing, I called out, "Um, anyone else's feet doing weird things?"

Heads swiveled as they turned to survey me.

"Weird things?" Fun Facts asked, brow furrowed as she looked at my feet.

"Yeah, like shooting pains or going numb?"

"Oh," Steve laughed, understanding dawning. "You've got drunk feet, man."

"Drunk... feet?" I asked, unsure I'd heard correctly.

"Yep, that's what I call it. When your brain shuts off recognition, but your legs keep going." He slowed to walk beside me, watching me plant my feet. "You'll have to take each step more carefully because you don't have much reaction time right now. Step wrong with drunk feet, you're much more likely to trip, stumble, roll an ankle... that kind of thing."

I looked over wide-eyed. I'd done a lot of hiking, but this was definitely something new. And rolling an ankle was an injury no hiker wanted. After the first roll, it becomes weak, bound to keep happening—hopefully without permanent, hike-ending damage.

With my attention focused on firmly planting feet at each step, we soon reached Dicks Creek Gap. We still had half a mile along a side road to reach the hostel, but I was grateful for flat ground and not a trail strewn with exposed roots and hidden rocks.

"This goes up to the Top of Georgia Hostel. It's probably full, but I pre-booked a reservation for two. Anyone want the other bed?" As I said it, I looked at Jukebox. I'd watched her stay at the group's back most of today, sometimes falling far enough behind with her slower pace that she was gone an hour or more before catching back up at snack breaks. She had a quiet demeanor not given to complaining, but I'd caught enough grimaces to know she wasn't comfortable. My offer came from a parental feeling that she needed a roof over her head most.

She glanced at Fun Facts, who nodded enthusiastically. "You should go. I'll be good with these guys." She thumbed at Huevos and Steve, who gave their own confirming nods. "We'll stealth camp here at the junction, hidden in the woods and out of the wind."

With a plan to meet at Dicks Creek Gap the next morning, Jukebox and I meandered to the quaint and very welcome sight of the Top of Georgia Hostel.

11

COLD AS ICE

"*The first week is officially complete,*" I wrote on the blog that night. "*In the past seven days, I've hiked 69 miles. A little over 3% down, and much more to come.*"

I pulled a pomegranate-flavored Clif Bar from the maildrop box I'd collected from the hostel staff. This was the first box Dana had mailed, and the system had worked perfectly. I was a little anxious opening it, unsure if the contents would arrive unscathed. But the food was just as I'd packed it. This box would last me four days until I resupply again at an upcoming general store.

I munched through the Clif Bar, listening to the sounds of twenty other hikers organizing gear for the night. It created a cozy, rustling atmosphere, even though the hostel itself was huge. Scrolling to comments on my previous blog posts, I sat up straighter at the name that appeared.

"*Hello, Neiman. This is Flower, your first trail angel from way back at mile 12! A friend who section hikes told me about a great blog she started reading last week and said I should check it out. Imagine my surprise when I did and saw you and your trail buddies! Can't wait to hear about North Carolina and beyond.*" I grinned widely at her presence in my corner of the internet, but also because a stranger thought my blog was worth sharing.

"Flower! Our day 2 hero. I'm so glad you found your way here, and thanks again for your generosity," I replied. That had only been days ago, but it felt much longer with everything I'd achieved since.

I stretched out on my bunk, sharing a small room with Jukebox and two strangers, enjoying the feel of dry clothes and soft surfaces. My legs ached and my feet needed a pickleball massage, but at least warmth had returned to my limbs. Tomorrow would be a short 4.5 miles to Plumorchard Shelter, the first after meeting the others at Dicks Creek Gap. I didn't need a full day off—a zero day as hikers call it—but given how beaten up I felt, a nero day (nearly zero miles) felt like a moment of planning genius all those months ago.

The next morning, Jukebox and I made our way back to the tramily. It was cold, so we bundled in all our layers, though the bright spring sun slowly warmed our faces as it ascended. We stepped back onto the trail and quickly reunited with Huevos, Fun Facts, and Steve, who were waiting for us.

"How was stealth camping?" I asked, scanning the three of them and noting stiffness in their movements.

"Cold," Huevos confirmed.

I grunted my commiseration, not sure I had anything to add after a warm night in a hostel bed.

"Let's get moving," Steve added. "I need to get blood flowing to my extremities."

I nodded. Trees blocked the sun's full warmth, and the resulting chill wove through our layers and limbs. The only remedy was hiking, which would get warm blood pumping.

The temperature continued dropping as we set out. Clouds covered what little sun made it through the foliage, and snowflakes began falling, landing on our eyelashes and sticking to cheeks painted red from cold. Beautiful as it was, it made the walk feel so much colder. After not too long, we were grateful to see the wooden sign etched with "Plumorchard Gap," and even more thankful for the one next to it indicating the nearby shelter. We dumped our packs onto the raised ledge at the entrance and immediately set about gathering firewood for the blazing inferno we'd make in the campsite's steel fire pit.

I pulled a log into the circle of warmth as a seat, setting down the stove and food I'd retrieved from my pack.

"Did you know twenty-five percent of thru-hikers quit before finishing Georgia?" I asked the group as I prepped my stove for dinner.

"Who's the one with fun facts now?" Fun Facts teased.

"Maybe we should call you Fun Stats?" Steve added, looking for a laugh but getting none as all focused on their dinner prep.

"I do love a good stat, but we can do better," I replied before Fun Stats could become a thing.

I turned back to the task at hand, falling quiet as gnawing hunger distracted me from the quiet conversation around me. The water was again taking longer to boil than my patience could stand. There was always talk in the hiking world about "hiker hunger," a stage of calorie deficiency where your brain tells you to cover everything in peanut butter and devour three days of rations at once. It kicks in when your body has burned through its fat reserves and starts to go after muscle. A typical hiker walking 15 miles a day can expect to burn between 5,000 and 6,000 calories. To stay on track physically and mentally, I needed to put that same amount back in.

But my daily calorie intake was still limited. I wasn't all that hungry and had eaten maybe half my pack's food so far, most of that being whatever I could grab quickest. The breakfast planned for week one was granola, powdered milk, dehydrated strawberries, and almonds. But when time came to prepare the meal, it had usually become just almonds. Coffee was still a staple, but that was all I could muster energy for in 30-degree mornings. Snacking on bars or trail mix worked best during the day, with only a subtle increase for lunch.

The exception was dinner. Each night, I was excited for a hot meal, so sitting around the campfire, waiting for water to boil in the extreme cold, while feeling the day's large calorie deficit, was becoming increasingly frustrating.

I muttered at my stove as the flame burned merrily. Words alternated between cajoling encouragement and curses carried on the wings of what was less hiker hunger and more hiker hanger—that unpleasant combination of tortured hunger and frustrating anger.

I pulled out a small bag of corn chips, my hors d'oeuvres to today's fancy freeze-dried dinner. Minutes later, chips gone, steam finally swirled from the pot of water. I knew I needed to wait for the bubbles to appear, but the hanger won out. I dumped the contents of my pasta primavera recipe into the water, already accepting another crunchy meal. When I loaded up my spork and took a bite, I expected the worst... but the extra al dente wasn't too bad.

"Setting up your hammock tonight?" Steve asked. "Looks like another cold one. Down to 15 degrees overnight."

"No," I responded, eyeing the shelter's loft area, theoretically away from the cold winds' reach. "I'll join you guys in the shelter. My quilts are only rated to 20 degrees, but maybe with joint body heat, we'll all be warmer."

"We can add a windbreak in front to help. I have a tarp," Fun Facts said.

Dinner complete, we set up sleeping arrangements for the night and filled the shelter loft with bodies. The girls cuddled on one side with Steve, Huevos, and me on the other. For insulation on extra-cold nights, I'd packed a lightweight foam sleeping pad. Not more than half an inch thick, but enough to fend off freezing wind gusts. But the closed-cell foam on the stiff shelter floor felt decidedly different than nestled between feathery quilts in my hammock. The thin layer of freezing plywood didn't help either. I spent several minutes shifting positions to find one that didn't feel like sleeping on a cold, hard wooden plank.

"You okay there, Neiman?" Huevos asked from his sleeping bag. I looked at the thin sliver of eyes, all that was visible, as the rest of his face was tucked deep inside his mummy bag.

"Yeah, just getting situated. I didn't really pack for ground comfort."

"Sleeping in the shelters wasn't part of your plan?"

"Not exactly," I confirmed, shifting again and deciding that starting on my back might be the only option. I pulled my hat farther down over my ears from where it had slid up in all my squirming. I was sleeping in all my clothes, as we all were, unwilling to remove any layers in the frigid temperatures.

"My fingers are frozen," Steve groaned from Huevos's other side. "These gloves are useless." I could see him holding up his hands in the dim light. "What if I get frostbite overnight? It's definitely cold enough." A few seconds of silence lingered after the question before Steve spoke again, "They'll have to amputate... I don't want nubs for fingers!"

Raucous laughter filled the shelter at Steve's exclamation, though the panic in his voice made us wonder if he meant it as a joke.

"Just keep them tucked into your... warmest area," I advised vaguely, trying to be sensitive to present company.

"Sleep with my hands in my crotch?" Steve asked, apparently having no such qualms.

Another round of laughter ensued while Huevos sighed, clearly implying he also took the advice.

We began to settle into pre-sleep quiet when a thought came to me. "Nubs," I said just loud enough for everyone to hear.

"What?" Steve asked, confusion drawing out his tone.

"Your trail name. It should be Nubs." I whispered. Verbal mumbles of agreement immediately sounded around the shelter.

"Nubs, huh?" Steve muttered. "Alright, Neiman. I like it. You know, that just leaves you. Still not feeling Fun Stats?"

"Nah," I confirmed, yawning. "But I'm sure you guys will come up with something."

Sleep that night was difficult. I couldn't get warm, comfortable, or the deep rest my body needed. I kept shifting, waking as cold thrust itself into new openings of my quilt cocoon. Then, trying to find a softer area on hard ground again, I'd balance whatever comfort I could find with minimal movements to contain the insulated heat my body desperately craved.

Dawn came early and bright, sun breaking through weathered cracks in the shelter's wood siding. I opened bleary eyes. Something pink was an inch from my nose. I blinked and then wished I hadn't when Huevos's face came into view. His eyes opened simultaneously, and we exchanged startled glances before I scooted backward in a noisy swish of sleeping bag against pad.

"Uh, good morning," I murmured awkwardly.

"Yeah, uh, right," Huevos responded in an equally awkward tone.

Now several inches away, I sat up to see the others doing the same. Mirrored in the tramily's heavy-lidded eyes was the sleep-deprived weariness I felt. No one looked rested or eager to leave comparably warm sleeping bags, but we all knew we had to get moving.

"How are your fingers, Nubs?" I teased.

He grinned sheepishly, wiggling them inside his gloves. "Still got all ten."

"Good to hear. That was by far the coldest night yet. I'd bet single digits," I replied, finally pulling myself from my quilt and peeling back the tarp we'd slung over the entrance. Snow dusted the ground outside, and a bitter wind blew through the gap I'd made.

"Hey, Huevos," I called over my shoulder. "Is that your water bottle on the picnic table?"

"Sure is," Huevos said, leaning to peer under my arm.

"I hope you like your water ice cold." I pulled on my boots and retrieved the bottle, showing him its contents. The bottle was frozen solid.

"Man, that's crazy," Huevos said, taking it to inspect closer. "I guess I should've slept with it in my bag."

"Neiman knows somewhere warm you can defrost that," Nubs commented, his blue eyes crinkled in mischief.

I shook my head, smiling. It might be below freezing, and I might've been crazy starting this hike so early, knowing most people wait until April. But I was glad my timing had coincided with this tramily, as it was certainly making for an entertaining adventure.

The day slowly warmed to a balmy 40 degrees as we crossed our first border and made our way into North Carolina by late morning. Layers of clothing were removed but quickly replaced when we began climbing Standing Indian Mountain. Even though uphill hiking was intense cardio, it was becoming easier on my body than downhill. My Achilles took pressure on the ups, whereas downhill pushed it forward to my fragile knees and ankles. Staying upright was also significantly easier going up, especially with my new poles distributing weight to more ground points. By the end of 12 miles, we'd climbed partway up the 5,500 feet of total elevation needed to reach Standing Indian's peak—our biggest achievement so far, and the highest peak before Great Smoky Mountains National Park.

Our accommodation that night was Standing Indian Shelter. I pulled out my hammock, having decided earlier that if I was going to freeze to death on a hard shelter floor, I might as well freeze to death in my much softer hammock. Plus, I wouldn't wake with my face in someone's nose.

I was rigging my hammock between two perfectly spaced trees with strong roots, pulling the straps tight around a trunk, when I heard the crunch of frozen leaves behind me. I swung around at the sound, fingers stilled mid-knot. Nubs and Fun Facts stood behind me, and from their glances at each other, I could tell they wanted to run something past me.

"What's up?" I asked, attaching the loop of my hammock's end to the strap, and sat to test the angle of its hang.

"We know you have a plan to get to the NOC in a few days," Fun Facts started.

"I do," I confirmed.

"But we're wondering if you'd be up for stopping by Franklin first. We could really use a resupply," she finished.

"And the weather looks terrible," Nubs added, showing me his phone's forecast for the coming days. Each picture showed rain or snow, with one day showing both under the same cloud.

"Ugh," I exclaimed. "That looks miserable. I'm seriously questioning why I started in March."

I didn't want to stop progress again and get off track from my plan. I was on a tight schedule, needing to complete the trail by August so Dana and I could move back east. There was also a wedding she and I planned to attend in June, costing me more days traveling off and back onto the trail. But it would've taken three tough 16-mile days to reach the Nantahala Outdoor Center, affectionately known as the NOC. With snow and rain factored in, covering that distance felt dangerous. And I'd already discovered how long days hiking Appalachia in rain sucked.

A memory of Dad's blog comment a couple days earlier jumped into my head. *"There is no one way to hike. Your brain might be saying, 'I've got to get to the top of the pass,' but your body responds with, 'Screw you, brain.' Sometimes there are no shortcuts, and you have to go with what's presented before you."*

"Alright," I agreed, handing back Nubs's phone. "Franklin it is."

Nubs and Fun Facts grinned, and our plans were settled.

12

FEELING GROOVY

Turns out, rain is a great motivator. With impending showers threatening, we woke early, stepping onto the trail at 8 a.m. to get as far as possible before rain hit. Our shelter options were 7.5 and 16 miles away. We'd decided over breakfast to press for the latter, but all agreed to settle for a short day if needed.

We readied ourselves and our gear for rain and set off along the trail in a line of rainbow-hued backpack covers. At first, the storm was supposed to hit at 9 a.m., but as we hiked the final miles up the side of Standing Indian, we remained dry. The meandering set of switchbacks, where the trail zigzags up or down the mountain, helping to make easy work of elevation changes. With still-dry ground ahead, I found myself settling into a contented rhythm. I was also grateful to the people of North Carolina for making such elegant trail designs that include those switchbacks, something Georgia noticeably lacked.

By mid-morning, we stood atop Standing Indian, munching on snack bars and taking in the beautiful mountain vista in every direction.

"Is that Clingmans Dome?" Fun Facts asked, removing one hand from braiding her shoulder-length blond hair to point at the furthest line of peaks.

I squinted in her direction. Low clouds sifted through the mountains, making it difficult to distinguish the distinct flat-topped shape of the AT's highest peak.

"Right there," Fun Facts announced as clouds partially cleared. "See that tall flat area between those two pointed ridges?"

"I see it," I exclaimed. Even though it was still 100 miles away from us, the level top sloping down on one side gave it the appearance of a perfect ski run. It stood monolithic above everything else. "That'll be an awesome climb," I added, shaking my head slowly.

"Sure will," Fun Facts confirmed, smiling hugely.

I laughed quickly. Fun Facts reminded me of The Captain, always up for a challenge.

"Looks like rain will hit around 1 p.m. now," Jukebox said quietly. She flipped her phone to show the wall of rain on its screen.

"Better get moving," I grunted, standing and settling my pack into place.

We fell quickly into our familiar hiking formation, with me or Nubs leading, accompanied by Fun Facts, while Jukebox and Huevos took turns as caboose. Around fourteen miles, the predicted rain still hadn't reached us, and the trail started ascending again. We'd reached Albert Mountain and its steadily rising 600-foot climb. We were making good time, so slowing to accommodate the second uphill jaunt added no pressure.

I was whistling along to The Beatles' classic "Here Comes the Sun," admiring the perfect triangles I made with my poles and feet when Nubs's sky-blue pack cover appeared in front of me.

"Whoooaaa," I said, elongating the word like a rider stopping his horse.

Peering around my back, Fun Facts had also stopped just before running into me.

"Uh... what's going on?" I tentatively asked.

Nubs lifted a pole and gestured at dozens of steps leading to a wall of rock. I could see the white blaze painted on a tree trunk at the base, and another distinctive white slash on the rock face above.

"Does that blaze up there mean we have to..." Fun Facts trailed off.

"Climb the rock?" I finished. "Sure does."

"Right," she replied, and I heard the hesitation in her voice.

This was an unexpected turn of events for any hiker who, unlike me, hadn't researched each individual mile of the trail before stepping foot on it, and I knew I needed to be the voice of reassurance.

"I know you love a challenge," I gently teased, elbowing Fun Facts's arm. "And this is a really good one."

She looked over, blue eyes that had been concerned now crinkling at the edges as she straightened. "You're right. We've got this!"

I took the lead, climbing thick logs pounded into dirt and pinned in place by smaller posts as steps. It didn't take long to reach the rock wall, whose top was made less visible from the dense fog dropping over it. Now closer, I could see that while incredibly steep, the rock face itself was craggy, providing plenty of crevices for hand and footholds. My mind flashed to earlier adventures with The Captain, as I collapsed and stashed my poles in my pack. This would require all four limbs.

"Follow me," I called over my shoulder and started lifting myself onto the rock.

Rock climbing with a backpack is strange. This pack that had become my trail lifeline, carrying everything needed to survive, was now attempting to ensure my feet never reached the top. Its weight counter-balanced, obeying gravity alone, making each step and hand-grab more precarious than I cared for.

Wet fog pressed around me as I painstakingly inched my way up. Icicles thick as a man's arm and sharp enough to flay a bear appeared from the gloom, hanging from rock outcroppings. My hands protested their new workload, even protected inside gloves. I didn't dare look down to see how the others fared, but grunts of determination and effort told me at least one tramily member was right behind.

A few hundred feet later, the lack of stone above indicated the end of our rock scramble. I pushed a foot into the last crevice my hand had just vacated and stood back up on the trail. It meandered ahead as if nothing had interrupted its gentle passage.

"Maybe I'm not so grateful for North Carolina's trail design after all," I muttered before taking several celebratory gulps of water.

Fun Facts's hands appeared at the top of the slope next, followed by the rest of her. Then Jukebox, Huevos, and finally Nubs, who'd taken the rear. We all sat for a few minutes to gather ourselves before making it to Albert Mountain's peak. The view at the top was supposed to be another stunning vista, but we immediately discovered that the heavy fog we had encountered on the rock wall also blanketed everything beyond the safety railing.

Instead, heading down the other side, we celebrated a different landmark. Sticks had been meticulously laid on the soft path forming a one and two zeros. It was official—I'd hiked my first 100 miles of the Appalachian Trail.

The rain remained unseen in thickening dark clouds as 1 p.m. came and went. Now 4 p.m. was the storm's forecast, so we kept hiking... and hiking and hiking. Before long, we made it to Rock Gap, just short of 20 miles from where we'd started our day.

"I wasn't expecting to record a twenty-miler so soon," I told the others as we waited for our shuttle to Franklin.

"I honestly can't believe I did that." Jukebox's joy-lit face shining with the pride we all felt.

"And my feet stayed sober," Huevos added.

"Hey, mine too!" I agreed. Actually, my whole body felt great. Though today's extra miles sat well for now, I was glad for tomorrow's planned nero day, as I didn't want to overdo it multiple days in a row.

Thirty minutes later, the shuttle arrived and out stepped a middle-aged man, his long brown hair tucked behind eyeglasses. He stretched his arms overhead before his mouth turned up in a lazy smile, as he leaned against the passenger van.

"You Zen?" I asked, figuring it wise to confirm his identity before jumping into the vehicle.

"The one and only, my dudes," he replied, reaching out to shake our hands. "Y'all ready to roll?"

"I guess so," I confirmed.

"Well alright then. Jump in and I'll take you home."

We hauled our packs into the beaten-up Ford's trunk and found seats.

Zen clipped his seatbelt and turned to us, grinning wickedly. "Buckle up, buttercups," he said with a throaty chuckle. I exchanged wide-eyed glances with the tramily, unsure what we'd encounter next.

Zen revved the van like he was gearing up for the Daytona 500, thus beginning our anxiety-inducing ride of hairpin curves at 60 miles per hour, clinging to our seats to avoid being thrown into the windows and each other.

"She's got quite the pickup, huh?" Zen yelled over the rushing sound of impending death streaming through his open windows. "People don't expect that from ol' Betsy here. I get these kids trying to pull up on my ass, and I just get my gun out and swing it out the window. They get the idea pretty fast I'm not okay with tailgaters." His hands motioned wildly with the story, never landing on the wheel simultaneously as it maneuvered fast turns.

Fun Facts and I looked at each other wide-eyed. Zen may have sounded chill at first, but between the death-defying ride and his raucous laughter that followed his story, we knew we'd have nightmare fuel all night. Assuming we survived the drive.

Somehow, despite the NASCAR-style driving, we eventually pulled up to what appeared to be Zen's childhood home, now converted to a hippie hiker hangout. The small brown house was half-hidden by a covered porch strewn with chairs, hammocks, a grill, and empty planters awaiting spring flowers. Another larger planter in the far corner held sturdy walking sticks, the kind fashioned from perfectly shaped tree branches.

"Welcome to Gooder Grove Hostel," Zen announced, turning off the engine and looking back where we remained frozen, hands gripping the seats. "Did you book the bunkroom?"

"We did," I croaked.

"Well alright. Grab your gear and I'll show you around." He headed inside but stopped and turned, smiling teasingly. "It's got a cool vibe in there. You may never want to leave."

He snorted a laugh before disappearing inside. After entering, we encountered a small living room and kitchen. A young guy stood near the stove, chopping mounds of onions. He stopped and grinned, waving a hello with the chef's knife in the air.

"That's Ground Score," Zen nodded at the knife-wielder. "He's doing work-for-stay. Really handy with a knife, if you know what I mean."

"Oh yeah?" I asked, my voice pitching several octaves higher than usual. I peeked at Ground Score, who was back to attacking onions. Work-for-stay was a trail custom for hikers on strict budgets, where a free night was exchanged for running errands, cleaning, repairs, and anything else the host devised.

I hurried behind Zen past the kitchen and down the basement steps. My head cleared the low ceiling, and the basement appeared, filled with a dozen wooden bunkbeds stacked close like a military barracks.

"Here you go," Zen trilled. "Home sweet home."

"It's great," I said, and meant it. For $21, it was exactly what we needed—a quiet space and real mattress. Earlier apprehension slipped away as I dropped my pack on an unoccupied bed.

Zen beamed. "Thanks, man. We only have three rules here: be kind, be kind of clean, and enjoy being." He paused for a prolonged moment at what I could tell was a personal mantra before adding, "Treat my home like your own and harmony will greet you. I'll let you get settled in. And let me know if you want us to do your laundry. Just six bucks."

Hungry for dinner, we let our eyes do the shopping as we made our way back upstairs, ordering five Domino's pizzas... one for each. I sighed, stretching in my hostel loaner clothes, happy to be wearing sweatpants with an elastic waistband while Ground Score ran our laundry. Even though I hadn't intended to take another nero day until Virginia, I was glad for one tomorrow. Especially with a full stomach of cheese and a full day of rain in the forecast. It would help my body rest in comfort, and I'd enjoy exploring Franklin, a town I hadn't researched since I'd initially planned to skip it.

We walked into Franklin the next morning to explore its offerings. It was a neat trail town, reminding me of small towns I'd grown up visiting along Minnesota's northern lakes, but with majestic mountains hugging the border instead of tranquil waters. Since it was Sunday in the South, most everything was closed, so we window-shopped Main Street, noting two outfitters for another time. Still needing to resupply food, we walked back to Gooder Grove and bought a shuttle to Walmart.

Once inside the massive superstore, I headed straight to the pharmaceutical section. A headache had grown in pounding intensity all morning, with nausea beginning to compliment. I was either coming down with something or experiencing delayed dehydration from yesterday's mega-trek. Hard to tell with similar symptoms, but I knew I didn't want to feel this way long. After stocking up on various pills, I purchased a bottle of fuel for my stove, a roll of toilet paper, and new Smartwater bottles. These disposable bottles had been my choice over popular but bulky Nalgenes since discovering their slimline design and lightweight durability. For my thru-hike, I'd even bought custom pockets to hold them on the front shoulder straps of my pack. They were great, the only downside being the need to replace them every couple of weeks.

My headache ignored the painkillers' efforts to quiet it, and the nausea doubled down, requiring extra effort to keep anything in my body. By lunch, I felt like absolute crud. Fun Facts had mentioned earlier that if we made this nero day a full zero, she could pick up her resupply box at the post office the next morning. So with that and my ailing body, we decided to stay another night at Gooder Grove.

Rest came deeply that night, and I opened bleary eyes the next morning to see Nubs's face in his phone on the next bunk.

"How are you feeling, Neiman?" he asked as I attempted to rub my eyes awake.

"Actually..." I paused, assessing my body. "Pretty good. Guess I just needed to sleep it off."

"Nice. Guess I'll start packing then."

We laid out the day's plans over breakfast, chatting with Ground Score, who looked less sinister when absent a large, waving knife. The majority wanted to visit Outdoors 76, one of Franklin's outfitters, before returning to the trail. I was eager to hike again, now that apparent dehydration had finally receded.

Gooder Grove was comfortable and provided a much-needed break, but I was finding hostels stressful for my hiker psyche. There's not much to do, every amenity costs extra, and each minute inside is another minute "normal life" slips back—watching TV, scrolling social media, snacking on junk food. Sitting idle didn't feel right, and after a shower, laundry, and good sleep, I wanted the trail under my feet and miles collecting behind me. Zen had been right initially, as it was hard to leave the hostel. But at this point, there was nothing I wanted more.

I was also beginning to realize a downside of group hiking—you weren't just a lone ranger caring for yourself. Sometimes you had to set aside your own interests and plans for the group's betterment. So we set off for another trip to Franklin.

Reaching the 100-mile marker on Day 10.

13

SAY MY NAME

After the lazy morning touring Franklin, we didn't rejoin the trail again until 3:30 p.m. That meant only a couple hours of daylight before needing to set up camp for the night. Moore Creek Campsite, a small clearing beside a creek, was a short 4.5-mile hike down the trail, making it the best place to stop and avoid hiking deep into the night.

"This weather forecast looks terrible again," Fun Facts announced as we gathered dinner supplies. There was ominous familiarity in that sentence. We'd experienced lots of weather-related plan changes in recent days. Some turned surprisingly better, but more often they'd slowed our pace to a frustrating crawl.

"I'm not sure I even want to know," I muttered, rummaging in my bag. I couldn't find my spork, which was odd because I always kept it with my cooking supplies.

"Temperatures won't get above twenty the next few nights, and rain's coming again," Fun Facts added, apparently not hearing my plea for ignorance. "The Smokies look treacherous too. Freezing temperatures, snow, high winds... Seems like lots of hikers are waiting out the weather at Fontana Dam, according to Facebook."

I straightened, admitting defeat in both the spork search and my ability to remain blissfully unaware. "When does the rain hit?"

Fun Facts's brow furrowed as she navigated to her weather app. "Friday, then every day until Tuesday."

Jukebox appeared, concern shining in her brown eyes. "Maybe we should get to the NOC and wait there until the rain passes?"

I felt objection rising immediately within me. I didn't want to delay with more unplanned zeros. But seeing genuine worry on Jukebox's face drew ire from my tone.

"I think we can make it past the NOC to Fontana Dam by Saturday. It's only 55 miles, so if we spend one night at the NOC, we can easily do the rest in time." Huevos and Nubs joined our circle, listening attentively with Jukebox and Fun Facts. "Look what happened last time rain was in the forecast. We did twenty miles in one day! I think we need to reframe our thoughts about rain and cold. Move from avoiding it to letting it motivate us to push through."

The tramily exchanged thoughtful looks, weighing my words. It was easy to forget on the trail that they were all young adults, and I was significantly older. But as they stood silently debating my argument's merits, the gap of experience between us stood out clearly. I felt I could push them, not just to keep my schedule, but because there was more in them than they knew. The only way they'd discover that was to stretch beyond their comfort zones.

"What do you say?" I asked, doubling down on the encouragement.

Huevos surprised me by answering first. "I think you're right. Let's make Fontana Dam and see what the Smokies look like then."

I clapped his shoulder excitedly and waited for the others. Jukebox and Fun Facts agreed, and we looked to Nubs. He was a strong voice in decision-making, especially when there was an option for off-trail food and beer. He pulled off his hat and scratched his dark curls, causing them to stand in all directions.

"You think we can reach Fontana Dam in five days?" he asked me.

"Absolutely," I replied confidently. "We'll go through maybe one day of rain, and that's if the forecast holds. Which, if we've learned anything, rarely happens in the mountains."

His gaze drifted over the campsite to where the creek gently trickled over its rock bed. "Alright," he said. "I'm in."

Decision made, we returned to dinner prep, and I returned to reality—I no longer had an eating utensil. In my ultralight packing desires, I had no backup, so needed some wilderness survival creativity.

My mind whirled with thoughts of what could scoop up my pasta. I scanned the campsite, eyes landing on broken twigs and branches from the surrounding trees. A long, thin stick stuck out, its end splitting into three small branches. Retrieving my Swiss Army knife, I began whittling the points to somewhat even ends. It wasn't ideal, but it looked enough like fork prongs to let me haphazardly twirl noodles. My dinner almost cooked, somewhat proud of my ingenuity, it was time to test out my invention.

"What's going on over there?" Nubs laughed, watching me dip the stick into my pot.

I twirled it between fingers, successfully hooking a few noodles. Lifting them to my mouth before they slid off, I paused before my next attempt to display my crude utensil to the eagerly watching group.

"Can't find my damn spork, so I improvised," I explained.

The group dissolved into hysterics as I began painstakingly digging out noodles with my inefficient utensil.

"Full points for ingenuity," Fun Facts commented between giggles.

Forgoing the stick for the remainder of my meal, I drank the last mouthfuls like soup. Cleanup was a quick rinse of the pot with purified water, then I stashed it away with my stick, which would need to work for a few more days until I could replace it at the NOC.

I settled onto my sleeping pad, using it as a cushion against the cold ground, and leaned against a fallen trunk of a tree set up as a bench around the campfire. It was time for a blog update. I felt the simmer of pride as I narrated my achievement up Albert Mountain and the subsequent milestone of 100 miles, then chuckled quietly as I detailed our stay at Gooder Grove Hostel next with its off-the-wall host. Blogging had become a way for me to process my experiences on the trail, just as much as it was about sharing the details of my adventure with family and friends. There was something about writing it out that brought a greater connection with what I was doing.

As expected, Dad had commented on the previous day's post. *"Bought my new stove and pot today. I thoroughly checked all options and opted not to buy the titanium teapot. I went with the GSI Halulite pot instead. It has a far superior handle and storage system, but it weighs 2.5 oz more. Bummer! Ordering new shoes in a couple weeks when REI has its annual member sale."*

Reading his words, that old acorn and tree adage came to mind. I could hear anticipation building for his time with me, and the excitement of strategizing the purchase of new gear for lightweight packing. It was comfortingly familiar.

"Keep going, Dad. The new pot sounds great," I responded. I knew this would be the first of many preparation updates, and my own excited anticipation built at the thought of him experiencing the joy of the AT.

The next day, we began by climbing two of North Carolina's famous balds—mountain summits with no trees. First was Siler Bald, which was underwhelming in view, but presented a snow-packed hill and some entertainment when Nubs and Jukebox tried sledding down on their sleeping pads. It didn't work, but did give us all a good laugh.

Wayah Bald next was significantly more beautiful. A lookout

tower stood sentry atop its pinnacle, and the mountain landscape view rivaled Blood Mountain at Neel Gap. At my suggestion, we took a long break, reveling in the beauty together. I knew Wayah Bald had a shelter only half a mile farther, and I didn't want to miss the opportunity to enjoy the splendor before me.

Nubs plunked down beside me. I looked over as I munched some trail mix, noting his thoughtful expression. I could tell something brewed in that sharp mind, and I didn't wait long to find out.

"You know how you've been waiting for your trail name?" he began.

"Uh-huh."

"And you know how you tend to, well, get lost at times?"

I winced, knowing he spoke the truth. More than once, including that very morning, I'd accidentally found myself on a blue blaze forking off the main AT. Keg and The Captain had also made sure the tramily knew about my mistaken southward turn the morning after our first night. I realized that I'd habitually become so preoccupied scanning my feet for loose rocks and tree roots that paying attention to trail markers tended to take second place.

"Yeah, I'm aware," I admitted, not liking where this was headed.

"And that spork you had. Not just you getting lost anymore, is it?" He followed.

His question was laced with rhetoric but was once again truthful. At this point, I knew whatever they devised for my trail name was unavoidable.

"Well, we thought Nemo might be fun, as in the Disney fish, because he gets lost in the ocean like you get lost on the trail. And your gear is all orange and black—"

"And Nemo is orange and black," Jukebox finished, grinning as she joined us.

I thought before answering, "Well, it's a nice idea. And some friends back home call me Nemo already, given my last name." If Nemo was suggested, I felt like it could work.

"Yeah, it was... but apparently there's already some bigwig in the trail community called Nemo, and when I casually mentioned it to Zen at Gooder Grove, he made it sound like you wouldn't want to rain on his parade by taking the same name."

Darn, the name had already started working into my mind as a perfect combination of home and trail life. But before I could respond, Nubs continued.

"So I thought more and realized Nemo has a nickname in the movie too, after his trial in the dentist's fish tank, almost like his own trail name. So we talked it over and... Sharkbait is your trail name," Nubs finished.

I chewed through another mouthful of trail mix as I let the name sit for a minute. I liked it—a trail name for a trail name, befitting me and my adventure. Turning to Nubs, I nodded. "Sharkbait it is. But on one condition..."

Nubs raised eyebrows. "Oh yeah? What?"

"Whenever it's mentioned, you have to respond with 'hoo ha ha' like in the movie."

Nubs snorted, laughing. "I think we can manage that."

We found the rest of the tramily and conveyed my trail name update. Enthusiastic agreement followed, so introductions would now be made as Sharkbait. Hoo ha ha!

A half-mile and short blue blaze later, we approached Wayah Shelter. Perched on a ledge with its back nestled into the mountainside, the terrain dropped away on two of three sides. It was decent-sized with a generous porch and a spacious sleeping area. And with temperatures forecasted in the teens overnight, it seemed best to sleep in the shelter again.

Dinner was a quick affair in the type of cold that permeates through every layer of clothing, no matter how well-designed. As soon as humanly possible, I snuggled into my quilt, bringing the material up over my head to protect the warmth as I wrote a quick blog update. Checking the comments, I saw another update from Edie. He mentioned that his son and a friend were closing in on my location, so I promised to look out for them over the coming days. Then I curled myself into a tight ball, sealing all gaps from within my quilt to the frigid outside world.

The night was cold, as if the air itself had frozen solid, and sleep was nearly impossible. Every toss and turn on the hard shelter floor exposed a crack in my fortress of warmth, and cold flew inside my cocoon, startling me awake. Adding insult to injury, we woke in the morning to the surprise of snow flurries on the ground. I skipped my usual routine of exchanging long underwear for hiking clothes and just added the layers on top, which was becoming a common trend. I pulled my Patagonia fleece hood tight around my head like a balaclava. With the addition of my puffy down jacket on, I was now ready to hike through the wind and snow.

We were almost at day's end, and spirits were high, knowing a soft bed and four walls awaited. We began our final few miles down to the NOC and quickly realized these would be the most challenging since Albert Mountain. The narrow ledge we navigated was crazy steep, rocky, and dangerous. The chatty conversations usually accompanying our days ceased as each tramily member focused on staying on the trail. I kept both eyes on my feet, placing each carefully, and watching for pitfalls. A grunt of exertion sounded ahead, and I glanced up just as I put my right foot down... right onto an exposed root's uneven angle. My ankle rolled sideways, and my arms windmilled in the air. My body tilted, and I slid over the edge of the embankment. Twenty feet of mountainside slammed into me as I lost footing.

"Sharkbait!" A panicked scream followed me down, but I was an avalanche of pack and poles picking up speed.

My hands dug at ground, grabbing plants, moss, and mud, but nothing stopped my momentum. Images of my broken body flared. Panic took over. Then pain punched through my ribs, and just as quickly as I'd jettisoned over the mountain, I stopped. I wrapped my arms around the tree trunk that stopped my fall, looking back to the ledge I'd just left. Snow-white faces of Fun Facts and Huevos peered over, wide-eyed and agape in twin expressions of horror.

"I think... I'm alright," I croaked, lungs attempting to expand past the pain of hitting the mountain and tree.

"Can you get up?" Fun Facts yelled, voice shaky.

I pushed against the trunk, using the leverage to get onto my backside. Keeping feet against the tree, I pressed on tender ribs, testing for broken bones. They were painful, but nothing felt severe enough to be cracked.

"Do you need help?" Huevos shouted.

I looked back up the steep incline. No way I wanted anyone else to risk their life flying down like I had. "If I take it slow, I think I'll make it back up." I pushed my hands into the ground and pain lanced through my chest. I groaned, settling back down. "Just give me a minute."

Several minutes later, I inched back onto the narrow ledge and into the tramily's company. After pale-faced declarations of concern that I'd become a statistic, we resumed hiking at much slower pace until we reached the NOC. I'd been grateful for a soft bed before, but nothing compared to the bliss of a mattress that night on my bruised ribs.

14

STAIRWAY TO HEAVEN

W hat was there to say about the NOC? The sole oasis at the US 19 road crossing resembled a poorly-designed theme park. Primarily an outdoor recreation center, its grounds hosted a restaurant, ropes course, general store, lodging, and a shower house. The cabins for thru-hikers like us were up a hill, a cold 100-foot walk to the shower house below. While the bunk beds had real mattresses, the cabins were essentially wooden boxes with shelves holding those mattresses off the floor. Hardly worth the $100 price tag, but it was also the only option.

Fun Facts, Nubs, Huevos, Jukebox and I set ourselves up for the night, squeezing the five of us into the box meant for four, and then headed to River's End restaurant. It was a long cabin-style room, overhanging the Nantahala River that ran through the facility. We quietly surveyed the menu of pub fare mixed with Italian food when hurried footsteps and a yell of surprise resounded through the restaurant.

I spun around with the twelve other hikers seated nearby to find the source. Ground Score's thin, muscular frame strode toward us, grinning widely through his considerable facial hair.

I stood in anticipation of his arrival and found myself in a full-body clasp. I smiled at his obvious pleasure seeing us again, while he moved on, embracing the other tramily members. An odd greeting for someone we barely knew, but then again, everyone out here quickly felt like family.

"You staying here?" I asked.

"Sure am. Didn't think I'd see you guys again so soon." His brown eyes widened as he lowered his voice conspiratorially. "I had to get away from Zen, man. That guy was damn crazy."

Nubs snorted a quick, mirthless laugh. "Yeah, we figured that out pretty fast."

"Want to join us for dinner?" Fun Facts asked. "We have to hear what happened!"

Heads nodded as Ground Score looked between us. "Alright. Sure."

He slid over a chair and sank into it, blowing breath out both sides of his mouth.

"Where to start?" He shook his head, pausing for dramatic effect. "I knew something was off right away, but the night after you left, he cornered me in the kitchen, demanding my plans for the rest of the season. I told him I was thinking about moving on... I'd been there a couple nights and was getting restless. He'd picked up the butcher knife and was wiping it on a dishcloth, but started waving it around wildly, saying, 'Who's going to prep dinner if you leave?'" Ground Score lifted hands in surrender as if Zen's knife was still flashing. "He was laughing like it was one big joke, but I was like, 'Dude, put the knife down.' That made him laugh harder. He had this weird look, and I honestly didn't know what would happen."

He paused and rubbed his eyes. "He eventually put the knife down and started to leave the kitchen. But at the door to the basement, he looked me dead in the eye and said, 'Maybe I'll just hide your things so you can't leave.' Then he laughed again and disappeared. As soon as he was asleep, I got my stuff and left. It was the middle of the night, but I didn't care. I hitched to the trail and kept hiking until I got here."

Beats of silence followed as we digested the dramatic details. Zen had seemed unhinged, and Ground Score's story backed that up, but I wondered if it could've all been his weird sense of humor with no harm intended. Hard to know.

"I'm so glad you got out of there," Jukebox said, her skin a few shades paler than normal.

Ground Score nodded slowly. "Me too." He stared at the table before looking up, grin back on his face and expression clear. "Mind if I join you guys on the trail tomorrow?"

Quick glances between the tramily confirmed unanimous agreement.

"You sure can," I answered.

"Thanks, Neiman," Ground Score replied, gripping my shoulder firmly.

"Actually, it's Sharkbait now."

Ground Score raised an eyebrow, lips curving in amusement. "Oh yeah? Sounds like I need to catch up on the story behind that one."

I grinned, settling back to begin the tale—

"Sharkbait?!" a young man's voice resounded in my ear. I swiveled to the table behind me. Two guys and a girl barely out of school stared at me with wide eyes.

"Yes?" I asked hesitantly.

"You're Sharkbait?" The voice belonged to a guy with hair cut short on the sides and an unruly mop on top. His face was adorned with the scruff of a week-old beard and wide-eyed questioning.

"Hoo ha ha," I responded with a smirk.

"No way! Hey Tarzan!" he yelled, smacking the guy next to him with the back of his hand. "It's Sharkbait. The guy with the blog."

Tarzan rubbed his arm, peering up from a low-fitted baseball cap.

Astonished, I turned my chair to face them. "Wait, you guys know about my blog?"

"Sure do." As he said it, Tarzan nodded so hard in agreement that I grew concerned about permanent neck damage. "My dad won't stop talking about it. Keeps asking why I can't even check in with a text while some other guy is blogging his whole damn hike. He keeps asking if we've seen you yet." He rolled his eyes while a wry grin turned up one side of his mouth.

"Hang on." I held up my hand while a memory resurfaced. "Is your dad Edie?"

"Yes!" he shouted, earning looks from other hikers around the room. He laughed and thumped his fist on the table, oblivious to the commotion. Stretching across the table, his hand reached to grasp mine. "I'm Jack."

His handshake was a vigorous workout, as enthusiastic as his general demeanor.

"This is Tarzan." Jack indicated the smaller, quieter guy beside him before turning to the girl on the right. "And that's Happy Feet."

She gave a little wave, a shy but warm smile appearing between curtains of long chestnut-brown hair.

I returned the wave before introducing the tramily. We joined tables and took the natural next step for new trail friendships—planning tomorrow's hike together. Which was simple once we discovered we were all heading to Sassafras Gap Shelter.

After a slow start that included an extended brunch, a resupply of provisions, and a trip to the general store for a replacement spork, we were back on the trail with our new friends. Unfortunately, last night's high quickly faded as we discovered the next two days would be sponsored by relentless uphill hiking and sub-freezing temperatures.

"Where are those North Carolina switchbacks I loved so much?" I huffed, attempting to force more air into my oxygen-depleted brain.

A grunt was all Huevos could manage in response from directly behind me.

After a decent day's hike out of the NOC, mostly uphill from the road crossing, the whole crew stayed at Sassafras Gap Shelter as discussed. The next morning, everyone packed up and headed out, hopeful the worst of the uphill climbs was behind us for a stretch. But we were quickly proved wrong. A few miles in, we hit an infamous AT section known as Jacob's Ladder—an apt name given the trail went straight up, with wooden beams driven into the ground like ladder rungs. It also felt nearly impossible to reach the top, like the old carnival game of the same name. When we weren't climbing log stairs, we were clambering over fallen trees and uneven boulder piles thrown down carelessly. It made our climb very slow and painful.

The biggest concern was getting enough water. I was still feeling the lingering effects of last week's dehydration, and each day I woke with legs close to cramping. Throughout the night's tossing and turning, I could tell I walked a tightrope between stretching calves and triggering a painful charley horse. I needed to strategically plan water breaks that day to ensure I didn't run out or run low.

Guthook showed only two known water sources between the base of Jacob's ladder and the mountain's other side, with 600 feet of elevation gain between. While the app clearly marked available water sources, that didn't mean they were conveniently placed or clean enough to drink from. The Aqua Mira drops I used to purify made the best of what was available, but it was basically a diluted chlorine solution, so even that wouldn't help if water was too difficult to collect. I still somehow needed to get enough into my bottles. To help, I'd started adding a sturdy leaf atop rocks in shallow creeks. It acted as a funnel for the water to run over, creating a steady, collectable stream. For now, it kept my water intake up and kept me moving without too much delay.

But the physical effects of climbing Jacob's Ladder couldn't be remedied by our midday stop at Brown Fork Shelter. The rest of the day was a significantly easier eight miles, walking mostly ridgelines or small hills, but we were so beaten up by Jacob that even easier miles hurt more than normal.

When we finally reached Cable Gap Shelter, I quickly strung up the hammock, downed a double dinner, and prepared for bed. Ground Score lit a fire, and I settled onto my sleeping pad, using it as cushion against the cold ground near the campfire.

Jack, Tarzan, and Happy Feet stretched similarly beside me, pulling off boots to massage feet as tired as mine. Despite the challenging day, I still felt in good shape, but the Smokies were ahead, and I knew they'd test my body's limits. Tomorrow's shorter downhill into Fontana Dam would be a welcome respite.

As I sat, I rolled the pickleball along my aching foot muscles. I'd need to be well-prepared and healed if I was going to make it through those mountains without serious injury. Rumors were flying that winds were whipping across the peaks at 25 miles per hour, with snow drifts up to 18 inches, and night temperatures in the minus digits. This was further confirmed on Facebook by hikers a few days ahead, warning of treacherous winter conditions they'd experienced firsthand in the Smoky Mountains. These facts rolled around in my mind. I suspected that level of cold simply wasn't going to end well for me, especially since that 90-mile stretch required that all thru-hikers sleep inside the park's shelters.

I watched the dancing flames as I let my mind wander ahead to those danger-strewn paths. The mental hike I took alongside the physical one was performed in balance. I knew I needed to look ahead and be prepared for what was coming. But I also needed to stay in the present. And there was the glaring fact I could only enjoy the present if I wasn't looking ahead at a foreboding shadow of danger. Planning had long been my solace when circumstances started to look uncertain, so I pulled out my phone and texted Dana a list of winter gear items to add to my next resupply box. Heavier gloves, quilt liner, and crampons sat in our spare room, just in case they were needed. Message sent, I tucked my phone away along with any apprehension about what was coming.

15

SMOKE ON THE WATER

The earlier forecasted rain was due the next day. Plans were to get up at 4 a.m., pack camp, and hike into Fontana Dam before sunrise. But as the saying goes, the best-laid plans of mice and men often go awry. When the alarm went off at 3:45, it was already raining, so I settled back into my quilts. *Why fight it?* I thought as I closed my eyes again.

Four hours later, the rain slowed to a patter, and I decided it was time. Fun Facts's hooded face greeted me as I slid from under my hammock's rain cover.

"I guess that rain finally found us," she commented, offering a wry grin. "Time to try your trick of reframing my thoughts."

I smiled encouragingly from beneath my hood. "Let's do this."

Immediately, as if responding to our optimism, the rain intensified. It drummed an accelerated beat against our coats, individual droplets joining streams running off every waterproof surface. I peered at Jukebox and Fun Facts through the curtain of rain, who shrugged back in silent resignation.

We trudged on for another hour in the downpour until the sun finally poked out and temperatures swiftly rose into the sixties. After five miles, we reached the road crossing leading to Fontana Dam. But before officially arriving at this resort village, we encountered a small marina on a nearby lake. We dropped packs and walked down to find a welcome surprise—at the marina's end was a small convenience store. A hot dog, a sleeve of Pringles, and a can of beer made for a fantastic lunch. Eating on the dock in the warm spring sun was even better. The many small moments like this were really what made this hike enjoyable. When else would such a lunch be my day's highlight?

At the trail and marina intersection, a signpost suggested calling Fontana Village for a shuttle to the Lodge. But with full stomachs and sun-warmed bodies, I suggested hiking the 1.7 miles to the dam and visitor center instead, as it'd be nice starting right from the dam the next day. The general consensus swayed toward yes.

Nubs clinched it with a well-timed comment and mischievous grin. "It's mostly just uphill and downhill anyway."

We laughed as Fun Facts, phone in hand, rose from the bench and announced, "I'm calling my cousin Lillian. She lives nearby and was planning to hang out tonight. I'll see if she can drive out earlier and take us to the lodge from the dam."

She strode off, soon lost in conversation.

"All set," she advised minutes later. The ride to the lodge from the dam would've been additional unofficial miles off the trail and all uphill, so Lillian was really saving us.

Fontana Dam was incredible. The viewing platform let visitors look down the full 480-foot height of concrete wall. The Little Tennessee River below wound between tree-covered hills, barely beginning its wake to spring's warmth. It continued against the towering backdrop of the Great Smoky Mountains, foreshadowing what lay before us next.

After a pleasant couple of hours enjoying the view and visitor center, Lillian packed all of us and our backpacks Tetris-style into her befitting Subaru Impreza. Thankfully, we soon pulled up to a sprawling two-story building nestled in the woods. It was a beautiful facility with a hotel, cabins, pool, laundry, and shops. Unlike the NOC, it was a well-maintained and dream resort. Hotel rooms were lavish and spacious, equipped with normal societal amenities. We split into two rooms, so the girls had their own space while Nubs, Huevos, Ground Score, and I bunked in the other.

First order of business was attending to wet gear. It badly needed airing out to avoid the damp rot smell that sets in and doesn't go away. After covering every inch of the room with tents, tarps, and quilts, we agreed laundry was the next priority. Everything I owned needed washing, so I stepped into the bathroom, quickly changed into my bright-orange rain jacket and a black rain skirt. I loved this innovative product because it weighed almost nothing, keeping me cooler with far less perspiration than restrictive rain pants. I shoved all my clothes into a stuff sack and reentered the room.

Nubs, Ground Score, and Huevos looked me up and down and burst into hysterical laughter.

"What? You don't like my backpacker tuxedo?" I asked, striking a runway pose.

"Is that what they call it?" Nubs asked, tears running down his cheeks.

The laughter continued as everyone donned their own tuxedos before heading to the laundry facility at the resort's base. We weren't alone, as many hikers were doing the same, so conversations were plentiful.

Picking up my second resupply box was next, which would restock rations for the trek through the Smokies. With dry gear, clean clothing, and food refills handled, I settled in for an evening around the large outdoor fire pit at the main lodge. Twenty to thirty hikers gathered in small groups, getting to know each other or catching up from earlier meetings.

I'd claimed a fireside seat in one of the Adirondack chairs, but seats became scarcer as evening wore on and crowds grew. Huevos, who'd been talking with a group of college-aged guys, joined me next to the fire. He squatted on his haunches but groaned and went down to his backside. A glance revealed him rubbing his knees.

"You okay, man?" I asked, knowing too well what he felt.

"Yeah, just some twinges." He quieted, watching the flickering flames. "Those guys just told me they heard over 1,000 hikers have registered at Amicalola Falls already this year."

My eyebrows raised at the number. "Really?" I blew out a breath, eyeing the many hikers around me and recalling my first day on the trail. "The ranger at Amicalola said this year would be crowded. Guess he was right."

Huevos nodded.

"The Smokies are popular with weekend and section hikers too," I added.

"Yep," Huevos commented quietly.

The lodge's crowd already showed that a bubble of hikers was beginning to create a bottleneck on the trail. I didn't know how I felt about record-high registrations, knowing many hikers also quit the trail early on, but I did feel urgency growing inside. *Get moving*, it said.

I woke well-rested the next morning and itching for the trail's white blazes. My destination was Mollies Ridge—only 12 miles away but 3,000 feet straight up.

Huevos's loud groans filled our room as he rolled from his bed. He shook his head, massaging his knees again. "That climb today is gonna really hurt."

I sat on the opposite bed, pulling on my shoes. I stopped lacing and eyed Huevos. "You think it's a good idea to push it?"

Huevos grimaced. "You think I shouldn't?"

"I don't know, maybe you need a zero day," I replied.

"You've got to listen to your body, man," Ground Score added.

Nubs and I grunted agreement as Huevos frowned at his knees.

He looked back up, resignation and frustration written across his furrowed brow.

"Yeah, you're probably right. I guess I could rest another day, then catch up."

"For sure," Nubs reassured, clapping a hand on his shoulder.

"I'll leave notes in the shelter logbooks so you know where we are," I advised.

Huevos had become an enjoyable friend sharing the trail adventure, and I knew we'd all miss his presence. But it felt like he was doing the right thing taking it easy now.

Minutes later, the tramily said goodbye to Huevos, our words full of hope that the split would be temporary. We left the lodge to start the day's hike with a dozen other hikers. It was a big group, and before long, it stretched out as each hiker found their rhythm. I found myself closer to the front, where Happy Feet kept pace.

"So what brings you out on the trail?" I asked. She was naturally quiet, and with larger personalities around, I hadn't gotten her story yet.

"Oh, well..." she hesitated, gathering thoughts. "I'm taking a gap year after high school. I guess I wanted to see the world a little before starting college." She side-smiled shyly. "And I don't know, it sounded fun to hike the AT."

A gap year was something my generation might've considered after college, but doing so after high school was new to me. Yet here were Happy Feet, Jack, and Tarzan, all feeling the need for a break so early in life. And it seemed a common thru-hiker theme out here. We walked in silence, content in our own thoughts, letting birdsong be the only sound filling the air.

"It's funny," I said a few minutes later as our boots clomped over a metal plank anchored into dirt walls bookending a shallow creek. "When I went to college, we just left high school and went. Like we thought we had to get all our education done quickly before experiencing the world. But your generation sees it differently."

A thoughtful hum sounded beside me before Happy Feet

responded. "There's just lots of pressure in high school now. I guess our response is to take a break and figure out what we like before more years of education."

I nodded slowly. I could see her point. I'd always thought the world had much to teach before stepping onto the escalator of pursuing a career path. I changed majors half a dozen times before graduating college, clearly not sure what I wanted to do with my life. Plus, having younger hikers on the trail meant more people supporting the community in the future.

"That's cool. I like your drive to experience the world firsthand. Is it all you expected?" I asked.

Her blue eyes sparkled up at me. "No. It's better."

We walked in silence a bit more, reaching Shuckstack Mountain in short time. The climb was strenuous but what awaited at the top made it worthwhile. I stared up at a 60-foot, and very likely 60-year-old lookout tower. At 4,500 feet above sea level, it was a mammoth structure with rickety stairs winding up scaffolding that swayed gently with the wind. The voice of self-preservation warned, advised, begged me not to climb it, but that other voice whispering of adventure won out.

I began climbing. Happy Feet was content to keep her two feet on the ground with our backpacks. The stairs had few handrails, and its steps were wooden planks mostly attached to iron rails at either end. It felt like one strong gust of wind would send it toppling over the mountainside. But I couldn't stop. I knew the view would be phenomenal. And it was.

My head eventually peeked onto the top platform, little more than a shack of broken plywood and shattered glass. I climbed the final step and took heaving breaths as I surveyed the 360-degree view. Fontana Lake's outermost edge dipped between rows of mountains. Clear-blue sky, broken only by airborne birds of prey, reflected the lake's blue back to itself. My deep breaths were no longer from exhaustion, but from the exhilaration of fresh mountain air and the natural beauty before me.

I returned to ground level, finding Nubs, Fun Facts, Jack, and Tarzan now sitting beside Happy Feet. Impossible to hide excitement, I described the view. After a quick trail lunch, where each slowly made their way up and back down the tower, we all decided to keep moving, knowing Mollies Ridge Shelter was still miles away.

I checked my watch as we approached the blue blaze to the shelter.

"Hey, guys," I called, halting the others who'd already turned onto the side trail. "It's only four o'clock. Russell Field Shelter is just another three miles. Want to try for it?"

Nubs responded quickly. "I'm pretty beat. I think I'm calling it a day."

The others agreed with Nubs, their hearts also set on an earlier finish.

"No worries," I smiled. "I'm going to do it. I'll start slow tomorrow so you can catch up."

The miles were easygoing. Wide trails, clear of roots and rocks, that had me sending grateful thoughts to the Great Smoky Mountains National Park rangers who maintained them. I was content meandering, taking in the park's wonder. As the last mile approached, I spotted a small gap in the trees surrounding me. A log had been laid on its side on the ground, and approaching, I saw why. The view from its perch was Blue Ridge Mountains as far as the eye could see. I shrugged off my pack and sat, wanting a few moments of silence to breathe it in.

Suddenly, realization hit. I wasn't out here for a respite from studies before life's difficulties began. And I wasn't like many others out here I'd met; retirees with hard-fought experiences behind them, looking to finally enjoy a simpler life. The main reason I was here was the simplest of all—I just loved hiking. I could walk for hours in the mountains, taking in sights, sounds, and smells, experiencing the world as it was built to be seen. I enjoyed hiking with the others, getting to know them, and sharing camaraderie. But that wasn't my main reason for being here. The AT's social scene felt so important before arriving, but now I wasn't sure how much that mattered. I sat for minutes more as the color began to fade in the sky, letting my new realizations settle. I could feel the beginning of a shift in my approach to hiking the AT, and I let that be enough for now.

16

JUKE BOX BLUES

Russell Field was my first taste of Smoky Mountains shelters, and it was next level. It fit 20 people, with walls of stone and an indoor fireplace with chimney. The roof of the large, covered eating area rose to the shelter's top. In the daylight, it formed a natural skylight illuminating the interior with a soft glow. Rangers had even rigged a large tarp over the open wall to help protect against early-season wind and cold. If I'd packed a thicker sleeping pad, I would've happily tried it out. With the fire and tarp, it looked like a cozy night was guaranteed. But my minimalist pad was still an issue on the hard floor, so when I found the shelter already full, I wasn't disappointed to set up my hammock outside instead.

Everything set, I pulled out my food bag and stove. This week's dinner was backpacker walking tacos, a meal I'd been excited about in my prep days. A unique twist on the quick meal I loved as a kid. Freeze-dried ground beef, dehydrated bean flakes and onions, a mix of olive oil, taco seasoning, and hot water, gloriously tossed into a bag of crushed Doritos. The nacho cheese kind, naturally. It was meaty, cheesy, hot, and delicious.

I waved at a few unfamiliar hikers already congregated in the eating area and set to boiling water. The great thing about this meal was that it didn't take much heat to rehydrate the ingredients, still a recurring issue with my stove. Practicing the art of patience as I waited for the water to boil, I pulled out my phone for a weather check and a blog update. The forecast revealed that tomorrow would bring another rainy hike. I shook my head at the sight of more rain but didn't dwell much. After all, if it rained, I'd be wet for a few less miles, now that I'd completed the extra ones today.

Pulling out my phone, I saw new comments on the blog. Dad had added his wisdom again, and though the post he'd commented on was days old, the advice was still relevant to current circumstances.

"*When it rains, it pours,*" I read, huffing a laugh at where this dad joke was heading. "*And you have to expect it will rain. Actually, it's likely to rain. In fact, you better acknowledge the obvious... it will rain. By the way, it will probably be raining soon. I hope that clears up the unknown factors to consider while backpacking.*" And there it was, that reframing attitude I'd clearly inherited. Rain on a thru-hike was inevitable, but letting it sour my mood didn't have to be.

I paused, checking my water. A frustrated grunt my only response to the lack of bubbles. I turned back to Dad's comment: "*About the spork you lost. I thought of upgrading my spoon, but if it's that easy to lose, forget it!*"

I smiled at how the words conjured his voice in my head. Tapping a quick response, I hit send before turning back to dinner. "*Want my advice? Buy two! Better safe than stick.*"

The next day was supposed to take me to Double Spring Gap Shelter over 16 miles away, but as usual, I scrapped that plan. I started, slow as promised, and took the day's miles alone, enjoying a day of solitary hiking. Solitary except for impromptu meetings with Jukebox. Somewhere over the past few days, her hiking had shifted from the slow-and-steady pace she'd begun with. Now there was a new pattern, involving fast hiking and long breaks. So when I stopped for my first snack a couple miles into the day, I saw Jukebox hike by. After another couple of miles, she'd stopped for a break, and I waved as I hiked by. This leapfrog hiking style was common on the trail, where hikers walked a similar pace but took breaks at different times, and we laughed each time our paths crossed.

As morning wore on, I summited my big challenge for the day—Rocky Top. Pending rain still hadn't appeared, so the view from the top was breathtaking. It was aptly named for various-sized boulders strewn around, leaving a well-worn trail zigzagging around them. As I stood gazing across the mountain ridges, a sudden urge came over me.

Gathering a deep breath, I bellowed "YO!" into the sky. The outgoing sound was thunderous, but the echo resonating off the valleys below made it truly satisfying. A second later, I realized it wasn't just echoes off the hills but the responsive howls from other hikers making their way down the summit's other side.

As I descended Rocky Top's peak myself, weaving through the boulders, I heard hiker after hiker reach the top and give their own war cry to the wilderness. I answered each with my own echo, chuckling the whole way. There was certainly something to love about the common thru-hiker bond out here, even when you think you're alone.

A couple of miles down, a grassy patch looked suitable for lunch. I pulled out ingredients for my simple BBQ chicken pizza meal—hardtack crackers topped with canned chicken, parmesan cheese, dried pineapple, and a small packet of BBQ sauce. I was munching away, intently focused on keeping the messy ingredients in place, when Jukebox came striding around the corner.

"Hey," I called, waving a piece of pineapple her way.

Her head lifted and eyes beamed at my call. Reaching me, she dropped her pack to the ground. Taking the pineapple I'd offered with a nod of thanks. After regaining her breath, she giggled.

"The funniest thing just happened." She said, smiling.

"Oh yeah?" I asked, intrigued.

"I was hiking up Rocky Top and heard this loud 'YO' bouncing off the trees," she began. I started smiling in return. "Then all these hikers ahead and behind started answering, howling, and shouting... it was wild! Did you hear it?"

My smile grew. "I started it."

Her eyes widened as her mouth gaped open. "You did the 'Yo'?"

"Sure did, it was one of my dad's things and just felt right," I confirmed.

She shook her head, brown eyes shining with amusement. "I did my own when I got to the top."

"Nice! What did you yell?"

Jukebox's light-brown skin flushed pink. "Remember when we gave you your trail name and you said you'd keep it as long as we said 'hoo ha ha' every time?"

"Yeah, of course."

"Well, that's what I said." She laughed, and I heard the hint of embarrassment in the sound.

"That's awesome!" I encouraged, seeing the pink deepen across her cheeks. "I think my dad would be proud. Everyone has their own 'Yo' in them." And I knew he would, but also that it would help clear any humiliation.

Moments of silence followed as we chewed and hydrated before Jukebox turned to me again. "Can I tell you something?"

"Of course."

She took a breath. "I don't feel like my trail name resonates with me."

"Really? You don't like Jukebox?"

"No, I do," she said quickly, brushing stray strands of the light-brown hair that had escaped her ponytail out of her face. "It's just, I don't feel it fits my whole trail experience. Like, I'm not out here because I enjoy singing." She paused and sighed, lowering her eyes to her fingers, flicking her water bottle cap on and off. "But I guess you don't get to pick your trail name. Maybe I'm overthinking it."

"I get it," I said quietly, and her eyes lifted to mine. "Remember when the guys suggested Fun Stats for me? It was funny but didn't feel like me. Like it was part of my story, but not the whole thing."

She nodded, a small smile lifting her mouth's corner. We sat in silence again, both minds occupied. Then an idea came to me, as fast as the one on Rocky Top.

I turned to her, wanting to see her reaction. I'd noticed she had a pacifist personality, wanting to go along with others even if not fully agreeing with their decisions. I didn't want that happening here.

"What about Leap Frog? You've been doing it to me all day, and it fits your natural hiking style."

I watched her eyes take on the faraway look of consideration before they filled with sparkling amusement again. "And you know, my backpack is green. Hmm, I actually love it," she announced, face lighting with joy.

"You do? Really? It was just an idea. You can think about it if you're not sure." I wanted to give her an out if needed.

But she shook her head, ponytail swaying. "No, I don't need to think about it. It's perfect. Thanks, Sharkbait!"

"Hoo ha ha," I replied, earning a smile in return.

Leap Frog and I hiked together a bit longer before separating for the day's remainder. At some point, I officially crossed into Tennessee for the first time. Even though I'd cross back and forth between it and North Carolina many more times throughout the Smokies, I still celebrated reaching my third state with a peanut butter Twix bar.

Tomorrow would bring another big milestone—crossing the 200-mile mark after descending Clingmans Dome. The summit appeared through the trees most of the day, and even though less than 1,000 feet higher than my current elevation, as the AT's highest point, it was still a challenge not to be underestimated. I was looking forward to adding it to my growing list of achievements.

I arrived at Siler Bald Shelter at 5:15 p.m. and did a quick check for Leap Frog, but there was no sign of her. Fog descended in thick layers, carrying damp cold, and chilly wind that whipped into more than a gentle breeze. I considered my options, devouring my walking tacos dinner. I could hike the extra 1.7 miles intended today in miserable weather, maybe finding Leap Frog in the process, or stay put and tack the miles onto tomorrow's hike. I'd checked the shelter on arrival and knew there'd be more than enough room. With a fire already lit in the fireplace and tarps covering the open front, it was tempting, even though I'd sworn off shelters until I could resolve my sleeping pad situation. Especially with the fog expected to shift to rain overnight.

As I deliberated, a soft voice called out, "Sharkbait!"

Expecting Leap Frog, I looked up and instead saw Fun Facts and Nubs strolling toward me. They hefted their packs down before embracing me in slightly damp hugs. And that made the decision for me. Siler Bald Shelter it was.

Fire, tarps, and exhaustion proved the perfect sleep-inducing combination. Even with a cold, hard floor, I was quickly snoozing deeply. Then suddenly, the bellow of creaking roof panels startled me awake. I opened my eyes to see the fireplace, its flames guttered wildly as cold air blasted down the chimney. The groaning strain of nails holding plastic shingles came again as the wind made another attempt to tear off the roof. Between gusts, I could hear the slam of rain against the snapping tarp. I turned to see Fun Facts beside me. Her wide eyes gleamed in the fire's glow behind my head.

"That's some wild storm," she whispered, keeping her voice quiet. Unnecessarily, I realized, noting the wide-awake eyes of the rest of the hikers who'd decided to spend the night.

"I wonder how Nubs is doing," I said. The big group alongside us appeared not long after Fun Facts and Nubs had arrived the night before, and the shelter had filled up fast. Nubs decided to set up his tent outside rather than attempt to squeeze in with everyone.

"Oh yeah," Fun Facts laughed, stifling the noise in her hand. "Not the best night for a nylon house."

The next morning, we emerged into the bright sunlight of a post-storm world. Water droplets hung along the edges of the trees, while the ground was littered with their branches and leaves.

Several tents around the campsite sagged with rainwater, but none belonged to Nubs. We rounded the shelter corner and saw him surveying his sodden gear and munching a granola bar, coffee steaming in his other hand.

He lifted his head in greeting as he saw us.

"Wet night?" I asked, perhaps too facetiously.

"You could say that."

"Looks like you chose the best spot though," I noted, patting the shelter's stone wall. "Using the shelter as a windbreak was smart. The other tents out front look like they took a nasty beating."

Nubs grunted his response, taking a long swig of coffee. As smart as he'd been picking the location, his gear was still soaked through. It was clear his night was nowhere near as comfortable as ours. So, changing subjects, I remembered something from last night's blog post.

"Did you know," I began, capturing their attention, "As of today, there are less than 2,000 miles to Katahdin?"

"Oh wow, you're right!" Fun Facts replied.

"We're on our way, guys." I grinned at them.

So many milestones had been achieved the last day, and so many more were still to come.

17

HEAD IN THE CLOUDS

After helping Nubs pack his gear, the three of us began the day's hike, but I quickly began pulling ahead of their pace. These days, I woke without the usual pain or soreness. Stretching at day's end and working my arches with the pickleball at night helped, but I could also tell I was finding my trail legs. Like I'd told Dad, there comes a point where the muscles strengthen and you can hike farther and faster than the average day-hiker. I was there now, and I didn't want to miss the opportunity to get serious distance behind me. Especially with the climb to Clingmans Dome ahead, the apex of the Smokies and highest point of the Appalachian Trail.

So I waved goodbye to Fun Facts and Nubs and loaded my playlist. Today felt like a female pop-star day. Miley, Taylor, Sia, and Gaga kept me company as I karaoked my way up the trail. Somewhere in between "Wrecking Ball" and "Chandelier," I reflected on what motivated me to keep pushing forward. A good tune didn't hurt, but small rewards had become key.

I often found my inner monologue focused on giving my body short-term goals: *Four miles to the next water source. Get there and down a bottle.* Or: *see that summit bald? At the top, you can drop your pack for a few minutes.* And my favorite: *When you reach the next gap, have some candy.* I hadn't fully appreciated Dad's root beer barrels on hikes growing up until I found myself reverting to the same sneaky gimmick.

The temperature rose as I walked, and I felt the prickly discomfort of overheating. Stepping aside, I shucked off my fleece, stuffing it in my pack's side pocket, and grabbing my orange handkerchief from my hip belt pocket. I slipped it over my forehead to keep the sweat from my eyes, and the breeze that accompanied me was blissful.

Taking a few chugs of water, I grabbed a Twix bar from my snack stash. At almost 300 calories, it would provide the protein and sugar boost needed to summit Clingmans Dome. The quick break also let me bask in the incredible scenery before me. This trail section was a luscious green forest of moss-covered trees. Sun slanted through evergreen branches, casting enticing patches of warmth across the path ahead. The trail continued free of roots and rocks, with springy undergrowth on either side—the picture-perfect image of a fairytale forest.

I noticed yellow peeking from behind grass clumps across the trail. Crossing over, I bent down to investigate. A single yellow flower emerged between three speckled green leaves. I pulled out my phone and took a photo. A quick Google Image search identified it as Yellow Trillium. I knew immediately from the images that it was indeed the same flower. This was the kind of knowledge Dad would have shared instantly in the Rockies, so I was thankful for modern technology to fill that void in the Appalachians.

"Cool," I said, reaching a finger down to gently poke at the Yellow Trillium's soft petals. "So that's what you are."

"Talking to yourself, Sharkbait?"

I looked up to find Nubs and Fun Facts grinning. I'd been so engrossed in discovery that I hadn't heard them approaching.

"No, just my new friend," I laughed, pointing at the flower.

Nubs's eyebrows raised. "I'm not sure if that's more or less weird." Then, chuckling, asked, "Are you ready to hike again, or do you need more time befriending the natives?"

I clasped his outstretched arm and rose, nodding my confirmation.

"Hey, have you guys heard from Huevos yet?" I asked, turning to look over my shoulder.

"Neither of us have," Fun Facts confirmed.

I pulled out my phone, and still seeing a bar of service, sent a quick text. A response pinged seconds later. I smiled.

"He says he just entered the Smokies," I called back. "Took a couple of zero days, but now he's feeling good."

"That's great," Fun Facts replied.

I didn't know if my path would cross with Huevos again, but it felt good knowing he was back on trail.

Two hours later, the trail flattened as we reached Clingmans Dome's peak. A short, paved side trail led onto a giant concrete ramp, delivering us to the observation tower perched high above the tree canopy. Promising epic 360-degree visibility, this was one of the most exciting and anticipated views from my early planning days. But as we cleared the trail onto the ramp, reality struck of what awaited at the top. Clouds had descended to meet us, laying such thick swathes of white that I couldn't see a foot in front of my face. My heart sank, but I willed my feet forward. As I'd suspected, the same view awaited us atop the observation tower, and I felt the surge of disappointment for missing the moment that I'd built up in my mind.

Pulling out my phone camera, I marched to a south-facing information board. It was a panoramic picture of the southern landscape, visible underneath a brilliantly blue sky.

"Here's what the southern view should have looked like," I narrated to my video, showing the board before flipping the phone up to reveal a wall of cloud. "And this is what I see!", I continued.

Marching to the next sign, I narrated, "Moving on, here's what the western view would have looked like." Again, I showed boards then clouds. I completed my rounds of the other two sides before ending sarcastically, "The goddamn view is just so beautiful up here on Clingman."

Nubs laughed along, and although I took the video mostly in good humor, I could still feel frustration simmering behind my jokes. Sending it off to Dana, I tried to console myself that the even more picturesque McAfee Knob overlook was only a couple hundred miles north in Virginia. Knowing its status as the most sought-after photo opportunity of the AT, if it turned out cloudy that day, I fully planned to set up my hammock right there and zero until it cleared. The problem was that getting those iconic photos was another big mental motivator to keep me going through all these miles. Without them, it was easy to get discouraged from the long, drawn-out day of hiking.

On the way back down, our situation turned sour fast. Raindrops began pounding the concrete around us, bouncing back up with surprising force. The trail came into view, which was now a flowing river of brown.

"Well," Nubs shouted above the sound of pouring rain and rushing water, "This complicates things a little."

I stared at the path before us. Rocks and logs littered the trail, which was now streaming with water over and around. I looked down at my shoes, a pair of Salomon X-Mission trail runners that were slightly sturdier than sneakers but just as water absorbent. One step into the water and my feet would be soaked, even with the supposedly waterproof socks I'd donned that morning to be safe. I looked back at the trail, and an idea formed to avoid the water.

I turned to Nubs and Fun Facts, who looked equally uneager to begin wading down the trail. "Who's up for trail hopscotch?"

Fun Facts turned to me, a single eyebrow raised as she caught my impish grin. "Trail hopscotch?"

"Watch this." I stretched cautiously forward onto a solid-looking rock jutting from the water, landing with my right foot as my left swung to a ledge of flattened rock just past it. Balanced somewhat precariously on both stones, I assessed my next move. Spotting a log just ahead, I carefully hopped first one foot, then the other, over to it. Finding more stability, I looked back.

"Your turn," I called.

Nubs's face was wide-eyed with caution but shifted to childish joy as he took his first leap onto the same rock. Fun Facts shook her head, but by the smile growing, I knew she would also take the leap.

And so we continued, hopping, skipping, and jumping our way along the trail until, somehow, whether by skill or luck, we made it safely to Newfound Gap's parking lot seven miles later.

Standing back on the relative dryness of concrete again, we surveyed our options. My waterproof socks had given up long ago, so my feet now squelched uncomfortably in my shoes. Every part of me was wet with either rain or perspiration, and I could see Fun Facts and Nubs weren't in better condition. It was only three miles to the next shelter, so I felt the question needed asking, even though I knew the answer.

"So, should we take a quick break, then try for Icewater Spring Shelter?"

Fun Facts shivered. "I don't want to see anything that has 'water' in its name."

Nubs nodded, smiling tightly. "You know that shelter has to be full by now."

"And it's supposed to get cold tonight, maybe even snow tomorrow," Fun Facts added.

"Yeah, it's already been a long day," I said with a sigh, pulling my phone out. "And a ride to Gatlinburg is just a phone call away."

Fun Facts and Nubs quickly agreed, so we called a shuttle service and booked a room for the night at Johnson's Inn, making plans to get back to the trail the next day after lunch. The hope was that warmer afternoon temperatures would allow us to make it to the shelter in a nero day.

That plan, however, was quickly shut down by Sherpa Matt, our shuttle driver.

"There's no way you're heading back to the trail tomorrow on this road," he informed us cheerily as he peered through the rain-soaked windshield. The wipers were trying to keep up but woefully failing. "They close it whenever there's heavy snow on the mountain."

"For how long?" I asked, seeing my progress being stripped away. I had hoped to be in the town of Hot Springs by now, so I was already 50 miles behind schedule. Another day would add another ten miles to that gap. I realized a zero day was necessary if the snow was going to be that bad, but it still sent a zing of panic through me to know I was creeping farther behind.

"Oh, at least a day, I reckon," Sherpa Matt estimated with a sympathetic voice. "Sorry, folks. But you'll love Gatlinburg. Tons of fun for young hikers like y'all."

For the foreseeable future, it seemed we were stuck in Gatlinburg. If it was going to be that bad, I certainly wanted to be in the safety of the valley. But my mind went to our friends we hadn't seen yet. I could only presume that both Huevos and Leap Frog were still on the trail, and I hoped they would find a way down to us before the blizzard found them.

18

A HAZY SHADE OF WINTER

T wo days later, I sat at breakfast with a large group of hikers who had all zeroed in Gatlinburg. After days of frigid whiteout conditions, the temperature finally rose, melting the snow. It was even supposed to peak at a tropical 45 degrees by afternoon. We had done everything possible to pass the time in Gatlinburg, an amusement park town that reminded me of summers in the Wisconsin Dells, and we were desperately ready to leave. We were all stocking up on food, hoping the warmer weather meant the road to the mountains would finally be open.

I listened to stories of extreme conditions from other hikers who had come off trail after us, some of them walking 15 miles down the snow-covered road to get here. One comment caught my attention, and I stopped shoveling eggs into my mouth.

"Oh yeah," said a young guy nearby in response to something. He jabbed his fork into a pancake dripping with syrup. "It was that huge family from Cincinnati. I saw it on their YouTube channel. All eight of them crammed in the bathroom at Newfound Gap's parking lot, looking like they'd just been through a miserable night. Can you imagine?"

"But why the bathroom?" the girl opposite him asked, disbelief evident in her tone.

"Because the road closed and the weather was too extreme for the youngest kids to hike through. I guess they thought it was their best option."

The girl stared at him, lines furrowing her brow in disbelief.

"Excuse me," I called over.

He looked over at me, pancake-filled fork paused in midair.

"Did you say a family with six kids? Is the youngest a two-year-old boy?"

"Yeah, that's them. Apparently, they do everything together—even homeschooling on the trail." He eyed me. "Why? Do you know them?"

"Not personally." I set my fork down. "I think they started the same time as me. I came across a family of eight on the second day after Sassafras Mountain. They stood out because they weren't your typical thru-hikers. The mom was carrying the toddler on her back, the dad carried gear for three of them, and the other kids carried their own."

I paused, remembering back to that night. I was concerned about kids so young being taken on a thru-hike, but also impressed by their efficiency at camp. They ran an impressive system. Immediately after dropping their packs, the dad set up a campsite while the younger kids pulled out textbooks with the mom.

"I remember this huge stockpot the dad pulled from his backpack. He handed it to the teenager, and she started cooking a massive pasta dinner for the whole family while the others completed school lessons."

"That's crazy," the guy said, his attention so captured by the story that the syrup dripping from his fork had pooled into a nice pile on the table.

"Do you know what happened to them? Are they still up in the bathroom?" I asked.

"Yeah, I think so." Then glanced around before leaning toward me. "But I was reading comments on their video, and it sounds like maybe not for long. A bunch of people were talking about reporting it to CPS as child abuse. I wouldn't be surprised if the cops are there to check on them the second the road opens."

Child Protective Services? I shook my head at the wild picture he was painting. Even as brief as my interaction had been, it didn't surprise me to hear such judgment accompanied their thru-hike. Especially knowing they were video blogging everything to the world. I just hoped they were all truly prepared for this and wondered whether a toddler could even make it all the way to Katahdin.

Around noon, we heard the road had finally opened. With a quick repack of our gear, we were soon back in a shuttle with Sherpa Matt and on our way to the trail. To pass the time, I made small talk from the back seat.

"So is that a trail name then?" I asked.

"Yep, some guys gave it to me a few years ago." He answered.

It turned out, Sherpa Matt had traveled the whole Appalachian Trail as well. Though he did it by car, helping his girlfriend do something called slackpacking—hiking with minimal belongings and rejoining someone who held all the gear at the end of the day. He chatted happily about their strategy as he navigated the recently plowed roads.

"It worked great," he said, grinning. "I took the big stuff and drove it to the next access point. She got to enjoy hiking with snacks and water."

"Sounds great," I replied. It wouldn't be my choice as I loved carrying my life on my back, but it was the perfect example of "hike your own hike", a trail mantra to hike the AT however it suited you, and to respect others doing the same.

"So, you guys ready for some serious snow?" He looked over, eyes wide. "I heard there's about 12 inches blanketing the trail."

I let out a low whistle. Besides the morning's stories, I'd also heard from Edie on last night's blog post that Jack, Tarzan, and Happy Feet had all reached Mount Cammerer—meaning they'd hiked through the snowstorm and were now a couple days ahead of us. They'd reported six inches of snow, only half of what Sherpa Matt was suggesting. I spent the rest of the ride preparing myself for the winter wonderland ahead.

Stepping from the car, the first gusts of ice-cold wind found every part of skin I hadn't yet covered. I shoved a fleece hat on my head, but I could still feel spiky tendrils of wind penetrating my collar. Pulling up the hood of my puff jacket, I then quickly added gloves to fingers already stiff with cold.

Nubs, Fun Facts, and I were joined by many hikers from the party at Fontana Dam. Besides the brave few who hiked through the blizzard, we'd become a bottleneck of hikers all hitting the trail again at the same time. Among us were new names: Chickapea, Zoltan, Trenchfoot, Caveman, and Culligan. And in all our winter layers, we were quite a sight as we set off into the frozen tundra.

We quickly discovered that everything green just two days ago was now bleached white and covered in a foot of snow. As we walked farther into the woods, I started seeing drifts along the side twice that deep. Much of the trail had been packed down by other hikers, but not enough. Snow began finding gaps in the tops of my boots and soon my socks were sodden and frozen. In the haste to get back, I'd forgotten to put my leg gaiters on—a minimalist item that helped keep insects, debris, and weather out of my boots. But it was too cold to stop and remedy it, so I consoled myself that this was just a nero day. As agreed earlier, we only had to make it three miles to Icewater Spring Shelter.

In normal conditions, it would have been a breeze, but in thick snow, those three miles were sluggish and monotonous. Every step was carefully placed on top of snow that was atop ice that lay across frozen ground. It wasn't worth the risk to hike fast.

We eventually reached the shelter, and I immediately set about changing out my wet socks for dry ones. Feet no longer quite as wet, I joined the others setting up camp inside the stone shelter. Nubs and Chickapea stood off to the side, talking excitedly before disappearing into the woods.

It wasn't long before we heard grunting, interrupted by shouts of encouragement. They suddenly reappeared with a thirty-foot tree that had fallen nearby. Nubs was bringing up the rear, and from my viewpoint, it looked very much like he was taking the brunt of the weight. His face red and shiny from exertion as he called out another round of support.

The part of Chickapea's mouth I could see underneath the riot of his red beard was pressed into a thin line. His eyebrows had almost disappeared behind his black-rimmed glasses, pulled down by the pain-filled grimace across his face.

They took a few more steps into the clearing before Chickapea dropped his end of the log in a resounding crash of splintering wood.

"I think that's good, man," he called, turning to Nubs, who was wiping sweat from his brow with his sleeve.

Culligan joined them, and a strategy for getting the massive log into manageable-sized chunks of firewood was quickly laid out. Between Culligan and Nubs, the log was hauled over to a boulder that stuck out with a point from the ground. They began to drop the log onto the point, and the clearing filled with the cracking and tearing of wood, the groans of working men, and the cheers of onlookers as more fireplace-sized chunks flew into the air.

After several minutes, they had a pile big enough to warrant a fire. Chickapea produced a Duraflame firelog he'd carried up from Gatlinburg, and Nubs and Culligan were able to get everything lit inside the shelter's fireplace. Unfortunately, keeping it going proved near impossible. The wood was waterlogged and frozen, meaning the fire required constant care. I had to hand it to the guys though, they made it work the best they could. The tiny shelter filled with warmth for enough time to eat dinner and set up our beds. We even had enough flame to get out ingredients for s'mores, which

Chickapea also packed in. Nubs sighed contentedly, eyes closed in blissful joy, as he took his first bite.

"That good?" I asked, chuckling.

His eyes blinked open, and he fixed his steely blue gaze on me. "Mmmm... the softly melted chocolate, the crunch of the cookie, the sticky marshmallow... I've never heard of this, but it's amazing."

I stopped just before taking my own first bite. "Wait. Is this your first-ever s'more?"

"Yeah," he smiled sheepishly. "We don't have this in Australia. It's genius!"

"Wow," I said at a loss for any more substantial words.

Nubs waved his s'more at me, his trademark mischievous grin illuminating his face. "But it won't be my last!"

As I sat enveloped in my quilt's warmth that night, but still grimly cold, I came to the brilliant conclusion that I didn't like camping in cold and snow all that much. At 6,000 feet in elevation, and no warm car to run back to, everything that had frozen earlier that day remained frozen. And it was really fricking cold. The kind of cold that went deep to your core and never seemed to thaw. The fire had long since died out, and although sleep slowly came, the icy frost woke me constantly as it permeated up through the floor and any crack in my quilt's protective sheath.

When I finally roused myself from bed, I discovered the water pipe at Icewater Spring Shelter was living a little too much up to its name. It had completely frozen over, which meant no water refills with breakfast. My bottles, which had hung from my pack overnight, had also become solid blocks of ice. And with temperatures not expected to rise out of the teens, the odds of finding running water weren't looking good.

Concern for dehydration built with each new realization, but I knew I had to shake it off. I had no control over the situation, only how I navigated through it. I shifted focus to getting the day's hike started as soon as humanly possible. Standing around was not an option. I had to get moving to get warm.

It was a quiet start with each hiker concentrating on taking careful steps and scanning the surrounding woods for any sign of water not trapped in icicle form. I also had another mission—looking for Leap Frog. Her parents had commented on my blog that they hadn't heard from her in a couple days and were getting concerned. The group I was with would not know her location, as they'd all been with me in Gatlinburg, but I hoped to come across some hikers who might have remained on the AT since cell service was absent to try a text. It was a slim hope because any hikers who hadn't zeroed in Gatlinburg should be at least a couple days ahead, but I still searched.

A mile in, a blue blaze appeared a hundred yards ahead, indicating a short side trail to Charlies Bunion. As we approached, I debated whether to say anything about taking the detour. I knew from my research this was an opportunity for incredible views across the Smokies, and unlike the day I summited Clingmans Dome, the sun shone in a brilliantly blue sky today. I also knew we were cold, and climbing up to an exposed outcropping wasn't going to help us get warmer. But I didn't want to pass this scenic vista without at least considering it.

I stopped at the blue blaze, turning back to Nubs and Fun Facts. "I'm going to take this blue blaze to Charlies Bunion. Are either of you up for joining me?"

Nubs's mouth curled into what I could see would be a "no," but Fun Facts immediately agreed. Nubs closed his mouth again and looked at her. I had noticed this lately. Fun Facts was steadfast, and even if you disagreed, you'd eventually concede to what she suggested.

Raising one eyebrow, I asked, "Nubs?"

He looked at me before his gaze slid back to Fun Facts. "Sure," he said, shrugging his agreement.

I grinned and took off down the side trail. The path narrowed to that of one person's striding legs as it carved along the mountain's edge. We navigated its icy slickness until we reached the boulder outcropping at its summit. As we scanned the crystal-clear horizon of peaks, I knew we'd made the right call. It had been worth taking time to appreciate the moment and not rush because of a little weather-induced discomfort.

We hiked back to the main trail, continuing our search for water while we tackled the remaining miles. It was fruitless, besides handfuls of snow, until about three hours later. I halted in the middle of the trail, causing a domino effect behind me. A faint sound of running water came from our right. Exchanging gleeful looks, we abandoned our packs in the snow. A minute of searching revealed a white pipe sticking out of the bank running alongside the trail. Somehow, the water had kept from freezing, still trickling out slowly but consistently! I finally got a bottle filled and quickly downed it, but it was too cold to wait and drink another. I was still thirsty, and it was a decision that included a certain amount of danger, but we had to keep moving to stay warm.

We covered the remaining 12.6 miles to reach Tri-Corner Knob Shelter in six hours. Given how hard it was to hike safely at speed in the snow, we'd made good time.

A couple hours later, the other shelter-mates from the night before arrived, but no one else. I checked the logbook, searching for Leap Frog's signature. Jack's quick scrawl appeared on a page from several days previous, but there was nothing from Leap Frog. If she'd passed through here, she hadn't recorded it.

19

I WILL SURVIVE

I peered out the shelter's tarp door the next morning, already knowing what I would see. I could hear the evidence rattling against the roof, but the optimistic part of my mind prayed it wasn't true. Then my eyes confirmed the heart-dropping proof as I watched pellets of sleet bounce off any snow-bare surfaces, covering them in a fresh layer of white. It was going to be another day of wet and cold.

Fun Facts appeared beside me, still wrapped tight in her sleeping bag, and surveyed the scene with determined resignation. She sighed. "We really need to make it out of the Smokies and to Standing Bear Farm Hostel in the valley today."

I nodded slowly. At 18 miles, it would be one of our longest days yet, but the thought of spending another freezing night in a shelter was not a pleasant one.

"Or die trying," Nubs added from behind us, his head still tucked tight in his sleeping bag.

I'd really enjoyed the first half of the Smokies, but doing the back half in these conditions was far from fun. It was hard to do anything other than trudge woefully through the day, consume calories as quickly as possible, and crawl into bed for a miserable night's rest.

"At least we'll drop 2,000 feet today," I said, attempting to add hope to the day ahead.

"And hiking downhill is a lot easier and faster in the snow with that soft landing for our feet," Fun Facts added, feeding off my attitude as she pulled more layers over her long underwear.

The tarp rustled open again, bringing a blast of icy air. Chickapea had slipped out a few minutes before to replenish his water supplies, and he now stomped his way back in. Defrosting ice pellets clung to his hat and beard, his cheeks starting to match the color of his facial hair.

"It's awful out there," he grumbled.

I felt the bubble of optimism burst with a resounding pop, but there was nothing we could do to change what we were facing. We simply had to do it.

Ten minutes down the trail, as predicted, everything was soaking wet. We were freezing cold. My boots were waterlogged on the inside and frozen stiff on the outside, an uncomfortable combination that got worse with every step. The sleet assaulted my face, the only part of skin I had dared to leave exposed, reminding me of the first day's hike with Keg and The Captain. It was strange thinking back that far. It had only been twenty-three days, and yet so much had happened that it seemed like a lifetime ago.

The eleven of us who'd stayed at Tri-Corner Knob Shelter were spread out along the trail, each locked into our personal world of perseverance. But we each needed to take breaks to refuel, so we ended up leapfrogging each other the whole morning, swapping curse words and woeful cries in the camaraderie of the shared awfulness.

The blue blaze to Cosby Knob Shelter appeared around lunchtime, so I hurried down the side path to take advantage of its covered porch. I was gathering the basic resupply meal I'd picked up at Walgreens in Gatlinburg—flour tortillas wrapped around string cheese and beef jerky—when I saw Nubs and Fun Facts appear along the sleet-soaked trail. They covered the last hundred yards and climbed onto the porch, dropping their packs and offering me a nod each.

"This officially sucks," Nubs said, rubbing his gloved hands together and blowing into them.

I stood and gathered my trash, looking around to make sure I'd left no trace behind. Satisfied, I added, "And on that note, I'm going back out. Standing Bear or bust, right?"

Fun Facts's quick laugh was without mirth, and I couldn't blame her. Yep, this sucked.

The elevation had indeed dropped quickly during the morning, and I was now at only 2,500 feet. The snow and ice had melted at this level, but the trail had unfortunately become a slick mud pit instead. So there was nothing else to be done. Leveraging my poles as extra limbs, I went into a second round of trail hopscotch. After eight miles of the strangest square dance Tennessee has ever seen, I reached the end of the Smokies and discovered the most welcome surprise... trail angels!

A middle-aged man and woman had set up a covered eating area at Davenport Gap off the back of their pickup truck by strapping a tarp to the cabin and lifting it above head with two poles about eight feet out. They both stood under the tarp and behind a table covered in food—a large crock pot of soup, bags of chips, bananas, fruit snacks, and soda. It was a banquet fit for a thru-hiker king.

"Hey!" the woman greeted me warmly. "I'm Janet. Are you hungry?"

She held out a cup of steaming soup, which I immediately cradled gratefully in my icy hands, letting the warm steam permeate my face's pores.

"Chicken noodle?" I asked, peering at Janet through a haze of steam.

Janet nodded while the man beside her said, "It's her own recipe. The best soup you'll ever taste." He put his arm around Janet, his eyes crinkling in amusement. "In my opinion, that is."

I took a tentative sip to test the heat before gulping down a few more swallows. "Oh," I groaned. "This really is the best soup I've ever tasted."

After two days in the freezing cold, living off quick and easy trail meals, this was heaven.

Janet beamed and gestured for my empty cup. "David here would eat half the pot if I let him."

"That I would," David laughed, patting his generously sized stomach.

After downing another cup of soup and a few extra snacks to round out the meal, I gave them both my profuse thanks and got back to the trail. The afternoon was marching forward, and thanks to these angels, I was now ready to close out the day and hang up my boots for the night.

The last three miles to the hostel began with a stretch that stayed close to a beautiful spring with plenty of mini waterfalls. I found my spirits lifting as I listened to the sound of running water again and felt the warmth of Janet's soup flooding my core.

It wasn't long until I heard a "hoo ha ha!" behind me, and turned, grinning, to see Nubs and Fun Facts charging along the trail.

"You guys check out that trail magic feast?" I asked.

"Just a quick stop. We're trying to beat the rain," Nubs huffed.

"Rain?" I asked. I'd been so lost in rushing out of the mountain snow that I hadn't once checked the radar in the valley.

Nubs lifted a hiking pole and pointed at the sky behind us. Sure enough, through gaps in the trees, I could see a darkening line of gray beginning to overtake the white cloud cover we'd had all day.

"Alright then," I said, planting my poles firmly. "Let's do this."

Soon, the trail intersected with a busy highway that we needed to hike along to reach the Standing Bear Farm Hostel. In the absence of trees, the blazes here had been painted on stop signs, guard rails, bridge struts—anything easy to see. It felt so out of place compared to our normal green tunnel, but it kept us entertained as we encouraged tired legs down the final stretch to that night's rest.

Asphalt turned to gravel, and wooden slats of buildings began peeking through the fresh green of trees just as the heavens opened again. Letting out a roar of effort, I pushed my body into a run for the last couple hundred yards, intent on reaching the dry safety of a porch.

Panting and feeling the strain in my hamstrings, I ran through a complicated jumble of dilapidated wooden buildings. It took me a moment to survey the surroundings, the rain beginning to pour now, but I spotted a riot of colors that turned out to be a brightly painted signpost. I strode over to see the bunkhouse was marked as a building just to the right. I turned quickly onto its covered porch, dropping my pack, just before Nubs and Fun Facts joined me. We laughed at each other's wet dog impressions as we shook ourselves dry. None of us taking the time to stop and don rain gear.

Safely ensconced in the relative dryness of the porch, I looked around at my surroundings, and what I saw left me beaming and scratching my head at the same time.

Rounded tree branches of varying sizes held up the roof above our heads. They looked like they were pinned together by a few nails and some garden lattice threaded with vines just awakening to spring. Along the wall that led to the bunkhouse door were wooden bookshelves stuffed full of worn books, most curling with damp from years of exposure to the elements.

Attached to the outside of the porch, sitting atop a long wooden plank, were a row of old hiking boots. They were filled with soil and an array of purple, yellow, and white flowers spilled out the top of each one.

The porch floor had a sloping feel, as if it was sinking back into the bunkhouse, and I had this boyish desire to drop a marble and watch it roll off the far corner.

The white, glass-paneled door leading into the bunkhouse creaked open, and I stepped back into the garden lattice, pressing against the porch railing as a guy with a shock of curly white-blond hair stepped out.

"Oh, sorry, guys," he smiled, staring at our wet packs on the ground. "You just get here?"

"We did," Fun Facts said.

"Cool. You staying the night in here?" He thumbed over his shoulder into the bunkhouse's dark interior.

"That's the plan," I confirmed. "Any idea where we check in?"

The guy laughed. "It's a little confusing when you first get here. But you'll soon figure out where everything is." He squinted off into the distance, over a fast-running river about thirty feet ahead. "See that guy over there?"

He pointed to a building across the other side of the river that looked more permanent than the rest. Its wooden siding was a beautiful warm brown, and its front was decorated with a rock garden edged with a red-brick path. The sole occupant of the space sat in a chair on the porch, leaning forward with his hands on his knees, watching the water race by.

"That's Hawk," he said. "He works for the owner and can show you the ropes."

We thanked our new bunkmate and went back out into the rain, which had now turned into a light mist. Hawk looked up as we approached, but although his dark eyes fixed on us, they held a faraway look that made me wonder whether our existence even entered his mind.

I cleared my throat. "Hey, um, we'd like to stay for the night." It came out as more of a statement than I had intended, as we didn't actually have reservations. But the man's spacey gaze was not eliciting confidence.

He nodded slowly and stood. His fleece-lined black hoodie hung off his thin frame, and a blue bandana wrapped around his jaw-length black hair, pinning an unlit cigarette to the top of his right ear. He silently surveyed us before climbing down the few steps off the porch.

"You want a tour?" he asked, his face not moving into any kind of recognizable expression.

"Uh, sure," I said. "That would be great."

He nodded again and walked back in the direction we'd just come, leading us on a quick circuit of the kitchen, washroom, shower, and privy before ending back at the bunkhouse. Wet clothes hung from fourteen beds, steam-drying in the heat from a large oil drum converted into a wood stove. It was tight quarters, but warm and cozy. And for twenty dollars a night, there wasn't much room for complaint, especially as I lay that night on my bunk hearing rain hitting the thin roof inches above me. Sleep came quickly, knowing I didn't have to endure the cold of another exposed night on the trail.

After what felt like seconds later, my eyes flew open, and I gripped my right leg as piercing shots of pain lanced from the top of my foot halfway up my shin. I panted through several rounds before the pain eased. Rubbing the tender muscle along the side of my shin bone, I stretched it slowly. My eyes drifted closed again, but within minutes, the shooting pain returned. Stifling a groan with my fist, I reached over to where my pack hung from the post of the bed. After weeks of aches in my arches, calves, ankles, and hamstrings, I'd taken to keeping a healthy supply of meds nearby just in case. Ibuprofen had jokingly become my daily "Vitamin I" to ease the day's pains, but these shooting daggers along my legs were worse than anything before. Much worse.

I scrambled around for the bottle as quietly as I could. Finding it in much slower time than preferred, I gulped down a few extra pills and tried to settle back into sleep. My eyes closed, only to fly open again as another round of pain rippled along my leg, only slightly dulled by the pain meds. This pattern continued throughout the restless night. By morning, when a rooster decided to announce the dawn to one and all, I was cranky with lack of sleep.

I climbed gingerly down the steps of my bunk, wincing at the pressure each step put on my legs. Gathering my clothes and shoes, I dressed quickly before hobbling over to the main house to access the Wi-Fi. Something was seriously wrong, and there was no way I could hike in this condition. I needed to figure out what the heck was going on.

20

DR. FEELGOOD

"Shin splints," I announced to Fun Facts and Nubs as I eased myself into a chair around the small kitchen table.

Nubs looked up from his oatmeal and lifted an eyebrow, but Fun Facts sat back to observe me.

"Uh-oh," she said, wincing sympathetically.

"Yeah," I sighed, scratching at the beard that had grown in over the last couple weeks. "Looks like what hit me last night is just the beginning stage. I think I need to take it easy."

Fun Facts continued to eye me, her gaze jumping from my face to the leg I stretched out between us. She had told me early on that she was a pre-med student, and I could see in the way she studied me now that her mind was whirring away. She remained uncharacteristically silent, though, as I consumed a quick breakfast. I was eager to get back to the bunkhouse because my internet search had also yielded results for stretching exercises that were supposed to strengthen the muscle causing pain.

A few minutes later, I hobbled back over to our night's accommodation and attempted to stretch my tight shins as diligently as possible. As I held each stretch, I could feel the pain slightly easing. I completed the full routine and walked the narrow gap between the two rows of beds without limping. Hoping it would be enough, I popped a couple more ibuprofen and got ready for the day's hike.

Fun Facts and Nubs were waiting for me outside, and Fun Facts gave me another careful look as I made my way down the steps.

"You're not limping as much," she commented, smiling.

"I found some stretches, and they seem to have worked," I replied, tightening my hip belt and settling my pack securely around my waist. The day was starting off milder, so I'd opted to leave my sweatshirt packed away. It also seemed I was cinching the straps just a little more snugly than at the beginning, even without the extra layers. "I'm just going to take it slow and evaluate my legs every couple miles."

The aim for the day was to make Roaring Fork Shelter 15 miles away, but I knew it wouldn't be wise to push the early signs of this injury.

My phone dinged, and I pulled it out, wondering if Dana had decided to get an earlier start than usual to her day. But Ground Score's name appeared on my screen instead.

I smiled and clicked the notification, anticipating a question about our location in hopes of catching up. We'd left him in Gatlinburg where he wanted one more zero day. But when the message appeared, I let out a soft groan.

Fun Facts had just started walking ahead but turned back, hearing my distress.

"Something wrong?"

"It's Ground Score," I began. "He's in the hospital."

"What?!" Fun Facts exclaimed, her hands going up to her mouth.

Nubs frowned and placed a hand on Fun Facts's shoulder. "What happened?"

"He says he slipped in the snow coming out of Newfound Gap and landed hard on his hip. Dislocated it." I checked the text again.

"He says he's sore and doing fine, but definitely off trail. He hopes he'll be back before the end of the season though."

Fun Facts shook her head, her brown eyes wide. "I don't think he'll be hiking for a while."

I held her gaze for a few seconds before looking back at my phone. Hitting reply, I typed, *"Rest up man, the trail will be here when you're back to 100%."*

Ground Score's news filled my thoughts as I followed Nubs and Fun Facts down the road that would lead us back to the trail. My ailments were worrisome but not hike-ending yet. Ground Score was out for the foreseeable future because of a freak accident he couldn't have seen coming. But I did know the potential consequences if I pushed my body too far with shin splints. We made our way onto the trail, littered with exposed roots and rocks, and I found myself keeping an extra careful eye on my feet.

Ten miles into the day, and I hadn't felt any new bouts of shooting pain. Every time I stopped, I took a few minutes to do the same stretches, which were helping to keep everything nice and loose. My confidence in reaching Roaring Fork Shelter was growing. The day was chilly but not obscenely cold like the last few. It felt good walking under a canopy of spring leaves, without a muddy river beneath my feet.

We reached mile 11 about fifteen minutes later, and pain immediately radiated up my right leg. It was quickly there and just as quickly gone again, so I pushed on, keeping the pain to myself rather than worry Fun Facts and Nubs. I figured I could set up my hammock at any point to rest if needed, but it was less than two miles to a summit called Max Patch. It would be a beautiful, clear bald, known to be a highlight of this section. I really wanted to see it. So, gritting my teeth and straightening my pack, I suffered the occasional shots of pain and moved on.

We reached Max Patch soon after, and I took a few minutes to do another round of stretches. The pain was getting more frequent, each one more prolonged. My leg was warning me it was reaching a tipping point, but my brain was goading me on, knowing it was only another couple miles to Roaring Fork Shelter. I could make it. Slowly. So I finished my last stretch, took another round of ibuprofen, and plastered a smile on my face when Fun Facts looked my way.

By the time we got to the shelter, my limp was much more pronounced again, and there was no fooling Fun Facts. She took one look at me lurching up the steps to the shelter's porch and ordered me inside for some amateur medical attention. I sat down on the floor of the shelter and, at her direction, removed my hiking boot and sock before rolling up my pant leg.

She rummaged in her bag, pulling out a roll of bright-purple tape.

"Uh..." I began, "What are you planning?"

She gave me a puzzled look before noticing my attention fixed on the tape in her hand. "Oh," she laughed. "This is KT Tape."

"Katie who?"

"KT Tape," she repeated slowly. "It's something I learned about at school. I wish I'd thought about it this morning."

She unrolled a long section and used the small scissors from her Swiss Army knife to cut it, then rounded its corners.

"That keeps it from catching on your pants and socks," she explained, noting my raised eyebrows.

Starting just below my knee, she applied the tape lengthwise down my leg to the top of my foot, stretching it tight over the bone. Two smaller pieces joined the long piece horizontally, one over my foot and the other at the top of my shin. It looked like a giant purple letter "I."

"There," she said, sitting back to survey her work and smiling. "That should keep you out of more trouble."

The tape pulled in a constricting layer across my skin, but not with any discomfort. In fact, it gave me a pleasant feeling of being held together.

"Thanks," I grinned, putting my sock and shoe back on. I took a few test strides across the shelter and immediately felt the difference with the tape's support.

A double round of stretches accompanied my granola bar and coffee breakfast the next morning. I needed to do everything I could to help my shins make it the 17 miles to Hot Springs, the oasis trail town coming up. It also had the side benefit of getting my body moving early in what was yet another morning of sub-freezing temperatures.

I was holding the last stretch for the full count of thirty when Fun Facts stepped out of her tent and made her way over.

"How is it feeling?" she asked, gesturing at my leg.

"Great, actually." I rinsed out my coffee cup and packed it away. "I think I should be good to get to Hot Springs today." Seeing Fun Facts's slightly alarmed look, I added, "Slowly, of course. Is Nubs still sleeping?"

Fun Facts nodded. "I'll probably be getting a late start too, but we'll try to make it to Hot Springs with you. Let's check the tape before you leave."

I pulled up my pants leg and let her inspect her previous night's work. Once she was satisfied and had issued several warnings about not overdoing it, I said my goodbyes and headed out. Knowing I'd be hiking alone for a while, I hit play on a new podcast I'd been waiting to get to. And with Fun Facts's words ringing in my ears, I slowed my pace way down.

Around noon, I reached Walnut Mountain, just about when Fun Facts and Nubs caught up. After a full round of questions about my pain level, we reconfirmed the plan to get to Hot Springs that day. It meant we could camp in town and take a full zero the next day to recover. We all agreed we could use the break to enjoy the iconic mineral spas at the resort on the far edge of town.

By late afternoon, we traded wooded paths for concrete roads as we followed the trail on its cut through town. The white blazes on tree trunks switched to Appalachian Trail emblems engraved into the sidewalks as we walked down Hot Spring's tiny Main Street. The KT Tape had not let me down; my leg felt great.

A resupply box was waiting for me at the Laughing Heart Hostel on one end of town, sent last week by Dana, so that was my first stop. Opening the box, I pulled out the ingredients for my new lunch of peanut butter and dried banana wraps and my next round of dinners, fancy mac and cheese with breadcrumbs, olive oil, and freeze-dried mushrooms.

I walked over to the town's tavern to rejoin the others for dinner. When I got to their table, I saw it would be a lot more than just the three of us. Zoltan, Trenchfoot, Culligan, and Chickapea (the guys we'd hiked out of Gatlinburg with) were joking and laughing with Nubs and Fun Facts. We caught up on each other's last couple of days and stuffed ourselves full of greasy pub fare. Dusk was beginning to draw in, and we decided it was time to find a campsite for the night.

"This isn't the stealthiest campsite I've ever seen," I commented a few minutes later as I surveyed the dozen brightly colored tents and hammocks before me. Stealth camping was legal in Hot Springs and, apparently, very popular. The campsite area was set up on the edge of town, along the eastern bank of the French Broad River. The trees surrounding us gave some idea we were still in the wilderness, but the traffic noise from the road behind left no doubt we were close to civilization.

Nubs snorted. "Stealth? Pretty sure everyone in town knows we're here."

All I knew was that after opting to sleep in the shelter again the prior night because of impending rain, I was very much looking forward to blissfully swinging in my hammock. As I settled into my quilts that night, I felt the gentle rocking of the wind whipping through the leaves above us. Nubs had disappeared into his tent minutes before, still muttering about the plethora of stones he'd be sleeping on all night. I couldn't help the small smile of satisfaction that grew on my face with the knowledge that I wouldn't be dealing with that rocky ground. The conditions were perfect for a great night of hammock camping.

And what a great night it was. I woke the next morning refreshed and ready to see the wonder of Hot Springs... which, given its short four block length, wasn't going to take long. The only downside I had seen so far was the complete lack of cell and internet service. The tavern the night before didn't have Wi-Fi, and the hostels only gave it out to guests, so I was feeling at a loss on how to get my blog posted, call Dana, and download some more podcasts.

I rolled out of my hammock and saw Chickapea emerge from his tent at the same time. Then a memory hit me of our brief conversation over dinner the night before. He had left early to try and locate anyone with internet so he could send a few emails.

"Hey," I said, turning to him. "Did you find anywhere to access Wi-Fi?"

"Oh yeah. Check out Hiker's Ridge Ministry Center. It's free there. And they have snacks."

I thought for a moment, an image surfacing of seeing that name on a building. "Is that the one opposite the outfitter?"

"That's it," Chickapea confirmed.

I thanked him and turned again to my hammock. It didn't take long to pack my gear, let Nubs and Fun Facts know where I was headed, and make my way to the ministry. It was exactly what I needed, seemingly existing solely to help hikers on their journey to Maine. I quickly published the blog entry for yesterday's hike and called Dana. Our conversations lately were few and far between, and not just because of my schedule. As I had predicted in our early discussions together, she was so busy with her studies and work that she typically only had time and energy for quick text catch-ups or responses to photos and videos I sent her.

It was good to hear her voice again, and I left the call smiling, anticipating our reunion in June to meet her for our friend's wedding.

Next on the agenda was laundry. Fun Facts and Nubs had made their way to Hiker's Ridge and still needed to resupply food, so I offered to wash their dirty clothes in exchange for them grabbing a few items I needed at the store. They eagerly agreed. So, backpack full again, I headed back up the road to the Laughing Heart Hostel, where I had seen a sign the day before indicating hikers could do a load of wash for five dollars.

The staff directed me to the kitchen, and I wandered in looking for the laundry room. Instead, I saw a young woman sitting at the table with her back to me, her dark brown hair pulled back into a casual knot. She turned, having heard me approach, and I froze in place, a cry of surprise escaping my mouth.

"Leap Frog?!"

PART 3

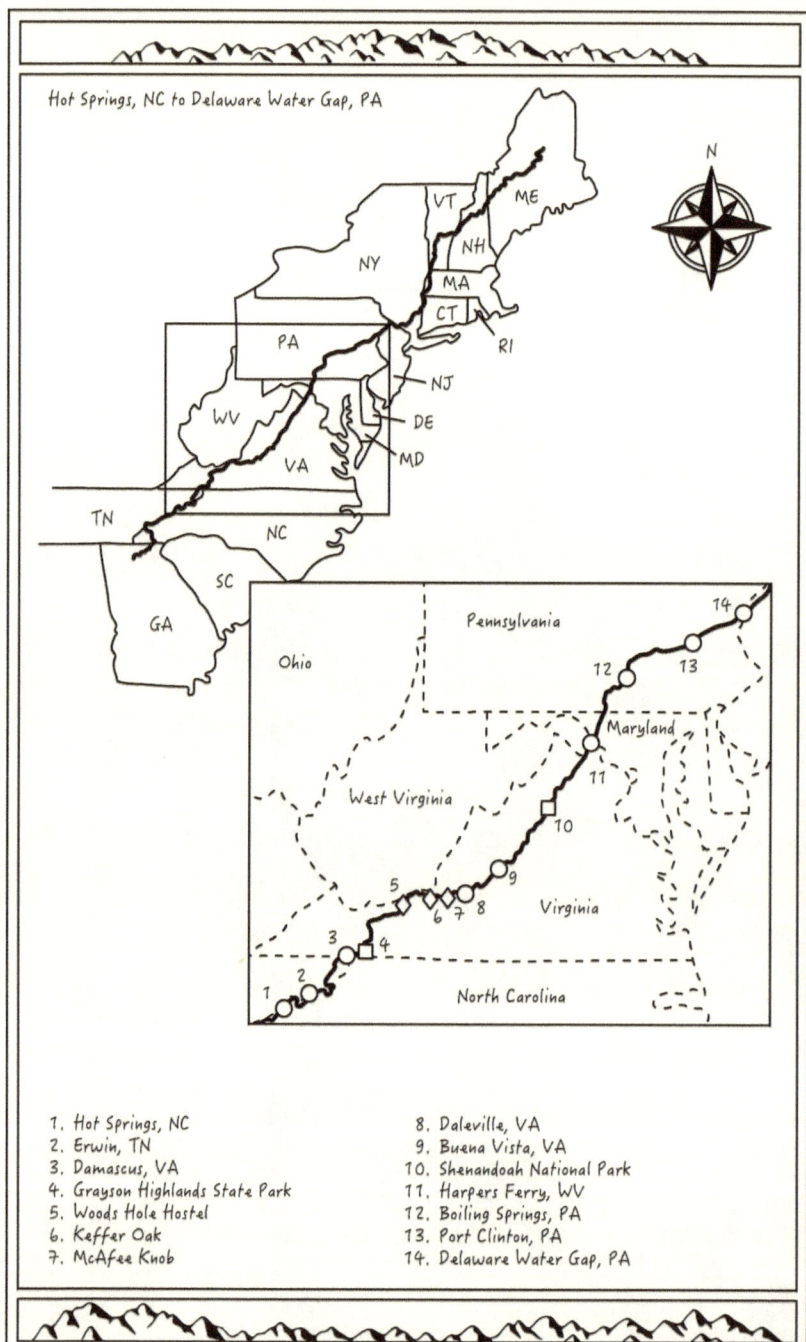

1. Hot Springs, NC
2. Erwin, TN
3. Damascus, VA
4. Grayson Highlands State Park
5. Woods Hole Hostel
6. Keffer Oak
7. McAfee Knob
8. Daleville, VA
9. Buena Vista, VA
10. Shenandoah National Park
11. Harpers Ferry, WV
12. Boiling Springs, PA
13. Port Clinton, PA
14. Delaware Water Gap, PA

21

GO YOUR OWN WAY

Leap Frog squealed and jumped out of her seat, reaching up on tiptoes to embrace me in a tight hug.

"I can't believe you're here," I wheezed as she squeezed my neck.

Releasing me, she laughed and winced an apology, having heard the result of her excitement. "I can't believe you are either. I wasn't sure I'd see any of you again. Are you staying here?"

I shook my head. "No. Nubs, Fun Facts, and I camped by the river. What about you? How long have you been here?"

"I got here two nights ago. Basically hiked thirty miles in one day to make it here alive."

"Thirty miles in one day?!" I exclaimed.

"Yeah," she said, rolling her eyes and giving me one of her shy grins that meant she was about to divulge something personal. "I don't know why, but I decided to stay in the Smokies when I heard about the snowstorm. I figured it was just mountain weather and would be over as soon as it started. That was pretty dumb, though, because I woke up the next morning to a foot of snow on the ground. I didn't know what else to do, so I hiked alone through the blizzard to another shelter and nearly gave myself hypothermia. The only other person I saw all day was some random guy who was on spring break. That night, I snuggled way too close to him, just to keep from freezing. That's when I decided I needed to make it to lower elevation and a warm bed. Thirty miles later, I crashed at Standing Bear Hostel, then just kept pushing until I got here."

"Wow, that sounds intense."

"It was."

I piled my laundry into a washer as we caught up on more details of Leap Frog's adventures. Then, switching her laundry from the washer to dryer, I shared about my own last few days with Fun Facts and Nubs before going into our plans for that night.

Originally, I was supposed to stay at the Laughing Heart Hostel too, then nero in Hot Springs before getting back to the trail in the afternoon. But I was also supposed to be here nearly a week ago, so when Fun Facts mentioned the Hot Springs Resort and Spa could put us up in a cabin and give us access to their outdoor mineral spa tubs if we stayed another night, I happily threw my plans out the window and jumped in. Literally.

Leap Frog was heading back to the trail later that day, but she was easily swayed by the unique hot tub experience as well, so she decided to join us for a few hours first.

I loved the first two weeks on the AT, but nothing compared to the next few hours of hiker heaven. We ate lunch in the spa; we drank beers and wine in the spa; we ran down to the river, jumped into its icy depths, and then ran squealing and laughing back to the spa. We slowly boiled ourselves into what Nubs lovingly called "hiker stew." The three hours we spent soaking in that hot tub were exactly what our beaten, frozen, and bandaged bodies needed.

As the afternoon washed away, along with any last trail dust, Leap Frog announced that it was time for her to hit the trail. We reluctantly watched her go, knowing that it was also time for us to check into our cabin for the night. The basic lodging we rented was situated along the river, far from extravagant. For sixty dollars, we got a roof, four walls, a space heater, and three beds. The quarters were tight, but no one complained as we drifted to sleep.

It was two hours into the next day's hike, and I was feeling sluggish. These days, my pace was around 2.5 miles per hour, but I had only gone three miles so far. As happened with most town visits, hiking out was significantly harder than hiking in. This was partly due to mental motivations pushing you towards town, like the promised comfort of a warm bed, shower, and hot meal. But the physical reasons made the real difference. On the way into town, my pack was typically ten or more pounds lighter since I had little food or water for the last few miles. And towns were usually downhill into a valley, easier for sustaining momentum.

That morning, however, had been an uphill climb from the moment we left Hot Springs. I was now carrying four days of food and two liters of water, and I still had five more miles of uphill before reaching Rich Mountain's summit. Even my optimism that the worst day on the trail was still better than the best day in an office couldn't ignore that it was a challenging day. It would have been very easy to call it quits in the first mile and go back to the comfort of Hot Springs.

Nubs and Fun Facts, also weary from the extra weight, slowly slipped behind me. I focused on getting past Rich Mountain, and when I got a text a couple hours later that they were going to stealth camp at the top, I knew my day would end away from the tramily again.

Not long later, my determination brought me across Chickapea just as he was finishing a snack break, and we fell into stride with each other. We hadn't talked much on the trail yet, besides his Wi-Fi advice the day prior, but as it was just the two of us now, conversation and curiosity eventually led to the origins of his trail name.

"Oh yeah," he chuckled. "That's a funny story. When I started back in Georgia, I was talking to some hikers about the homemade hummus they had packed. One of the girls was saying she missed fresh cucumbers to dip instead of dry crackers. I told her I loved hummus, and she asked if I had ever made it. Said she had and it was super easy. And I was like, 'Well, no, I haven't. Don't even know where to buy chick-a-peas.' And that just set everyone off. I wasn't sure what I had said that was so funny until they told me it was pronounced 'chickpea' instead."

He shrugged and laughed along with me, not at all concerned that his trail name was mocking him or based on one misplaced comment.

"I suppose I never really thought to look at a label," he added. "I ate the hummus and enjoyed it for what it was. I mean, I've eaten way more crazy things than hummus before. It just never crossed my mind what it was made from."

My curiosity piqued further. "What kind of things have you eaten?"

He laughed innocently. "Well, I should probably start by saying I grew up in a rural part of southern Illinois. Real rural."

"Okay," I said, waiting for him to go on.

"We would just wander around and gather things to eat. We'd go fishing, hunting, forage mushrooms, whatever. But my favorite was gigging."

"Did you say gigging?" My confusion was obvious; I'd never heard the word before.

"Oh yeah, man, gigging is great. You go out at night to a lake or a pond with a twelve-foot pole. It has prongs sticking out the end, so it kind of looks like a giant spear. We would creep around the edges listening for the croaks of frogs, and then when we spotted one, we'd raise our spear up into the air..." He paused, raising his hiking pole way above his head. "... before stabbing it back down and collecting the feast." He jabbed his arm down into an imaginary frog. "Then you cook 'em up and eat 'em."

"Eat them? What, like frog legs?"

"Nope, the whole thing. Body, head, legs... everything."

I couldn't stop a faint grimace from passing across my face, and Chickapea laughed heartily as he took note of my reaction.

Moving quickly to less unsettling topics, I asked one of the most common questions: "So, what brought you out on the trail?"

"Oh." Chickapea paused, and we walked several steps before he took a soft breath. "My brother passed away last year—"

"Man, I'm so sorry." A quick hurt settled on me at having brought up something so painful. "We don't have to talk about it."

"Nah, it's okay. It's hard to talk about him, but I like talking about him, too." Chickapea offered me a tight smile. "After it happened, I was really shook up, and I wanted to do something about it. I decided to walk across the US. From Virginia Beach to San Diego."

"Wow. Very Forrest Gump-like."

"Exactly like that," Chickapea laughed. "I pushed a cart of supplies and worked with local police departments to find legal places to put my tent up at night. I didn't want people to think I was just some homeless wanderer, so I declined any free handouts or money and asked people instead to donate it in his memory."

"That's such an awesome way to remember him." I found myself re-looking at Chickapea. His story gave me a fresh view on the perceptions I had formed of the person hiking beside me. And that was one of the reasons I loved hearing others' stories on the trail so much. Each person was comprised of building blocks that represented their experiences, character, and motivations. Stacked up, they formed a person, but it wasn't until conversations like this one that you could take one of the blocks and admire it in all its beautiful individuality.

"It was a cool experience, and it helped me walk through some of my grief. But I liked the drifter life too. It inspired me to look at other long-distance trips, and the AT seemed like a good challenge next, so here I am."

Chickapea grinned widely this time, lifting the shadow that had passed over his face. We shared more of our lives as we kept walking, and before I knew it, we were at Spring Mountain Shelter. It was still only 4 p.m. and we both felt good. Guthook showed me a campsite another 3.5 miles mostly downhill at Allen Gap, so it was an easy decision to keep going. Although I missed the relaxed comfort of Nubs and Fun Facts's well-worn company, I didn't want to slow down. It was 50 miles to Erwin, the next town stop, so they had plenty of time to catch up.

The next morning heated up fast as Chickapea and I hiked the six miles out of Allen Gap up to Whiterock Cliff. I quickly stripped off my Patagonia fleece, securing it around my waist in the "Neiman Wrap," a design Dad jokingly claimed to have patented, where a sleeve was tucked into itself in front to avoid an uncomfortable knot.

Each new day proved I was losing too much weight, as my hip belt no longer fit snugly. I was grateful for the extra padding of the wrap, since something had to help the belt take pressure off my shoulders. Lately, they had been doing a lot of extra work.

I kept an eye out for Leap Frog, wondering if I would catch her as she was only half a day ahead of me. Fun Facts and Nubs texted they were stopping at Jerry's Cabin Shelter for the night, which Chickapea and I would pass around lunchtime. I was still being mindful of the shin splints, even though my leg had felt close to perfect since arriving in Hot Springs, so figured I'd push on.

Our scenic lunch on Whiterock Cliff was eaten while dangling our legs over the fifty-foot cliff, bathed in a cooling wind. The rest was well-earned, and we were refreshed and ready to take on the ridgeline walk to Big Firescald Bald next. But this section began with a stark warning, a sign that read, "Exposed Ridgeline Trail." And as if not enough to foreshadow the danger, someone had unofficially written in ink below, "Unending Rock Scramble."

Chickapea and I exchanged apprehensive looks before moving past the sign. The ridgeline was a one-mile stretch of consistent 360-

degree views looking out across 100 miles of mountainous terrain. It was also very narrow and all boulders. The whole ridge was about three feet wide with a severe drop on either side. It required cautious footwork to keep from sliding off the acutely angled rock slabs that some trail-blazing simpleton decided could be called a footpath. With the combined danger and beauty involved, that mile was both the most scenic and most difficult I had hiked so far.

Even with the beauty surrounding us, I was glad to eventually reach level ground. The much smaller boulders and roots lying haphazardly across the trail seemed friendlier than they had before the rock scramble. In fact, the next 12 miles were pretty easygoing. Not too much up and down, with one notable and hilarious exception.

"Does that say, 'Big Butt Bypass'?" I asked Chickapea, squinting ahead at the wooden sign.

Chickapea squinted with me before busting out a long laugh. "It sure does."

"My nephews are going to love this. I've got to send a picture." My sister, Devorah, was going to join me on the trail with her three boys and husband for a couple days when I got to Virginia. I adored my nephews and liked to think I was a pretty fun uncle for them. And this was the perfect uncle material to keep that image alive.

We made our way past Big Butt Bypass and onto Big Butt Mountain. The top revealing its namesake. Two large, rounded gray stones sat next to each other with a narrow crack running between them, looking to all the world like a giant rocky rear end. I climbed up to lean against one of the giant rocky butt cheeks where I could point into the sizable crack while Chickapea snickered behind my phone camera.

Retrieving my phone from him, I grinned widely. "Oh yeah, they're going to love this."

Posing at Big Butt Mountain on Day 29.

22

DIXIELAND DELIGHT

The blue blaze trail to Flint Mountain Shelter came into view just as the golden rays of the evening sun threw their final shafts of light through the surrounding tree trunks. I followed Chickapea into the shelter to claim my spot for the night, too tired to set up my hammock. Dinner needed to be my focus, with the little light and energy left.

I pulled the stove out of my backpack and paused. It was going to take a good fifteen minutes before my fancy mac and cheese would be ready, and I was not in the mood to wait. Looking over at Chickapea, I felt a pang of jealousy as I watched him get his Jetboil canister stove into a quick boil with the simple click of a button. I poured a couple ounces of alcohol into my stove before lighting it, tapping my spork as I waited for it to prime into a steady blue flame. Chickapea, on the other hand, was already stirring the contents of his meal.

It was becoming clear that my stubborn passion for the lightest stove possible was losing the battle to the reality of its inefficiency on these cold, weary days. I looked up to see the deepening gray of approaching night and sighed deeply as I pulled out my headlamp to finish cooking.

The shelter's logbook sat close by, so I distracted myself with an entry and blog tease while waiting for the water to slowly hit its boiling point. Turning to the last written entry, I saw Leap Frog's neatly printed name with a note stating she'd stopped for lunch earlier in the day. With Fun Facts and Nubs a few miles back at Jerry's Cabin Shelter, me at Flint Mountain, Leap Frog some miles ahead, and Huevos in an unknown destination behind us all, the original tramily was now dispersed along the trail. A drastic change from our first few weeks of taking every step together. I missed the camaraderie of the group, but I also appreciated the miles I was putting behind me.

I was dimly aware of rain drumming along the roof as I turned from side to side in my quilt that night. But I was acutely aware of it when I left the shelter the next morning, fully donned in rain gear. After three days of beautiful weather, Mother Nature returned her attention to wet for the foreseeable future.

The trail was already a mud bath. Chickapea had left earlier, so I was hiking alone. I let out a huff of breath, which plumed white in the icy air, and set my mind to the task ahead. An immersive fantasy audiobook my sister had recommended helped distract me from my surroundings, but it wasn't long before I switched to '80s music to keep my feet moving.

There could have been incredible views at High Rock, Bald Mountain, and the many peaks in between, but I had no idea as fog descended along with the rain and blanketed the scenery.

When I finally arrived at Bald Mountain Shelter, Chickapea was already there, rainwater dripping from his sodden beard. We grunted a greeting as I unloaded my wet pack next to where his was already hanging from the shelter's awning.

"I'm sick of playing defense. I'm calling an audible for

tomorrow," Chickapea announced, scraping the last of instant rice from the bottom of his pot.

"What are you thinking? Statue of Liberty play?" I asked. I was miserable, but not so much as to miss a chance to add on to a good analogy.

"Ha, you could say that. I have to get out of this rain, man. I booked a shuttle to the Super 8 Motel in Erwin tomorrow. It's six miles to the pickup point, then I'll come back and hike the remaining twelve the next day back to Erwin."

I nodded as I munched half-hydrated macaroni noodles, considering his idea. "It's a solid play. Mind if I tag along?"

"Not at all," Chickapea said, grinning. "A Hail Mary takes at least two players..."

So, at 10 a.m. the next morning, we were on our way to the not-so-bustling metropolis of Erwin, Tennessee. We checked into the motel and immediately exploded our packs across every available surface. Raincoats hung from curtain rods while soaked shirts and socks draped over lamps.

I showered amid the chaos, then sat on the bed with my phone to review blog comments. I'd started to amass a group of consistent followers who enjoyed celebrating my wins and gently mocking me in my hardships. Dad, whose smattering of comments ranged from excitement over his new boots to eagerness to hit the trail with me, had now mentioned the jogging routine he was getting back into. At 71 years old, I wasn't sure whether to tell him to take it easy or applaud his tenacity, so struck for a middle ground.

"*Go for it. But you always say to listen closely to your body, too. You know the drill,*" I typed.

Next, I set out for Erwin. My route through the business district took less time than lunch at one of its many fast-food restaurants. A one-road town, it was eerily quiet for a Saturday afternoon. Every store was either closed for the day or boarded up for good. I finally spotted a shop whose faded red "open" sign hung crookedly on a slightly ajar glass door. The peeling white lettering above announced it as a comic book and collectibles store. Pushing the door open, I entered the dark interior, my eyes taking a moment to adjust.

What greeted me was a scene from a post-apocalyptic movie. Racks lay in overturned disarray, random items strewn between them. Dust particles I had disturbed from long-term slumber lifted in the few rays of dim light sneaking in. Trash lay where it had been dropped, and I couldn't think why the place had been left unlocked. Backing slowly toward the door, I fumbled for the metal handle, knowing I couldn't turn my back on a place like this. I had seen enough zombie movies to know the walking dead inhabited dark spaces just like this, waiting for prey to wander into their domain.

The door clanged behind me, and I strode away quickly, trying not to break into an all-out run. Later that day, over dinner at Bojangles Famous Chicken 'n Biscuits, I detailed the events to Chickapea. His laughter reverberated around the dining area, followed by an echoing hiccup. He clamped his hands over his mouth and snorted, "Man, you've got to stop. I can't breathe."

"Okay." I held my hands up. "I'm going to text Fun Facts and see if she and Nubs want to meet us at the shuttle drop-off site tomorrow. Perhaps we can even bring them some Egg McMuffins as trail magic."

Fun Facts's reply pinged onto my phone in seconds.

"YES," I read, showing the all-caps response to Chickapea. "I think they like the idea."

The final 12 miles back to Erwin brought me to the front steps of Uncle Johnny's hostel, an institution in the AT community, which I saw immediately was not an exaggeration. The trail led up to its location on the banks of the Nolichucky River. Underneath white awnings, I could see a soda machine, BBQ grill, and picnic tables. Signs advertised "free shuttle rides to town for guests" and "40¢ Snickers bars." This place knew the way to a hiker's heart, though I wasn't keen for a return to Erwin.

Finding an unoccupied picnic table near the front, I spilled the contents of my backpack across the ground. While I waited for the tramily to catch up, I needed to seriously shake down some of my gear. And first up was my cooking setup. I loved my little alcohol stove, but it had officially lost the battle against more efficient canister stoves. I had seen a tiny one-ounce stove in the store that would screw onto a fuel canister. With great sadness, I set my alcohol stove aside, hoping an enthusiastic hiker might pick it up and continue its journey up the AT.

Next, I reorganized my stuff sacks. When I first planned my pack, small stuff sacks holding similar items seemed best. All clothes in one, all toiletries in another, all electronics in a third... and so on. But in practice, this just led to me taking most of my pack to bed with me. If everything I needed after dinner was in one place, I wouldn't need to search. At night, I could simply pull out one bag of nighttime gear—headlamp, charger, toothbrush, long underwear, sleep socks, earplugs—and leave everything else in my pack.

Once complete, I tossed any gear that had proved to be dead weight into a nearby hiker freebie box—an extra bandana, backup length of rope, camp shoes, the just-emptied stuff sacks, and the alcohol stove.

Packing back up the rest, a shadow appeared over me, blocking the sun. "We have got to stop meeting like this."

I grinned. "Leap Frog." I stood and clasped her in a hug.

"Are you doing a shakedown?" She nodded at the piles still on the ground.

"You could say that. I needed to make some changes and get organized. Are you stopping in or staying the night?"

"Planning to be here until tomorrow. Is anyone else with you?"

I caught her up on the tramily's movements, and it wasn't long before Fun Facts and Nubs walked up. Leap Frog joined me on the bench while they checked out the facilities.

A few minutes later, Nubs flopped down beside us, followed by Fun Facts. "Those bunkhouses are crowded," Nubs said.

"And pretty rustic," Fun Facts added.

"They've got a cool setup in the yard if you want to tent camp. Did you see it?" I asked.

"We saw it," Fun Facts said, shaking her head. "There are already a lot of people there and, I don't know, I feel like I want something a bit more... luxurious."

I sighed, knowing where this was heading. I had already slept in a bed last night and was excited about the new hammock hangout area I'd seen near the back, but the others clearly weren't sharing that enthusiasm.

"Go ahead, say it." I knew exactly where this was headed.

Fun Facts exchanged a look with Nubs. "We were thinking about that Super 8."

I wasn't sure at which point Super 8 had become synonymous with luxury, but apparently, we were at that stage.

"Well... I was hoping to check out the hammock area. And they offer free shuttle rides into town. We can get whatever you guys want for dinner." I tried to inject some excitement but there was no shift in their expressions, so in a last-ditch attempt to win them over, I added, "And did you see they're doing a deal on Snickers bars?"

Nubs's one-sided smile told me he knew my game. I shrugged, a corner of my own mouth lifting.

"What do you think?" I turned to Leap Frog. "You said you were planning on staying here, right?"

Her eyes shifted between us. "I don't mind the Super 8 idea either. I mean, this place is great, but the Super 8 would be more comfortable."

The decision had swayed unanimously. I could still choose to stay at Uncle Johnny's alone, but they were my tramily, so I reluctantly agreed to another night in Erwin.

23

THE TRAIL OF THE LONESOME PINE

A plan was formed over breakfast at Super 8 the next morning. I was ready to start hiking but the others wanted more time in town. Leap Frog jumped in with me on getting an earlier start, and we agreed to aim for a campsite 14 miles away at Unaka Mountain's base. But we didn't get far down the trail before we quickly remembered the very different cadence of our hiking pace, so once again, I found myself hiking alone for most of the day.

Upon arriving at the Unaka campsite, I spotted the back of Chickapea's fiery red head. He was standing in a circle with some other hikers, pointing intensely at something hidden from my view. My approach caught Chickapea's attention, who turned and waved me over. "Hey, Sharkbait. Come take a look at this."

A tall, skinny hiker shifted to make room for me. I smiled my thanks before turning to the object capturing their attention.

"Oh, cool. It's a Christmas tree," I remarked. And indeed it was, a small pine tree adorned with colorful decorations. I looked back at the faces surrounding me, who all watched me, apparently anticipating a different reaction. Confused, I looked again. It was then I realized that the ornaments weren't just of the Christmas variety. Interspersed with the usual shiny orbs and twinkling icicles were notes and pictures. I took a step forward and lightly pinched one of the notes between my fingers. It had been laminated to protect against the weather—a clue that this tree wasn't a seasonal addition accidentally left out too long, but a much more permanent feature.

I scanned the note and dropped it back into place. "Oh," was all that I managed.

"Yeah," Chickapea said, with such sadness that I stepped back to his side.

The note was written to someone named Max, a hiker who had passed away a couple years earlier. The tree had been decorated and left at the campsite in his memory. I glanced back to see stones also stacked on the ground under its branches. They looked like tiny, eternally-waiting gifts for a Christmas morning that would never come.

An uneasy feeling settled in my gut. As beautiful a memorial as this was, I didn't feel like sleeping beside it. I looked back at Chickapea, who was still staring with paler-than-usual skin at the tree.

"Want to stealth camp tonight instead?" I asked. "We could be at the top of Unaka Mountain in ten minutes."

He inhaled briefly and nodded.

"Alright then. Let me leave a quick note for Leap Frog in the logbook, and we can head out."

Unaka's summit stands at 5,100 feet, so it wasn't a light half-mile of hiking, but neither of us complained. We reached the top to see three tents already set up with plenty of room between them. It was a completely wooded top for once, and the forest of mossy-green pine trees welcomed us with a comforting embrace of peace and quiet. There was no wind, no rustling leaves, no trickling river, and no sounds of civilization. Just pure and serene forest silence.

As I settled into my hammock for the night, I sighed contentedly at the quiet around me. I thought about Max briefly, and how different his story was now compared to mine. Gratitude swelled within me for all I was able to experience while hiking this trail... and a reminder of how fragile this life truly is.

The next day ended up being an unexpected 20-miler. When I woke that morning in the same peace and quiet, the plan was to hike a modest 11 miles to the Greasy Creek Friendly Hostel, a short half-mile from the trail. I could pick up the resupply box waiting for me there and get a good night's sleep. But when I arrived, I quickly made other plans.

As I walked through a jumble of rundown homes and crumbling barns, a feeling of disappointment grew. I had planned a stop here based on promising reviews during my early planning. The atmosphere was supposed to be warm and inviting, like a communal family, but that wasn't the impression I was getting. And when I arrived at the front door, it swung open effortlessly, with nothing but empty silence inviting me inside.

A sign near the front door gave instructions on how to wash my hands or purchase candy bars, but the small home was otherwise unrecognizable as a hiker hostel. Everything was covered in a layer of dust as if untouched by time. I spotted my resupply box stacked in a corner of the living room with several packages. Taking it to a small kitchen table, I organized my food while deciding what to do. After another thirty minutes of silence that stretched tightly between me and the emptiness, I was done considering.

I walked back to the front door, my eyes darting around for anyone I might need to explain my actions to. Then, perhaps just to appease myself, I cleared my throat and declared, "So..."

The soliloquy hung awkwardly. "I, uh, I think I'm going to keep hiking. The day's so beautiful and I still have hours of daylight left..." I trailed off to silence again, realizing I didn't need an excuse, but feeling somehow content that my departure sounded justified.

After making a quick exit, I got back to the business of thru-hiking. I decided to walk as far as I could, perhaps even to the shelter on the top of Roan Mountain, the highest shelter on the AT at 6,250 feet, some 12 miles away.

It was mostly uphill for the entire afternoon, but with clear skies and majestic views, I was a happy hiker. Around 7 p.m., I was only 1.8 miles away from the top. I approached a campsite before the final climb, intending to walk through. But as I passed, I heard a familiar voice. "Sharkbait!"

I looked through the trees, and there, just a few feet away, was Chickapea's head poking out from his familiar green tent. Among the dense foliage, he was almost completely camouflaged.

"Wow, talk about stealth camping! I didn't even see you there."

Chickapea grinned. "Like a renegade hiding in plain sight. Are you stopping here too?"

"I wasn't planning to. I thought I might check out the shelter at the top. But it is getting kind of late."

Seven o'clock was past bedtime for most hikers, so the chances were high that the shelter would be full. The wind was whipping my hair into a frenzy at this lower elevation, so I suspected that a night outside the shelter farther up would be even worse.

"You know," I said, "I think I will stay here tonight. Twenty miles in one day is more than enough."

I had chosen to ignore the 80 percent chance of rain, trusting my odds to the trail gods. But it turned out that trust was severely misplaced. Rain started not long after I got cozy in my quilts and pelted my tarp all night long. Any hopes of waking early were quickly dashed as soon as I felt the chilly, damp air the next morning. At first, I thought I could wait out drier skies, but the wind laughed at that idea, knocking moisture from the trees down on me with every gust.

I left my tarp up and sat under it to heat my coffee, trying to stay dry until the last possible moment. Finally rolling up my wet tarp, I shoved it into the top of my pack and made it out around 11 a.m.

Chickapea joined me, and we started our miles in earnest. Thankfully, the sun came out, making the cold and wind slightly more bearable. We summited the top of Roan Mountain, a grassy meadow surrounded by swaying trees. Stone stacks appeared in the distance, and as we got closer, we saw they were man-made structures used to contain wood fires, like chimneys. My mind tried to make sense of it, ranging from ideas of the decayed remains of a caveman's ancient home to some ritualistic temple of human sacrifice. An informational board nearby dispelled those notions. We had come across the ruins of the Cloudland Hotel, a luxury resort from the nineteenth century.

"You just never know what you're going to come across in the woods," I commented to Chickapea as we paused to read the resort's history.

"You sure don't," he confirmed.

By 3 p.m., we made it to an old barn that had been converted into a shelter. Chickapea had been feeling his feet the last few miles, so decided to stop. But with a few hours of daylight left and a group of spring breakers crowding the shelter, I decided to continue on.

As I hiked, I realized something had shifted this last week, and I suspected the catalyst was my second night in Erwin. I no longer felt as concerned staying together with others, but more with hiking my own hike. I wasn't purposefully leaving my hiking partners behind, but I was really enjoying the stamina I had built up and the excitement of seeing as much of the trail as possible each day.

And it wasn't just me. As I crossed paths with groups along the trail, I noticed they were less static and more fluid in their members. Everyone was moving more at their own pace, making temporary plans to meet up, but not holding each other to them. I didn't yet know what that would mean for my onward journey, but I did know it felt good to be out on the trail under my own steam.

24

MOVING RIGHT ALONG

I spent the night at the Mountain Harbour Hostel, a half mile from where the trail intersected Highway 19E in Roan Mountain. It was a complete reverse of the questionable Greasy Creek Hostel the day prior, and by far the friendliest, cleanest, and most luxurious hostel I had come across.

After sleeping late and enjoying two helpings of Mountain Harbour's famous family-style breakfast, I was feeling a little weighed down. The trail followed a river, meandering through the hillsides, and I groggily meandered along with it. I stared at my feet as I hiked to keep from tripping in my sluggish state. The plan was to make it to Mountaineer Shelter about nine miles away, or maybe a campsite I had seen on Guthook six more past that.

I rounded a bend to see a massive oak tree stretching its limbs fifty feet in every direction. I could tell, even from a distance, that someone stood at the base staring into the upper branches. Increasing my pace, I closed the gap and soon could see the features of a recognizable hiker I'd camped with a few times. He was usually with another hiker, and although they kept a much faster pace than mine, they also took much longer breaks and more frequent town stops. I had last seen the two of them heading out of Hot Springs a few days earlier.

"Yo, Ripple!" I called out his trail name. "Where's Legs?"

Ripple turned and opened his mouth to speak, but a much louder voice boomed from above, stealing the words.

"Sharkbait, hoo ha ha!"

There was no question, the voice belonged to Legs, who stood nearly at the top of the massive oak. He was aptly named for his exceptionally long, skinny legs. With his slightly pointed ears sticking out of a tight black cap, he looked like an elf that had wandered out of Tolkien's Rivendell and found himself a new home in Appalachia's woodland mountains. Legs quickly scampered down, reinforcing his elvish persona, and dropped to the ground with a silent thud beside his friend. Ripple was average height, but with his long black hair, heavy thru-hiker beard, and small frame next to his stretched-out friend, he was the dwarf to Legs the elf.

I set my pace to match theirs as we started down the trail again, detailing our last days of hiking and our plans ahead. The sun shone brightly as we walked, removing some chill from the air, and daffodils bloomed in yellow splashes along the edges of the path. It felt like spring was getting into full swing, and my hope soared for the perfect hiking conditions this milder weather would bring.

We were trekking along the flat trail under the warm afternoon sun when I realized just how fast we were going. I did some quick calculations and realized we were pacing at 3 miles per hour rather than my usual 2 or 2.5. Sometime after lunch, we passed my original shelter goal for the day and by mid-afternoon were edging past a campsite 14 miles from my day's start.

"Hey. Where are you guys thinking of stopping tonight?" I asked.

"Moreland Gap Shelter," Ripple replied.

"It's about four miles from here," Legs added, glancing my way. "Have you got that much left in you today?"

"An hour and a half? No sweat," I said, grinning and increasing my stride.

When we arrived, the shelter was occupied by one sole resident and his pile of gear. He was a giant mountain man with thick brown hair swooped back and flowing freely in a lion's mane style. And his lighter-colored, equally thick beard completed the king-of-the-jungle look. When he rose to greet us, the kindness in his blue eyes told me he was a gentle giant—a kindhearted king.

"Hey," he greeted us, using his foot to shove some of the clothes and gear out of our way. A foot that, I noticed, was bedecked in Merino wool socks and sandals. "I'm Ridge."

We relayed our trail names before setting up to eat dinner at the shelter's fire pit together. Ridge, another thru-hiker, filled us in on his hike as we ate. He had started a few days after me, but his pace had been much faster in the beginning. Which got me thinking about the terrain ahead.

"So, I've been hearing people talk about twenty-five to thirty-mile days once you hit Virginia," I started.

Legs shrugged. "Seems doable to me."

Ripple and Ridge grunted their agreement, and I chewed my rehydrated beef and vegetable fried rice thoughtfully as I looked at them. These guys were used to hiking big miles in a day. I didn't think of myself that way, but looking back, my daily distance had started to increase. Especially now that my knee and shin troubles were behind me. I could tell my body was adjusting well, so perhaps it was time to consider some longer days to make up lost time.

Legs, Ridge, and I started out the next morning together, leaving Ripple still sleeping at the campsite. We were eager to be on our way and were rewarded with incredible views as the sun slowly rose in the clear blue sky. The still relatively flat trail continued alongside the river, leading us across wooden bridges and between towering cliffs of layered rock. It ended in grandiose fashion at Laurel Fork

Falls, a fifty-foot wall of unrelenting water that flowed incredulously fast down a gauntlet of rocky chutes.

We took our time eating lunch, even climbing to the top for an epic view that rivaled anything on the trail so far. The rest of the day was spent steadily gaining and then losing 1,500 feet of elevation, which brought us to a road intersection for Hampton, Tennessee, at the mouth of a massive lake.

"This has to be our stop for the night," Ridge commented.

"Oh yeah?" Legs replied, not looking the least bit interested in stopping.

"We're going to be hiking around Watauga Lake next. They shut down all the shelters and campsites for the next seven miles because of bear activity," Ridge confirmed.

I remembered this lake from my research. The next available campground after the zone Ridge mentioned was five miles beyond, and the next shelter was another five miles after that. So it was either stop here or hike through the night.

"We'll be out there after dark if we take it on now," I said.

Legs looked beyond us to the trail ahead and then at the sign pointing back to a campsite 200 yards behind us. He sighed. "You're right, but I hate having to double back."

It seemed the decision had been made for us by the National Forest Service, so we gathered our gear and did what no thru-hiker likes to do. We retraced our steps.

During the night, rain began to patter down along my tarp. I rolled my eyes in long-suffering silence, resentful for the wet gear I'd have to pack up in the morning. Eventually, the raindrops ceased, and I snuggled deeper into my quilts as the cold around me intensified. I woke the next morning to white plumes of my own frozen breath, which could only mean one thing: freezing temperatures. Stepping out of my hammock, I quickly realized that the rain had not in fact stopped but instead turned to snow. I stared in astonishment and some mild disgust at the thin layer of white that blanketed everything in sight, while my hopes for milder spring conditions wilted like the snow-covered blooms of the daffodils I had seen just the day before.

I checked my watch, noticing it was still only 7:15, but with the cold, I had no interest in hanging around. So, packing up gear, I once again threw my wet tarp on top and clocked in for the day's hike before eight o'clock. Legs joined me, and we hiked quickly through the bear-frequented area. I was hoping to see my first bear in the early hours of flat hiking around the lake, but we didn't spot even a sign. Rain and fog covered the lake, so even that was mostly invisible. The one benefit of the cold conditions was the motivation it gave us to take on another huge mileage day. It would be 24 miles by the end, my longest day yet.

We eventually made it to a campsite above US 321, Ridge showing up shortly after. None of us were keen to set up our wet tents or hammocks in the winter wonderland, so I once again huddled on my thin, useless sleeping pad on the cold shelter floor.

Damascus was our goal for the next day, the next big trail town on the edge of Virginia. We were 19.3 miles away, and after our mammoth day yesterday and the prospect of a zero day ahead, I was feeling confident that nothing could stop me from a warm bed that night. The day began incredibly cold, but as the miles sped by, the sun warmed the air and began melting the snow. Soon, Legs, Ridge, and I were entering Virginia, my fourth state of the Appalachian Trail, and the state with the most AT miles in it—over 500, encompassing a quarter of the entire length.

Damascus sat just over the border, and I was very excited to see it. It was an institution in the thru-hiking community, both because the trail ran directly through it and because of the "Trail Days" festival, which drew crowds of more than 20,000 people supporting the AT each year. I'd always wanted to visit the festival. To be able to talk with the hikers, shop the vendors, and just be a part of the excitement. But unfortunately, it was scheduled a few weeks from now, when nicer weather and more thru-hikers typically pass through. Damascus was also a big sign of respect among thru-hikers, because it was widely known that half the hikers who start in Georgia quit before reaching there.

"You know," I announced to Ridge and Legs as we exchanged wooded trail for paved path, "Damascus was supposed to be the first zero of my thru, but by my count, it will be the fourth."

Ridge chuckled. "Yeah, plans sure do change once you get out here. I thought I would be in Maryland by now."

My accommodation for the night was Crazy Larry's Hostel, which had me traveling through most of the town, while Legs and Ridge had chosen other hostels. So, we made loose plans to find each other at dinner or meet up over the next couple days and then went our separate ways.

I quickly checked in at Crazy Larry's, meeting the infamous older gentleman who carried the same name, and set myself up for a restorative sleep in a warm bed inside the quaint home.

Crazy Larry woke us all the next morning at 7 a.m. as he started preparing breakfast. My morning now wide open, I decided to check out the three well-stocked outfitters Damascus boasted. After almost 500 miles, I had been feeling the sharp edges of every stone and root I stepped on, so I knew it was time to replace my hiking boots, which had done their duty since leaving home.

After surveying the options, I chose another pair of Salomons, very similar to my X-Mission model, but with a slightly stiffer sole and reinforced toe box that would help with the rocky trail conditions constantly tripping me up.

I also walked out with a real treasure, one I had waited far too long to acquire. The closed-foam sleeping pad I begrudgingly laid below me in shelters was officially trashed, as I found a great deal on a new Nemo Tensor sleeping pad. It packed down smaller than a water bottle and weighed less than a pound, so I couldn't resist splurging on the replacement. I still didn't like the idea of sleeping in shelters, but at least now I might actually get some sleep if I do.

Between the pad, shoes, and hostel fees, this was turning into an expensive stop. I had read it is common for hikers to often quit in New England because of financial issues, and was starting to see why. I was trending far over my initial budget, so I hoped I could tighten the purse strings now that I was past much of the winter cold and gear issues.

Shopping complete, I spent the rest of the day eating, relaxing, and chatting with Legs and Ridge. Ripple soon made it into town, and not long after, Leap Frog turned up as well. It was a good, relaxing zero day with friends. My legs were rested, my feet were happily reshod, and my mind was recharged for the next chapter of the AT. The enormity of Virginia stretched before me, but I was ready.

25

THE SOUND OF SILENCE

The next morning, it was time to head out of Damascus and back onto the trail. It looked like the others wanted to stay another day, but Ridge and I were ready to move. We met up early and quickly discovered a popular tourist attraction for Damascus, a 30-mile bike path called The Virginia Creeper Trail. This nicely paved road cut through town, following the Laurel River in its winding northward path. The trail also parallels the AT for a few miles, and while the scenery was gorgeous all morning, the close proximity was distracting and confusing.

A few miles in, Ridge and I had already made our second accidental detour onto the Creeper Trail. I let out an exasperated sigh as we turned around once again.

"You know that trail name of yours is a bit too accurate, Sharkbait." Ridge joked. "The soothing river and paved road just a bit too distracting?"

It was true. The scene coming out of Damascus was beautiful and not nearly as straight uphill as the usual exit from town. I was looking everywhere but at the trees for white blazes that would keep us on the correct path. Ridge was right, getting this disoriented reminded me of my early days in Georgia getting turned around with Keg, The Captain, and the tramily.

Where were Nubs and Fun Facts now? I wondered. It had been over a week since we last hiked together and I missed their company. I made a mental note to text them or ask around if any hikers caught up to me from farther back, but also had to admit how content I was continuing at my new pace.

Even with two detours and the addition of a third later that morning, we made it to our destination of Lost Mountain Shelter in good time.

"Three o'clock," I said, checking my phone. "But Guthook says the next few miles are all up the side of Mount Rogers."

"Yeah... I don't like the sound of that," Ridge grimaced. "Isn't Rogers the tallest mountain in Virginia?"

"Sure is. Want to stay here instead? Take it on tomorrow with fresh legs?"

Ridge nodded, and I went back to Guthook to review tomorrow's new route. I scanned through the miles and stopped when I saw the icon for a special point of interest at Grayson Highlands.

"Ridge," I called out to him as he attempted to get a campfire started. "If we do 24 miles tomorrow, we'll go through Grayson Highlands State Park. You know what they have there, right?" I paused, then answered myself, "Wild ponies." My excitement was too great to give him time to guess.

Ridge's head whipped over. "Wild ponies? As in free range?"

I smiled at the boyish excitement on his face. "Exactly."

"I'm going to ride one."

"I doubt you'll get within ten feet of one."

"Wanna bet?"

I shook my head, laughing as Ridge flashed me a mischievous grin. It was only my first day hiking alone with Ridge, but I could tell I liked him. With The Captain at home, he brought just the right amount of competitive spirit I missed on the trail.

We approached the US Route 58 road crossing the next morning and took simultaneous sniffs of the air.

"Do you smell that? Almost smells like..." I began, sniffing again.

"Pancakes!" Ridge finished, his voice an excited squeak.

We exchanged thrilled looks and quickened our pace to discover a couple standing by their truck, grilling up hotcakes and eggs. A table laden with bananas, candy bars, and hot cocoa sat in front. It was a massive spread, and after introductions, we happily dove into the feast.

These trail angels were Grumpy and Gucci Girl. Grumpy had been a thru-hiker this year but an injury had taken him off-trail early on. Now, they were spending the season doing short day hikes and giving out trail magic. It was inspiring to hear how they'd turned a bad situation into a gesture of generosity.

Bellies full and warm, we climbed the six miles straight up Mount Rogers. It was a 2,500-foot climb that never seemed to end. But when it finally did... then came the ponies.

We weren't even in the state park when I saw the first flash of brown and white ahead. A moment later, a furry head topped with pointed ears popped up, and the pony began making its way toward us. The ground here was mostly scrub brush strewn with boulders, but the pony navigated the obstacles with impressive ease.

We slowed, letting it come up to us in its own time. Its head was level with the hip straps of my backpack, and it took the opportunity to shove its nose into the pockets there, sniffing noisily. Clearly, it was used to being fed by hikers, whether it was permitted or not.

Another smaller, white pony joined shortly after, butting its head against the other's side to claim more space beside me.

I looked over at Ridge, whose dreamy-eyed expression matched the one he'd worn upon hearing of this wonder the night before.

"Which one are you getting on?" I asked, chuckling at the thought of his giant frame climbing onto the diminutive ponies.

"Ha ha." He remarked sarcastically. "So, maybe I won't ride one, but you still lost the bet."

The smaller pony shoved its head into my hand. "I'll happily lose if it means I get to experience this."

We continued strolling through the park, seeing a dozen more ponies come and go. There were big ones, small ones, baby ones, old ones, even pregnant ones. Some stood back and surveyed us as they swished their tails, and some approached us, searching and sniffing out our snacks, but none of them were afraid.

The final stretch of our day's hike was challenging. The scrub grew less and less, and the trail became littered with increasingly large boulders, necessitating a change from hiking to rock scrambling.

Looking at Guthook, we'd reached the 500-mile spot, so I was surprised it didn't have a celebratory marker like previous milestones I'd seen. Instead, our reward was a rock tunnel called Fatman's Squeeze. I encouraged Ridge to go first, knowing if he could fit, then I'd have no problem. While he hugged the rock face, I quickly laid out sticks in the shape of a five and two zeros on the ground. He disappeared into the crack, and I heard a couple of grunts before he yelled, "I'm through!"

I navigated my own way through the tight triangular gap, trying not to slip on patches of ice beneath me. Once completed and a third pony-petting session had taken place, the dream of hiking 24 miles evaporated. It was 4 p.m. and we still had 11 miles to go to keep to that plan. So, we decided to stop at Wise Shelter on the park's boundary instead.

As I settled into my hammock, I couldn't wipe the grin from today's excitement off my face. I pulled out my phone and started typing the day's blog entry: "*Day 42. Wow, today was epic. I'd go so far as to say it was a highlight day of the trip. I had it all... blue skies, calm winds, high peaks, trail magic, and the damn coolest ponies you'll ever see...*"

The next two days treated me to a wide range of terrain. I tripped across awful boulders, trekked through wide-open fields, came across towering waterfalls, and pushed onward through the ever-present company of the forest canopy. Sometimes Ridge and I hiked together, and sometimes I was alone for large portions of the day, but the one constant companion was my earbuds. A podcast or music had become the soundtrack to each mile's progress. That is, until the morning I woke up at Chatfield Shelter.

I untied my food bag from where I'd stashed it in a nearby tree and pulled out the gallon Ziploc containing the day's food. Coffee and Pop-Tarts in hand, I sat in a sunny patch to eat breakfast. Leaning my head back, I basked in the spring warmth like the little orange salamanders I'd recently started seeing on sunbaked rocks. The weather was continuing its trend toward spring, and I was ready for it.

Around nine, I knew it was time to hit the trail if I was going to make it the almost 20 miles to Knot Maul Branch Shelter. Ridge's tent was still up and silent, so I got my gear packed and headed out alone. About a mile down the trail, I called Dana to check in. She was still working late hours and studying with any free time she had left, but it was good to hear her voice.

Hanging up, I checked my phone's battery life. Good enough to keep the earbuds in and continue my podcasted radio show. A bird trilled loudly above my head, and I paused just before hitting play. Putting something on to pass the time had become such an automatic action, and I realized it had been a long time since I hiked with only the sounds of nature.

I put my phone away and decided to simply let myself be in the woods for the day. There was an element of mental stamina needed on the thru-hike that I hadn't required on other trips. The knowledge that I would be walking 20-mile days over and over had made me want to manage the mental fatigue with manufactured noise. But today, I felt like reminding myself why I was out here in the wilderness, traversing mountains I loved to climb.

As I walked, I paid attention to my surroundings. On a rock beside the trail lay a long black snake warming itself in the sun. Up above, a hawk circled, searching for its next meal. A pond I came across was surrounded by bullfrogs, leaping into the water as I approached. I noticed, smiled, and reveled in the joy of nature. And I realized that by distracting my mind with music and audiobooks, I'd also distracted my eyes from seeing these amazing details. I couldn't help but think, *how many times had I missed all this in the past?*

I took the quiet time to reflect on what made me happy in my life back home, what wasn't bringing the kind of joy I was feeling now, and what changes I could make to encourage more. It felt refreshing to take a break from the get-through-it mindset I'd slipped into.

By mid-morning, the sun was beating down and sweat was trickling in streams down my back. The trail was heading through the small town of Atkins, where the asphalt reflected heat back up to me. A gas station appeared ahead, and I knew it was time to get a sugary, refrigerated drink. The simple joy of having every option at my fingertips made the choice seem overwhelming. But then I spied the piña colada-flavored advert hanging above the Icee machine. And sitting in the shade, slurping its frozen sweetness, I let myself slip into an existential level of bliss.

With renewed vigor, I returned to hiking, but by 2 p.m., my feet were beginning to complain. A campsite off the trail offered access to Reed Creek, so I veered onto the side trail. A few minutes later, I slipped off my socks and shoes and dangled my feet in the water. The icy creek water washed away the pain and five days' worth of dirt almost instantly. Completely relaxed, I slid into a quick nap that revived me for the day's final ten miles.

The final spectacular moment of the afternoon was a hand-painted wooden sign nailed to a tree. The modest-looking display made it official—I was one-quarter of the way into my AT thru-hike. A celebratory selfie with the sign marked the occasion, and then there was nothing to do but get on with the other 1,644 miles.

26

PEACEFUL EASY FEELING

I woke up the next morning, hoping to hike 20 miles to Jenkins Shelter in a pleasant valley next to a creek. As I sipped my instant coffee, pleased with how efficient the new stove was, I checked my weather app and let out an audible groan. Rain was expected again by mid-morning. The thought of hiking another day in the rain killed any motivation for a long day or early departure. So, I boiled another cup of water for a refill and made a new plan to get to Chestnut Knob Shelter instead, only ten miles out, hopefully before the skies could dump another deluge.

Fortunately, my lazy morning didn't come back to bite me. Chestnut Knob Shelter was an old ranger cabin converted into a shelter. It was huge, holding six beds and a picnic table within its fully enclosed walls. And just as I shut the door, the rain started. Hard. I breathed a sigh of relief as I heard it thrash against the thin cabin roof.

Ridge waved at me from across the shelter, where he was setting up to eat lunch with a hiker we'd seen off and on over the past few days. His trail name was Shelter Dog, but I secretly thought it should have been Zoolander. His black, spiked hair was always perfectly styled. With his tanned complexion and sophisticated dark beard stubble, he could have easily been Ben Stiller's character stepping off a runway photoshoot for Backpacker magazine.

"So, what are everyone's plans?" I asked as I set my gear down and pulled out lunch.

"I wanted to get to Jenkins Shelter," said Shelter Dog, running a hand through his hair, which somehow just made it look even more styled. "But this weather, man. I think I'm crashing here tonight. I'll lose half a day but at least I'll be dry."

"Did you see there'll be snow tomorrow?" Ridge asked.

"Yeah. If my stuff's dry, I think I'll be good to hike in the snow," I replied, though wasn't sure I actually wanted to.

"I'm probably going to push on," Ridge said. "I want to get in some more miles."

"I'll join you," I added, not wanting to lose ground, and using the challenge to keep up as motivation.

We only made it a few miles before I realized that hiking in the wet and cold down a mountain was as miserable as I remembered. We were close to a road crossing where Guthook told me the Mountain Garden Hostel would pick up hikers. I shared my plan with Ridge to make the call, but he wanted to keep fighting his way to Jenkins Shelter, so I waited for the shuttle alone.

The Mountain Garden Hostel was... pricey. What sounded welcoming quickly turned into a checklist for upcharges. Three dollars for the trail pickup, forty dollars for my bed, ten more for dinner, five for a beer (how silly of me to think the host would offer it on the house), and five more bucks for breakfast in the morning emptied my wallet faster than the goodwill in my heart toward the farmhouse owners.

I grumbled quietly as I handed over a few more bucks for a ride back to the trail the next morning. Getting out of the shuttle, I was glad to see the trail again, even with the layer of snow and sub-zero temperatures that greeted me. I cinched my backpack strap as much as I could. A weigh-in on their bathroom scale showed I'd lost fifteen pounds since beginning my hike. No wonder my pack was fitting so loosely.

The day breezed by because I was on a mission for hot food. I wanted to make it to the Brushy Mountain Outpost, where I knew I'd get an excellent dinner. It was set up as a small convenience store with a couple shelves of hiker-oriented food, but it also had a grill station and a reputation for killer ice cream milkshakes.

I barely stopped, hiking the 16 miles to the outpost in just five and a half hours. When I arrived, I found Ridge there with Shelter Dog already, looking in no hurry to leave. We each downed a burger and fries before sucking down a cold shake, not caring that it was still freezing outside.

Heading out together, we began the next two miles with a slow-and-steady walk down the road and back up a mountain, but the main event was a river crossing that the past two days of snow and rain had eagerly fed. Rocks and logs lay in a haphazard path across water flowing fast around and over them. I went for another round of trail hopscotch, leaping from one to the other, but with my final step, I miscalculated. A shrill shriek erupted from my mouth as I landed calf-deep in the icy river with both legs.

A deep roll of laughter sounded from the other side of the bank. I looked up to see Ridge doubled over, his pack shaking with laughter.

"I'm glad someone finds this funny," I grumbled, frustrated that they were somehow still dry and my wet socks and boots would now be frozen solid in the morning.

At the shelter that night, I defrosted in my hammock under my quilts, and my mood thawed as I read a well-timed comment from Dad on my blog: "*I ordered some new boots today, they're waterproof. But I'm starting to wonder if I should just pack chest waders for all this rain instead!*"

The next day's 24 miles brought me within an easy 7.5 of Woods Hole Hostel, the next off-trail accommodation I'd planned. I slept well and woke the next morning with the decision that I would take my sweet time hiking those miles to really absorb my surroundings again. I even took my time leaving camp, opting to spend a lazy morning writing a blog post about my typical daily routine on the AT. After seven weeks on the trail, even my daily privy use was consistently on schedule.

With that out of the way, there was nothing to worry about except leisurely putting miles behind me. I visited every side trail and vista, took numerous photos and videos, slowed my pace to a leisurely 2 miles per hour, and soaked in the sun that had returned in earnest. When I finally came to a road intersection, I turned right and hiked the half mile down to the scenic, red-roofed cabin nestled among farmland and forest.

Animals immediately appeared from every corner. Dogs, cats, goats, and even a goofy-looking pig. A larger black-and-white dog dropped a stick at my feet, its tongue lolling out and its tail wagging in eager anticipation for a game of fetch. I threw the stick across the open field, watching him gracefully snatch it up and race straight back. I threw it again, smiling at the simple pleasure.

Do dogs play fetch because they enjoy it, or because they think we do? I wondered.

"You know, you'll be there the rest of the day," a voice called from the cabin's porch.

I shaded my eyes and squinted down the path to see a petite woman about my age descending the stone steps. "I've already played at least 20 rounds with this guy today," she added, ruffling the dog's ears as she reached us.

I laughed, picking the stick up again. "Then I guess I've got a few more rounds to keep up. Are you staying here?"

"Yeah, you could say that." She said with a mischievous smile. "I stayed here last night, and I'm staying again tonight. In fact, I think I'll be staying for a long time to come."

Before I could respond to the confused look on my face, she laughed and continued, "I'm Neville, welcome to Woods Hole Hostel. This is my home, but I'm glad for you to make it yours as long as you want. It's hard to leave Woods Hole. You'll see."

She took me into the main cabin, and I realized quickly she was right. Neville was the warmest, most welcoming host I'd come across so far, exuding a peaceful calm that was easy to get caught up in. She filled me in on the hostel's amenities she hosted: yoga in the afternoons, meditation at night, and licensed massages in between. Then one of her staff brought out a freshly made fruit smoothie and a plate of homemade cookies. I wasn't sure if I was thru-hiking or at a spa retreat, but I gratefully accepted two cookies and the smoothie. As I took a bite, she raised both eyebrows with a grin as if saying, "I told you so."

Neville led me out of the cabin and pointed out the other facilities, which included a large garden, a hiker bunkhouse, and newly built platform tents. Everything was clean and decorated with friendly, freshly-painted information signs.

"We have a wonderful community here. People like to help out, so you'll see other hikers around lending a hand where they can." She pointed across to the platforms where three hikers were setting up large canvas tents. "There's an optional job jar in the bunkhouse with suggested chores if you'd like to give back to the community too."

She smiled serenely before adding, "Dinner will be at six. Go get settled in and check out the place."

I spent the afternoon organizing the resupply box I'd picked up in the lobby and playing a guitar I found by the fire pit. It was the rest for my body and soul that I needed. In fact, it was the most relaxed I'd felt since the spas in Hot Springs. Neville was right; it would be easy to slip into spending a few unplanned zero days in this relaxing oasis. She had something special, and I felt grateful to be here.

27

ON TOP OF THE WORLD

As yesterday had been a beautifully hot, sunny day, the next morning had, of course, started with rain and cold. It was obviously too much to ask for multiple consecutive warm days. I contemplated staying another night at Woods Hole and taking on some optional chores, but I wanted to keep my momentum up while the terrain was relatively flat. I was still about 100 miles behind schedule. After studying Guthook and the AWOL Guidebook, if the weather cooperated, I had a good chance of catching up before my next break at Harpers Ferry in West Virginia.

So, I enjoyed a delicious communal farm-to-table breakfast from Neville, reveling in the feeling of tranquility and community one last time, and helped clean up the kitchen and bunkhouse. Then I headed back to the trail for my fiftieth day of hiking the AT. It struck me as I walked out of town just how significant a milestone that should be—fifty days straight of walking. But it barely registered, except as a number to include in that night's blog post.

The town of Pearisburg was 12 miles away, known mostly among hikers for having a Dairy Queen. I contemplated stopping for a celebratory treat, but as I got closer, the thought of hiking a mile down the road and back for ice cream in April didn't sound enticing. Pulling out two Snickers bars, I clinked them together in a cheers to myself and enjoyed that as my reward instead.

The 18 miles I'd planned for the day were completed by 5 p.m., but knowing I had more to give, I kept hiking. I didn't really know my destination, but a few hikers were still ahead of me and I noticed plenty of campsites strewn about. About two hours later, I saw a familiar green tent blending into the trees. Ridge was here, and he was already in bed. I set up quietly next to him and enjoyed a quick dinner before settling in myself.

The next day started bitterly cold, again testing my resolve to exit the hammock. My body was begging for the warm comfort of my quilts, but I knew the chance of achieving my 25-mile goal decreased with each minute I stayed put.

Around 8:30, I finally gave in and got to work. Ridge's tent had disappeared, so I knew I'd likely be hiking alone. The trail was mostly narrow ledge-walking with a significant 1,500-foot drop followed by an immediate climb back up. That wasn't the hard part, though. The path was strewn with rocks, and every misstep led to a rolled ankle or stabbing pain in my feet. After 18 miles of this, I spotted a blue blaze for War Spur Shelter and called it quits.

As I sat that night looking over the terrain for the next couple days, I realized I was now only 45 miles from McAfee Knob. This was one of three photo poses every AT hiker documents, with the other two being the Amicalola Falls arch and the sign atop Katahdin's summit. McAfee Knob was included in this prestigious list because it provided the illusion of hanging hundreds of feet over the vast valley below, while offering the most stunning view of the Appalachian Mountain range. In all my years of research on the Appalachian Trail, nothing was more inspiring and iconic than the countless heroic poses I'd seen captured at McAfee Knob.

My weather app also showed that five days of clouds and rain would start later that week, meaning that if I wanted to get the photo and see the view, I had two days to hike 45 more miles.

I grunted my frustration. If I'd hiked another seven miles to the next shelter last night as planned, I'd have a better chance of arriving before the weather turned bad. But my feet were beaten up by the rocks, and they were calling the shots.

Knowing I was on a mission, I set an alarm the next morning for one of my earliest starts. I was on the trail before 7 a.m. and quickly caught up to three of the four other hikers I'd shared last night's campsite with. I didn't know them, but one glanced over his shoulder, looked me up and down, and quickly stopped.

"Cool fleece, man." He laughed, stretching out his own bright green fabric.

I was wearing my orange Patagonia fleece with the three-quarter zip and hood. I loved this layer because it was so versatile in constantly changing weather conditions.

"Is that an R1?" I asked, spotting the Patagonia logo and similar zipper.

"Sure is." He laughed again. "I guess we share good taste. My name's Remy."

"Sharkbait," I said.

I noticed then that Remy was also wearing an orange bandana around his head and similar dark-gray cargo pants that converted to shorts. With our matching outfits, dark hair, and trail beards, Remy could have easily passed as my slightly shorter twin brother.

It seemed only natural we'd hike together, so falling into an easy rhythm, we used the time to learn about each other's lives. Remy from Atlanta, just out of college and starting graduate school in the fall. Like many others his age, he was out on the trail to do some soul searching. Like me, he'd started his thru-hike on March 1. But somehow, he hadn't crossed paths with me once in the time we'd both been out here.

Around midday, we passed a giant tree—over sixty feet tall and wider than my nearly six-foot height. I knew because I stretched out on the ground as a measuring stick and couldn't reach end to end. It was the biggest tree I'd ever seen and realized it must be the famous Keffer Oak—the second largest tree on the AT. I read about this famous monument, but for some reason, had expected a bit more spectacle to go with it. A protective fence, a group of tourists waiting in line for photos, or at least a signpost directing passersby to see a wonder of the world as legendary as the world's largest ball of twine. Instead, if I hadn't been paying attention, I would've walked right past. It just sat plainly in an open field. And given no one was collecting tickets or taking photos, it was the perfect place for a lunch break.

I got up to leave, brushing the last few crumbs of peanut butter crackers from my pants, but froze when I noticed the smallest of red dots making a trail up my arm. I looked closer and recoiled in disgust. It was a tick! And not just any tick... a deer tick, unmistakable by its distinct size and reddish hue. This was the first tick I'd seen on the trail, probably aided by how I'd pre-soaked all my hiking clothes and hammock in Permethrin to deter any stray blood-suckers with its potent insecticide qualities. Only it wasn't on my clothes; it was on me. I must have uttered a distressed sound because Remy was suddenly beside me, curiosity on his face.

He watched as I picked the tick off my arm and put it on my thumbnail. Getting out my knife, I executed a clean kill by beheading and tossed its headless body to the ground.

"Let that be a warning to all your little friends," I shouted down to it, adding some flair of my best Al Pacino Scarface voice.

Remy laughed, adding his own Scarface quote. "So say goodnight to the bad guy!"

The rest of the day was a scenic ridge walk along the Eastern Continental Divide. Water on one side of the ridge flowed to the Mississippi River while the other side would eventually lead to the James River and down to the Atlantic Ocean. The view during the five-mile stretch was breathtaking, and if it hadn't been for the continued presence of obtrusive boulders on the ground, it would have been a perfect hike.

We made our way past Niday Shelter, where we'd originally planned to stop, but now occupied by a dozen or so 12-year-old giggling and screeching Girl Scouts—no thanks. Continuing up Brush Mountain, we searched for another decent place to camp. As we reached the summit, the sun was setting behind the distant ridgelines. The last flash of orange painted the bottom of the sky while wisps of clouds darkened from daytime white to dusk-tinged gray.

Remy and I watched in silent wonder until the last color dipped out of the sky and the hush of night surrounded us. Then, with a click of our headlamps, we illuminated our way down the other side of Brush Mountain to the road and a makeshift campsite next to a parking lot.

I'd hiked 26 miles in thirteen hours of day and now moonlight, and I was ready for my hammock's gentle embrace.

I read over my blog comments the next morning, where Dad continued his comments of excitement about joining me in New York. His new boots had arrived, and he was restarting a jogging routine. He'd also purchased a new tent and, discovering its fiberglass poles were heavy and fragile, replaced them with lighter aluminum ones. He ended by expressing concern at the number of rocks on the trail. I huffed my agreement as I finished the last of my coffee.

It was time to get started. McAfee Knob should be waiting at the day's end, but it wouldn't be the only great view today. Dragon's Tooth was another elite view that, along with McAfee Knob and Tinker Cliffs, made up what day-hikers referred to as the triple crown of Virginia hikes. Tinker Cliffs, the furthest of the three, would be tomorrow's achievement, but I was looking forward to the other two monumental clear views today.

Dragon's Tooth turned out to be very aptly named—a summit crowned by two jagged crags, with one shaped like an upwardly pointed tooth. We climbed the tallest rock, opening our view to a panorama of the surrounding countryside. It was incredible but we knew it was just a preview of what was to come at McAfee Knob.

However, since the weather was holding up well, we opted for a quick side trip first. Both Remy and I were low on food and needed a few supplies before reaching the town of Daleville. A short blue blaze down the mountain and a speedy gas station trip in Catawba completed the task. Before long, we were back at Dragon's Tooth and on our way to McAfee Knob's famous overlook.

And when we arrived, I knew it had all been worth it. Yesterday's long hike, the camp setup in darkness, and the quick side hike to a quick resupply. The weather forecast had updated to show rain as early as 9 a.m. the next day. But right now... we had the clearest, most fantastic views of these majestic Appalachian Mountains stretching to the farthest horizon.

McAfee Knob was quite the impressive vista, clearly showing why it was so popular. With its large rock shelf and vast valley below, a hiker could stand on the end and appear to be hanging off the side of the world. Which I did, ensuring I got several photos in various poses before trading photographer duties with Remy. We'd also timed it perfectly to watch a glorious sunset of red and orange blaze its way across the sky. I marveled in the moment because in years of preparations for this hike, I'd seen so many triumphant poses captured on film at this exact location. I could not contain my pure joy as a smile stretched across my face while I watched the last vestiges of color leave the skyline.

Looking out from McAfee Knob on Day 53.

28

RAINDROPS KEEP
FALLING ON MY HEAD

The following day started with a single mission: get to Daleville before it rained. A warm and dry bed was waiting at the finish line, and small goals like that were very good motivation. Remy and I were up at 6:45 and on the trail less than an hour later.

The path meandered along the ridgeline for a few miles before reaching the last stop of the triple crown, Tinker Cliffs, then turning west dove down the mountain to our next stop. Daleville was relatively large compared to our usual trail towns, home to roughly 3,000 people and a common trucker stop, given its proximity to Interstate 81. It also marked another big milestone, the one-third completion mark for the AT. So, when we got to Daleville, Remy invited me to celebrate our achievements together at lunch with his grandmother.

She'd driven up from Atlanta to meet him, and as we approached her diminutive Honda Fit in the parking lot outside the Three Li'l Pigs BBQ, Remy threw out a warning to watch for her sharp humor. A sprightly, white-haired lady emerged from the hatchback, a broad smile lighting up her face as she enveloped her grandson in a firm hug. Extricating himself, Remy kept his arm around her shoulder as he introduced us, and she clasped my hand in a vise-like grip.

"How long did it take you to get here, Grandma?" Remy asked, providing me with enough distraction to slip my squashed hand from hers.

"Oh, not long. Maybe seven hours." Her brown eyes crinkled. "How long did it take you two?"

Remy chuckled as he held the restaurant door open. "Well, slightly longer... about fifty-five days."

I shook my head in disbelief. That was the reality of the temporary nomadic life we'd chosen. What was typically an afternoon drive was a few weeks' walk on our feet. The realization of how long this journey takes felt so much more real in that moment.

The restaurant was simple and clean with enough tables to seat about forty people. A few were already full, and one was occupied by two dirty hiker faces I recognized.

"Tarzan! Happy Feet!" I called out, making my way over and clasping their shoulders.

"Hey, Sharkbait," Tarzan replied. "I didn't know you were on our tail."

I'd seen their entries in the logbooks and knew we were closing the gap, but I didn't expect to find them at the same random town restaurant. "Where's Jack?" I asked, referring to the enthusiastic friend who'd been so excited at the NOC when he heard my trail name.

"Oh, he goes by Starman now. He was going on one night about some comic book superhero with his same name, so the alter ego stuck. He's a couple days ahead still. We keep trying to catch him, but he's pretty fast," Happy Feet said.

We caught up on the typical hiker conversation—who we were hiking with, how many miles we were averaging, and where we were heading next. Then just as quickly, we parted so they could get back to the trail and I could rejoin Remy and his grandmother.

I woke up the next morning in my bed at the Howard Johnson Inn to the sight of rain outside my window. It was disappointing, even though I knew by now that rain was never far away. But I had a new mission that wouldn't be stopped by rain. I was going to get to a town called Buena Vista in three days to meet up with my sister. She'd be driving her family down from Maryland, and if I made it in time, I'd have the reward of a nice zero day together. It was 78.6 miles from Daleville to Buena Vista, and at my current pace, that felt easy to accomplish.

I started preparing, performing the routine that had become all too familiar. I zipped up my rain jacket and donned my rain skirt. My backpack got its own rain cover, and I finished by putting on my waterproof socks and gaiters. I wasn't overly optimistic for dry feet, knowing the rain was likely to last all day, but I had to try.

I met Remy in the lobby, and the two of us headed out. The trail turned out to be well-maintained and easy terrain. Most of it paralleled the Blue Ridge Parkway, famous for its panoramic views, but the weather hid any of them. About five miles in, we came across a blue blaze to a shelter. Remy, who'd been withdrawn under his raincoat's hood, declared he was done with the wet and would be stopping. I was tempted to join him, if not for my Buena Vista deadline. So, I said my goodbyes instead and continued down the trail alone in the rain.

The motivation of family kept my feet moving steadily forward, except for the multiple stream crossings. The rocks and logs typically used for crossing calm streams were now swollen and overrun by the flood of rainwater. They were all troublesome, but one in particular was extremely dangerous and made me stop dead in my tracks to ponder my options. The only crossable area must have had a bridge at one point, because the water was far too deep and fast-flowing for any sane person to consider crossing. But if it did, that was long gone, and there was only one way across. I already had soaked feet, but I didn't want to completely waterlog them by walking through shin-deep streams.

I pulled at my still-too-loose hip strap, hearing Dad's voice of caution in my head: *"Remember to unclip your pack in case you fall. The combined weight of the pack and the rush of water might make it difficult to get back up."*

Free from the belt constraint, I cautiously stepped forward onto a large boulder. Water rushed around my toes, and I realized getting my feet wet wouldn't be the issue. Avoiding being dragged downstream by the force of raging water would be the real challenge. I spotted the next giant boulder, but it was nearly five feet away and under flowing water, so it was bound to be slippery. I knew that once I committed to the step, there was no going back.

I backed up and searched the bank, walking a few feet in both directions for another path. Nothing. Holding my breath, I stepped back onto the giant boulder, said a quick prayer, and reached my toes across. My boot landed firmly on the next rock's surface, and I let out an audible sigh of relief. From there, it was a lunge to the other bank where I immediately hugged a white-blazed tree, shouting several thank-yous to the sky.

Lifting my feet to see just how much sloshing around I'd do for the next mile, I noticed my DexShell waterproof socks had done their job impressively well. My feet weren't nearly as drenched as I thought they'd be. I made a mental note to thank the manufacturer in the day's blog post.

I continued my way down the trail, filling my ears with some '80s rock tunes and filling the silence with questionable singing.

Bobblets Gap Shelter appeared shortly after 6 p.m., and I stepped dripping onto its vestibule, before shuffling to the corner. I turned around to apologize to the other two people who'd already set up, only to see Tarzan and Happy Feet smiling up at me.

"Hey," I said, smiling back. "Do I know you? Because you look like some friends I saw yesterday who should be much farther ahead by now."

Laughing, they waved off my ribbing, indicating the water stains from their own wet gear on the wooden floor.

"I thought you two would be way ahead. Didn't you leave Daleville right after lunch yesterday?" I asked.

"We did," Happy Feet said, her fingers working her brown hair into braids for the night. "And we should be. But this rain is no joke; it's a total momentum killer," Tarzan added.

I nodded, contemplating my own rainy-day experience, which hadn't felt that bad. Was there something wrong with me that I'd enjoyed being out in the rain all day? Remy had decided to avoid it, and these two clearly weren't enthusiastic either. But pulling off my wet clothes and climbing into dry ones, I realized I'd had a pretty great time. Perhaps it was the springlike temperatures rather than the awful cold of rain and snow in the sub-thirties. Whenever things got rough as a kid, I recall Dad would jokingly quote Young Frankenstein: "Could be worse. Could be raining." But out here? On the trail? I would take this warm rain over snow and frigid conditions any day.

The next morning, I woke with a sense of déjà vu. Rain continued to pour, and I remained determined not to let it affect my mood or plans. I checked my blog, seeing Dad had already read last night's post and left his thoughts about the stream crossing: *"Yikes, I don't relish crossing a stream like that. I'll have to really mustard the courage to even attempt it without my Tevas. In fact, you'll just have to go on without me until I ketchup."*

Only Dad could take a dad joke that far, but it still made me laugh. Not to be outdone, I typed back, *"Thanks, Dad, I'll try to quit hot-dogging it until you arrive!"*

I heard the rustle of sleeping bags and looked over to see Happy Feet rubbing bleary eyes. "Good morning," she said, sitting up. Tarzan followed her, and we began the typical discussion about the day's plans.

"Twenty-four miles?" Happy Feet exclaimed after I'd explained my thoughts for getting to Buena Vista in two days. "I don't know if we'll make that."

And as I went to sleep in Thunder Hill Shelter 23.7 miles later, Tarzan and Happy Feet were indeed nowhere to be seen. I hoped I'd see them again at some point though. They were fun to be out here with. Also, a check of the shelter logbook revealed no recognizable names written in the entries before mine, so that meant I likely didn't know anyone else ahead. It was weird to think I'd passed every hiker I met and would now be chasing those who'd started weeks before me. The realization came with a stab of loneliness, and I thought of the tramily. Were Nubs and Fun Facts still together? Did Huevos latch on to a new group? I enjoyed walking alongside others on the trail, but it seemed most of those companions were behind me for good.

It was a sad thought, but I was also comfortable with it, as I had started to enjoy the quiet calm of hiking alone. Besides, in two days, I'd be in Buena Vista with family. I hadn't seen anyone from my pre-hike life in almost two months, and I was looking forward to that sense of familiarity.

29

WE ARE FAMILY

"Hiking is weird," I muttered to myself as I pulled my medical supplies from a small stuff sack. I was in my ninth week of hiking without a single sign of blisters. Until today. After waking up alone and setting out, I instantly realized something was wrong with my feet. My usual long stride turned into a limping hobble until I reached the shelter where I now sat inspecting the damage.

I sucked in a breath as I removed my socks. There they were—bright pink and puffy blisters emerging on my little toes. No wonder the first few miles had been uncomfortable. After all the rain I'd hiked through, I wasn't surprised, but I couldn't let it continue either.

I wrapped some of Fun Facts's spare KT tape around the hot spots, hoping to ease them down before they popped, but the afternoon proved the damage was irreversible. By the time I arrived at John's Hollow Shelter at 2 p.m., my little piggies made it clear they were done for the day.

A nearby stream provided the perfect ice-cold soak my feet needed, and I treated the blisters more fully, hoping an afternoon of rest would heal them quickly. I could have done the full 25 miles today, but it was smarter to stop at this 16-mile point to let my feet recover. It felt right but now meant I needed to do a grueling 20 miles before 5 p.m. tomorrow if I was going to meet my sister on time.

I greeted the trail early the next morning, ready to put footsteps behind me. But the rain continued, and the damp weather didn't aid my blister recovery. They hurt almost instantly. By lunchtime, I knew I had to air out my toes and stop for another inspection. One of the stream crossings seemed perfect.

As I dangled my feet in the icy water, I considered my options. All my hiking socks were in various stages of wet, ranging from slightly damp to soaked through. The only pair left was my Injinji toe socks, a special pair I kept for bedtime and walking around camp in flip-flops. They fit my toes like gloves, rather than the more traditional mitten-like fit of typical socks. I knew the next two nights would be spent indoors, so the best option seemed to slip them on and gamble the need for them later.

Within minutes, I knew it was the right decision. With every toe wrapped in its own wool sheath, the rest of the day felt like walking on new feet. My speed returned to normal thru-hiker pace, and I made it to the US 60 meet-up location with an hour to spare. I dropped my pack and rewarded my tenacity with a well-deserved nap atop a nearby picnic bench.

Before long, my family arrived, screaming for joy at the sight of me. Spending time with my sister, brother-in-law, and young nephews was exactly what I needed to recharge my mental batteries. We laughed, joked, laughed at our jokes, and caught up on life in the outside world. Since Keg and The Captain left me in Georgia, I hadn't seen anyone from home, and it felt good to be with people who knew me as more than just Sharkbait. I regaled them with stories over dinner, realizing when they filled in some of the details themselves, they were all well-acquainted with my journey from the blog.

The weekend game plan was set over dinner that night, and the next day, they dropped me back at mile 807.8. I was going to try slackpacking 25 miles with just a few essentials in a daypack they'd brought. I was confident I could fly through the woods in time for our 4 p.m. rendezvous. After all, I was used to hiking 20-plus miles with thirty pounds on my back!

So, with assurances to my sister that I was going to practically run up and down the mountains I would climb today, I set off with hiking poles, water, snacks, and six hours to complete 25 miles. Easy.

Wrong.

The day started with a steep three-mile climb straight up Cole Mountain, then 15 miles of ups and downs on rock-laden trails before climbing five miles back down to the parking lot. By the time I began that final descent, it was nearly 6 p.m. and I felt horrible knowing they were waiting almost two hours for me.

But there was nothing to be done except continue on. In the end, it took eight hours—the same as with my regular pack. My sister texted that they'd decided to hike toward me, and soon I heard the sound of boys at play in the woods. I readied my apologies, but their smiling faces showed none were needed. They were having a blast being free-range in the woods. On the way back, my nephews excitedly showed me the sticks they'd arranged as signs for me, the trees they'd peed on, and the creeks they'd hopscotched through. I was proud to see how quickly they took up the carefree thru-hiker mentality.

The next morning was slow as we were reluctant to admit it was time for them to return to Maryland and for me to return to the mountains. We made plans to connect the following weekend if schedules worked out, then gave goodbye hugs. But it was still 35 miles before stopping in Waynesboro, where a hostel bed and resupply box awaited me, so I knew there was nothing to do but get walking.

Almost immediately, the trail became indiscernible from the boulders strewn across it, and it was on an incline, making the risk of stepping on the wrong rock and causing a small landslide a very real possibility.

I gritted my teeth, slowed my pace, and adjusted my expectations for the day. I was hiking alone and I was glad for it. Sometimes I needed to release screaming fits of frustration at the trail conditions, cursing the lack of trail maintenance in this part of Virginia. But even with the trail doing its best to cripple me, I showed up at Maupin Field Shelter as expected that evening. A couple of hikers I'd seen recently were setting up a campfire, and more kept trickling in. It ended up being a legitimate hiker party, bringing back memories from the early days with my tramily.

I pulled up my blog to write a new post and looked for Dad's latest comment. I was looking forward to his reactions and preparation details for our time on the trail together more and more each day. And true to form, his name appeared at the top of yesterday's comment section.

"I switched out my tent's zippers for glow-in-the-dark ones," I read. "It's always nice to find your zippers in the dark without having to search. I set up the tent with its new poles, too. I was a little surprised to see how small it is... I'm sure it's an illusion though because it definitely said two-person on the box."

A shadow of worry flickered across my face, my jaw tightening with tension as I imagined camping next to him in a makeshift bivy sack with customized poles and illuminated zippers. It seemed his gear research was falling short in practice, and I hoped he was doing better at preparing for what to expect while hiking these mountains. I made a mental note to ask if he'd researched our New York section next time we talked, then began typing the night's blog entry.

30

OH SHENANDOAH

The day began to warm fast, and I could feel my need for water increasing. And while the trail gave plenty of rocks to cuss out, it was scarce on water sources. After eight miles without water, I began feeling the concerning effects of dehydration—dry mouth, headache, dizziness, rapid breathing. Just as I started to worry, a creek finally appeared, and I eagerly filled my bottles, adding the few drops of Aqua Mira solution to purify the water. Then I waited.

Those fifteen minutes were torture, but after rechecking my watch for the hundredth time, it was finally time to drink. I chugged half the contents, gasping for breath. Water had never tasted better.

As I hiked on, I kept an eye out for creeks the rest of the day, refilling at every chance. Dehydration was a constant threat on these warmer days, and I didn't want to get as close as I had that morning.

Waynesboro soon came into view, and I sped up, eager to see it. As a well-stocked town on the edge of Shenandoah National Park, its reputation for being a haven for hikers preceded it. Dozens of trail angels willing to drive hikers from the trail were just a phone call away, happy to give back and be part of the AT support community.

Leaving the trail at Rockfish Gap, I halted as I took in my surroundings. It was a dilapidated road stop where only a food truck called King's Gourmet Popcorn remained. The remnants of a gas station and fast-food place haunted the background, looking like they hadn't seen customers in twenty years. It wasn't quite the first impression I expected. I ordered a cold drink and a hot dog at the food truck, then called a trail angel to pick me up and take me to Stanimal's Hostel, my lodging for the night.

Thirty minutes later, I strode into the hostel. It was nothing more than a converted house in the middle of suburban Waynesboro, on a block encircled by highways. Not the most picturesque, but only thirty dollars for a bed and convenient to everything I needed for rest.

I got settled in the bunk room and went to find my resupply box. Stanimal, the owner, pointed me toward a stack of boxes in the kitchen waiting to be claimed. I rifled through, but mine was nowhere to be found.

"Hey, do you have boxes anywhere else? I can't seem to find mine. The name is Neiman." I called out.

Stanimal took off his hat and ran his hand through his matted hair. "Hmm... let me check the mailroom."

I stood up to wait, and the door jangled open beside me. I looked over and immediately recognized the shaven head, strong jawline, and athletic shape of the endurance runner standing before me.

"Poncho Villa?!" I held out my hand to shake.

His brown eyes filled with recognition as he gripped my hand firmly.

"Oh wow! Hey, it's good to see you." A slight frown creased his forehead as he surveyed me. "Was it... Michael?"

"That's right. You've got a wicked memory." I smiled, knowing he'd appreciate the Boston jargon. "Although it's Sharkbait now."

"Sharkbait, huh? I bet that comes with a good story."

I laughed. "Yeah, I was hiking with this younger tramily for a

while. They loved the Disney connection to my color scheme and...
tendency for getting us off track."

Stanimal reappeared, nodding to Poncho Villa before turning to
me. "I don't see any boxes with your name. Are you sure it was here?
We have another hostel over in Glasgow, about an hour away.
Maybe you sent it there?"

Dread swept over me as I pulled my phone out to check the
tracking number online. Sure enough, I'd instructed Dana to send it
to the other location.

I groaned, and Stanimal apologized at my reaction. "Sorry, man,
but don't worry. I can have it shipped forward to you up the trail.
The post office doesn't charge for bouncing boxes."

"Thanks. I appreciate it." I thought for a moment. "I'll give you
my sister's address in Maryland. I'm headed that way after
Shenandoah and will buy some food in town to get through."

"That works, there's a Dollar General we can drop you at,"
Stanimal replied, then added, "Though you may want to go light on
resupply here. There are well-stocked concessions at the waysides in
the park. And trust me—you want to leave room for the blackberry
milkshakes."

My eyes widened at the sound of hot food and cold shakes. Add
the warming weather and I had a feeling I was going to like this
national park much more than the Smokies.

After the arrangements were worked out, Poncho Villa handed
me a cold beer and invited me outside to catch up. So much had
happened since Keg, The Captain, and I had met him back on that
first day in Georgia.

"I saw your entries in the shelter logbooks. You were making
incredible time, always farther and farther ahead of me. But they
disappeared recently. I thought maybe you threw in the towel or got
injured." I said, easing myself into one of the green plastic
Adirondack chairs. I was curious about Poncho Villa's hike because I
fully expected him to be through Pennsylvania by now.

"Yeah." Poncho Villa scratched his salt-and-pepper beard as a flush of red appeared on his cheeks. "Unfortunately, it's the latter. I slipped on some slick rocks a couple weeks ago and messed up my ankle pretty bad. I've had to take it slow since then. It sucks, man. I'm only getting about ten miles a day now."

"Damn, I'm sorry. These rocks are the worst. I read they'll be bad in Pennsylvania, but the last few days were brutal too." Seeing how dejected he was, I added, "But hey, at least you're still on the trail and pushing forward."

He sat back, pushing at the dirt with his sandal. "Yeah, that's true. Hoping I'll be back to full strength soon. I don't want to still be out here come fall!"

He gave a short laugh, and I smiled. I had my own close calls already, but I didn't have that luxury of time. If I didn't summit Katahdin by August, my thru-hike was over.

The next morning dawned bright. As I watched the early sun peek through the bunkroom windows, I knew it would be another hot day. Poncho Villa and I got dropped back on the trail together and officially crossed into Shenandoah National Park. Immediately, I felt the shift into better trail conditions that government funding provided. The path was well-maintained and wide, with clearings on both sides for us to hike side by side. And more importantly, it was soft on the feet. No rocks!

It wasn't long before I could tell Poncho Villa was slower than me, so when he mentioned stopping for a snack, it seemed a good place to break away and hike at my own pace again. I wished him farewell, and the rest of the day was spent walking alone through a lush forest awakening to spring's gentle touch.

The big concern was again the lack of water. The first few miles were fine, but then the trail quickly dried up until noon. I knew it was coming thanks to Guthook, but with the sun beating down, I still had a hard time stretching my two bottles for the last 12 miles. Going four hours with just 1.5 liters was painful.

In the last mile to Blackrock Shelter, I heard the delightful rushing sounds of water. And when I saw the blue blaze intersection, I pranced down the 0.2-mile side trail with visions of cannonballing into that river. But like a bad dream, when the shelter came into view, the river was nowhere to be seen. There was only a single pipe sticking out of the ground. The small dribble of water that trickled out hit the ground and immediately soaked into dry earth.

No river. No cannonballing. No guzzling down quick gallons of water. But it was still water, and that's all that mattered. I guzzled two liters after impatiently waiting the required fifteen minutes for my water treatment, then downed another liter while I ate dinner.

My thoughts turned toward tomorrow, which would have another eight-mile stretch without water. However, Loft Mountain Campground would be my mid-morning rest stop, featuring a wayside restaurant with the blackberry shakes Stanimal had teased as incredible. It felt like the motivation I needed to get up early and get in miles before the full heat of the day hit.

Stanimal was right. The milkshake was worth the early rise and extra miles. The first sip of purple elixir put a huge smile on my face, and the rest was consumed in huge gulps while sighing in ecstasy. The creamy treat complemented the salty grease of my burger and fries perfectly, and after three bottles of Gatorade, I finally felt ready to step back into the burning heat outside.

My belly full of sloshing liquids, I wound my way slowly down Weaver Mountain. I turned the corner of a switchback, looking ahead at what the trail was bringing next. As my right foot poised to land, I saw a shifting movement and yelped as I stopped, my foot still midair. A snake, five feet long and black as night, slithered across the trail and away from where I'd been about to land my foot. I stood frozen in an impressive *Karate Kid* crane kick pose as the snake disappeared into the woods.

Releasing my held breath, I continued along, taking caution now to scan the trail around each switchback in case I disturbed any more slithering serpents.

I finally rolled into Hightop Hut around 4:30, ate a quick dinner, and set up for bed. Days like this were new for me. Hiking 20-plus miles in cool weather had become easy, but doing that distance in the blazing heat of summer was exhausting. It was still only early May, but Virginia had skipped straight to the sweltering inferno of summer in this section of the trail. I needed a good night's sleep to get up early tomorrow so I could get miles in before the sun rose too high. My leisurely approach to mornings was too much of a luxury now.

31

SOLITARY MAN

I stood at a crossroads, my head pivoting between the white and blue blazes before me. Following white would keep me on the official AT and an easier path, but following blue would take me on a scrambling adventure to incredible heights and views. Never one to resist a good rock climb, I deviated from the official path for the first time and turned towards the blue blazes.

I quickly discovered this was Shenandoah's version of Neo's red-pill vs. blue-pill decision in *The Matrix*. I thought I'd experienced the full reality of jagged rocks, but as I looked up at the cliff, I realized my previous encounters had only hidden the truth.

The blue blazes were painted on the rock cliff in an almost vertical pattern, and I climbed past most on my hands and knees. It was hard, but I collapsed my poles and stashed them in a side pocket to give me full use of my hands again. And the 360-degree view at the top made the strenuous climb worth it. My "Yo!" war cry of triumph echoed around the treetops, and a flock of nearby birds took flight in cawing alarm.

I slugged water from my bottle, taking time to enjoy the view and the feeling of accomplishment, when a rustle and grunt sounded behind me. Turning, I caught sight of a hiker climbing the last piece of rock onto the summit. He grinned up at me, and I nodded a greeting back. Pulling up alongside me, he grabbed his own bottle from his backpack.

"What a climb!" he exclaimed before swallowing a gulp of water.

"Incredible," I confirmed.

"Are you thru-hiking?" he asked, pointing his bottle toward my backpack between us.

I nodded and gestured toward his faded, navy-blue JanSport backpack. "Are you out here for a day hike?"

"No, I'm thru-hiking too. The name's Thirteen." He held out his hand to shake, and I grasped it in stunned silence. How was this guy thru-hiking with the equivalent of a grade school book bag?

As I shook his hand, I offered my own trail name and turned back to the view, but curiosity surged within me. "I have to know, what's your base weight with that thing?"

"Thirteen pounds," he side-smiled and raised an eyebrow, clearly familiar with the question.

"Ha, I should have guessed that's what the trail name meant," I laughed.

"Yeah, everyone goes crazy when I tell them I don't have a tent, water filter, or stove, but I hiked across New Zealand last winter without 'em, and it worked out fine."

I hadn't seen Thirteen's name in any shelter logbooks, which meant he must have started after me. It also meant he had to be averaging a lot more miles per day. I asked him about his speed with such minimalist gear, and he confirmed my suspicions... he was averaging over 30 miles a day.

"Have you seen any hikers going by the trail names Fun Facts, Nubs, or Leap Frog?"

Thirteen took another giant swig of water. "Actually, yeah. Leap Frog doesn't ring a bell, but I saw Fun Facts and Nubs a few days ago at McAfee Knob."

"Oh yeah?" I was excited to hear more.

"I remember them because they were with this huge group. I couldn't figure out what was going on. I mean, there were a ton of kids and four adults. At first, I thought it was two separate families, but after talking to them, I realized your friends were just hiking with the parents and all their kids."

I knew exactly which family he meant. It had to be the same one the guy in Gatlinburg had been talking about—the family that spent a frigid night in the bathroom at the trailhead parking lot in the Smoky Mountains. I laughed, picturing Nubs and Fun Facts with all those children.

"It seemed like they were hiking together for a while," Thirteen added.

"That's awesome. I hiked with them early on and wondered where they were at."

Thirteen and I started the final six miles over Hazeltop Mountain and down to Big Meadows Wayside together, but I soon saw his speed in action. After watching him zoom off into the distance, it felt like I was moving at a snail's pace, even though I was clocking my usual 2.5 miles per hour. But I trekked along, eventually making it to Big Meadows Campground.

I lay in my hammock that night, listening to the campsite settling down around me. Each day, I was edging closer to Harpers Ferry, the unofficial halfway point of the Appalachian Trail, and it made me wonder if anyone I knew would catch up after my rest break there. I had planned a nero and zero to be with Devorah. If Nubs and Fun Facts were hiking with the family Thirteen mentioned, it was unlikely I'd see them any time soon. But Leap Frog, Ridge, Remy, or Happy Feet and Tarzan might be within two to three days if they'd kept up their pace. It would be fun to see familiar faces again, though I still felt content setting my own pace even if it meant hiking solo.

I left Big Meadows Campground at 8 a.m., amid the early rays of warm sunshine and gorgeous views of the Shenandoah Valley. I approached Hawksbill Gap shortly after and heard a loud, "Be prepared, and...?" from an adult, followed by, "Do your best!" in a raucous cacophony of boy voices. I'd seemingly stumbled across a Cub Scout group, and by the looks on their eager faces, they were on their first-ever backpacking trip.

A water break provided me an opportunity to eavesdrop on the scoutmaster's safety lesson, as well as a perfect view of the boys' lengthy attempts at wrestling their monster backpacks onto their backs for what I learned would be just a two-mile hike to their campsite.

Slinging my own pack on, I left them to their adventures, chuckling at the memory of that first fateful backpacking adventure I took in Montana with Max and my 75-pound pack. Hopefully, they'd make it more than the fifty feet I had before needing the first break.

I strolled into Beahms Gap at 4:30 p.m. and strolled out again early the next morning for the hike to the town of Front Royal. By this point, I was so close to Harpers Ferry I could almost see it, and I wanted to take advantage of Shenandoah's well-maintained trails to get good miles in. So besides a quick stop at the final wayside for one last blackberry shake, I didn't stop walking all day. I snacked as I hiked and filled my bottles from streams connecting with the trail. It was a great hiking day. At least until I hit mile 21. After that, conditions changed quickly.

I still had 3.5 miles to Front Royal, but I'd reached the end of Shenandoah National Park. There wasn't a ranger station, parking lot, or any designation marking the end, but I knew the moment my feet left the Park's boundary. The wide, well-groomed trail immediately transformed into a narrow, rocky semi-path that began winding unnecessarily up and down hillsides. And on top of everything, it began to rain. Heavily.

The last hour was spent reminiscing about the "good old days" of Shenandoah as I carefully stepped over wet rocks in an increasingly sullen mood. Walking 20 miles a day suddenly seemed monotonous rather than joyful. My untrimmed beard and unwashed hiker gear felt like I was nothing more than a wandering, homeless beggar, and the solitude I'd previously enjoyed was now cumbersome under my rain jacket's tented hood.

Front Royal and its BBQ restaurant were a welcome sight for my weary feet, and a dry hotel room with a TV set to the Kentucky Derby lifted my spirits considerably. So did the knowledge that I was now only 54 miles from Harpers Ferry, where I could take my planned break to revive my body and soul.

After eleven hours of sleep at the hotel, I devoured a giant pancake and egg breakfast at the diner in town and got back to the trail around noon. The intention was to do a shorter 15-mile day, but it accidentally ended up being 23 miles instead. The sun set at 8:08, and I rolled into Rod Hollow Shelter at 8:15 just as the last slivers of daylight faded. There was just enough light to see the eight mummy bags already occupying the shelter made for ten. I considered setting up a hammock, but it was still wet outside from yesterday's rain, and the radar showed more coming the next morning. So I quietly asked if there was room for one more inside, to which a kind female voice whispered, "Of course."

She cleared her strewn gear from a section near her, and I scuttled into the space, murmuring thanks as I tried not to wake the sleeping hikers around me. I still hadn't eaten dinner though, and I was ravenous, so I quickly set up my bed and backed out to eat a double portion of cold snack rations. As I was hanging my food bag, another couple of thru-hikers appeared. Where had all these people been? My only guess was that there'd been a hiker bubble a day or two ahead, and I'd just caught up with it.

I settled into my quilt, feeling the drifting heaviness of impending sleep. All was quiet until the loud rip of someone passing gas echoed throughout the shelter. I shook with silent laughter as everyone who the massive flatulence woke shuffled their positions and fell still again. As was typical for this vagabond thru-hiking culture, no one cared in the slightest, ignoring it in favor of getting sleep. I thought about how this same scenario would play out in a conference room at work or a family dinner at a fancy restaurant. But then I realized it didn't bother me out here in the least either, and my giggles soon subsided into my own slumbering silence.

32

TAKE ME HOME, COUNTRY ROADS

"Son of a—!" Three hours into my hike, and frustrated exclamations filled the air. I'd stopped at a creek to fill my bottles, but reaching for the Aqua Mira chlorine drops in my backpack's hip belt pocket, I made an unpleasant discovery. The bottle had leaked and somehow the concentrated solution burned a hole through the lining. And that wasn't all. As I followed the path of destruction, I came across a formerly dark-orange shirt that now displayed a white-and-yellow tie-dye splotch.

I let out a sigh. What was done was done, but I'd been drinking this stuff in my water for weeks. If it did that much damage to nylon and wool, what the heck was it doing to my internal organs? That settled it—a new water treatment plan had to be top priority when I reached Harpers Ferry.

The Aqua Mira had a few drops left, just enough for my two freshly filled bottles. I grimaced as I lifted them to my lips. The water I'd happily downed at breakfast now seemed perilous, but I had no choice. Until I could get to an outfitter, I had to go with what I had or risk the dangers of Giardia and other waterborne parasites.

I repacked my bag, shoving the empty bottles into its depths.

Settling it on my shoulders, familiar twinges of pain ran along my shoulders and down my spine. I'd been feeling increasing discomfort with my bag lately, especially given how much weight I'd now lost. The bathroom scale at Stanimal's had revealed I was now down twenty pounds since leaving home. And worse, my waist had dropped at least two inches, making it now too thin for the generous hip belt of my Osprey Talon backpack.

There was no question, the whole backpack had to be replaced. And fast. After researching popular alternatives and considering what other hikers constantly talked up, I had a couple of good but expensive options. Both were from small cottage vendors that did not sell in retail stores, so I ordered one of each to my sister's house. I figured I could convince her to meet me on the trail with them somewhere in Pennsylvania and test which I liked better. They each promised an important design feature—interchangeable hip belts. If the weight loss and waist thinning persisted, I could just throw on a smaller belt.

I began walking again, trying to ignore my shoulders and back's complaints and the discouragement of my water situation. But the next ten-mile section did nothing to improve my mood. The familiar rocky enemies were back, and even though I tried to make my way carefully over and around the boulder-infested path, I tripped, slipped, or clipped a foot more times than I cared to count.

By mid-afternoon, the bottoms of my feet, now raw from the villainous terrain, made it very apparent they were done, but I still had several miles before reaching Harpers Ferry. Stubborn determination alone propelled me forward until, finally, the Shenandoah River came into view, signifying my destination and the fulfillment of a 30-mile triumph. I crossed the river and made the final short climb into town, where I knew I'd find a special landmark —the central office of the Appalachian Trail Conservancy.

As the unofficial agency overseeing the trail, the ATC provides support, education, and resources to the AT community year-round. I'd stopped to register with them in Amicalola Falls, recording myself as #436 for the season and receiving my orange 2018 AT badge. I was excited now to check in at Harpers Ferry and the unofficial halfway point, where I could see how far up or down the numbers I'd gone.

I sped up as the office came into view, eager to see how my recent speed would impact my number. But this small sliver of West Virginia that the AT cut through had other plans. I soon learned that everything in town closed at 5 p.m., including the ATC office. My 7 p.m. arrival meant I was walking through a ghost town. I couldn't even find an open restaurant for an adult beverage to celebrate. It was disappointing, but out of my hands. I'd just have to come back after my zero day.

After my quick tour through the empty town, Devorah met me at the train station and drove us back to her home for my much-anticipated day off. And after a massive breakfast the next morning, we drove to the local REI to resolve my water filtration woes. I surveyed the many options on the shelf, from heavy hand-pump filters to ultralight iodine tablets, then selected the BeFree filter. It was compact, lightweight, and easily screwed into different-sized water bottles. With a two-liter soft flask attached, I'd be able to instantly filter water for both of my Smartwater bottles at once. No more waiting fifteen thirsty minutes for treatment drops, and no more chlorine concentrate burning through my gear and, undoubtedly, my insides.

With a couple backpack orders on the way and my new filter in hand, I was ready to take on the second half of the trail. I arrived back at the ATC office the next day to officially check in, receiving hiker #137. I knew the typical dropout rate at this point was 75 percent, and it seemed this year would be no different. Either the trail was knocking out people at its usual rate, or my speed really was outpacing the rest. In yesterday's blog, I'd written of the astonishment and pride my first 30-mile day had given me, asking hypothetically whether that may become the norm going forward. Today, I saw Dad's response in the comments: "*If you plan to do 30 miles while I'm there, you'll have to carry me on your back too!"*

The following day brought a new state—Maryland. By now, the trees were fully adorned in the light green of newly unfurled leaves, and they formed the roof of a natural tunnel that rustled pleasantly in the breeze as I walked through it. Giant turtles sunbathed along the river, but I was content to stay in the shade's cool cover.

As I settled that night in Rocky Run Shelter, I calculated that Allenberry Resort was only 82 miles away. During my Harpers Ferry break, I'd solidified plans for Devorah and the family to meet me there on Sunday with my new backpacks, which meant I had three days to walk those miles. It was a stretch, but I felt confident I could do it.

But as usual, the next day did not go to plan. I was slow to get going in the morning, and my pace matched that slow start. A few miles in, I decided to take a short side trail to see the original Washington Monument—an 1827 stone tower that, I learned from signposts, had been built a couple decades before its more well-known D.C. sibling. I hoped embracing this lesser-known piece of American history would help shake the lethargy that had crept over me. But although the top afforded a magnificent view of Maryland's Appalachian mountain range, it also offered a very clear view of quickly approaching storm clouds, which did not help lift my mood.

The rain began in earnest soon after, falling hard and heavy. I'd also lived in the D.C. area for a bit after college, so I was used to the common humidity-induced shower of summer. But this storm was different, leaving only to return a short time later.

The upside to the day was that I was not in it alone. A new influx of hikers on the trail provided camaraderie in the form of grunted hellos, eye rolls, and comments on the weather as we passed each other. A lot of these were thru-hikers who'd just started their journey north to Katahdin at Harpers Ferry. In recent years, a new thru-hike strategy was gaining popularity known as flip-flopping. The ATC was also promoting it heavily to lessen the human impact of overcrowding on the trail, as well as to give their HQ in Harpers Ferry a chance to impart wisdom to excited hikers before they set out. Once the flip-floppers reached Katahdin, they'd fly down to Georgia and start the hike north again to end back where they started at Harpers Ferry.

My stop that night, Raven Rock Shelter, provided the perfect opportunity to get to know some of the season's flip-floppers, as it was filled with at least fifteen hikers by the time I was ready to eat dinner around the campfire. I laughed to myself as I listened to them talking proudly about everything they thought they knew but had yet to experience. I'd also started with my own untested, naïve enthusiasm, thinking that with the years of planning I'd done and my previous backpacking experience, I knew it all. Although I was well-educated, I soon realized nothing could compare to being out here experiencing it firsthand. I'd already got a lot wrong, and I was sure there would be more lessons to come.

"When it comes to thru-hiking," I wrote on my blog later that night, *"Nothing can prepare you except a thru-hike. You simply don't know until you know."*

I woke the next morning with renewed vigor for the day ahead. Maybe it was a side effect of soaking in all that newbie enthusiasm, maybe it was the sun peeking over the horizon, or perhaps I was motivated by the proximity of a real bed again. Whatever it was, I more than made up for my slow pace the day before.

By mid-morning I was standing on the Pennsylvania state line. I was about to enter my seventh state. It was also marked by a large brown sign signifying the Mason-Dixon Line, which made it feel like an appropriate place to rest and ponder the significance of history I was walking through. Along with this line that had divided America in its day, I also saw signs for Antietam, Gettysburg, and other relics of the nation's troubled past. It was both humbling and inspiring to hike through landmarks containing so much history, one on top of the other like layers of sediment beneath my feet. And here I was adding my own story to this piece of land, just as other thru-hikers had done before me and would continue to do after. As I crossed into the North, a deep thought ate its way through my mind—wasn't that what life was all about? Walking out our stories in the time we've been given, leaving imprints on those around us and on the places we've been.

I got back down to the business of walking out that day's story, and the side trail to Quarry Gap Shelter came into view around 5 p.m. The next day would be a big one: I'd pass the AT's actual halfway point, and I was going to commemorate it in a celebration only thru-hikers could have come up with.

33

HALFWAY TO HEAVEN

I chuckled into my coffee the next morning as I read Dad's updates on his hike preparations.

"Our basement looks like a glorified garage sale. My unassembled gear is in piles across the floor, your mother has threatened to toss all of it (and me) in the dumpster," he wrote. *"I'm taking the night off from prep hikes to organize it (and stay married) but will resume tomorrow with some more weight. I've got to condition my body if I want to keep up with you!"*

I appreciated the planning stage Dad was in, having been there only a couple of months ago myself. His excitement, and knowing I'd reach the trail's halfway mark today, provided the boost I needed to put 18 more miles behind me to Pine Grove Furnace State Park.

By 1 p.m., a wooden pole appeared down the trail, topped with the familiar AT logo. One sign pointed back south 1090.5 miles to Springer Mountain, the other pointed onward to Katahdin, another 1090.5 miles north. This was it! Halfway? Officially? I almost couldn't believe it, so I stopped to take a dozen celebratory photos exhibiting the crazed joy only a thru-hiker feels at such a signpost.

From there, it was only three miles more to the State Park, so I picked up the pace, already anticipating the general store with its stocked shelves of junk food and cold drinks ahead. After a short time, I heard the sound of trampling boots and what appeared to be familiar voices ahead.

Drawing in a deep breath and cupping my hands around my mouth, I yelled out an elongated, "Yooooooooo!" Unlike my war cry from Rocky Top in the Smoky Mountains, this version was Dad's all-too-familiar greeting on the trail to warn hikers and animals alike of his location. If those voices were who I thought they were, it was about to be returned even louder.

"YOOOOOOOOOOOOOO!" came echoing back down the trail in a multitude of voices, with the gusto Dad would've appreciated.

My nephews came barreling into view, racing to be first to wrestle-hug me into a pile of limbs and walking sticks. Devorah and her husband, Kevin, followed at a more sedate pace, grinning at the carnage.

"Help?" I called out, stretching an arm toward them, but it only elicited wider grins instead of rescue. Finally disentangling myself from three excited boys, we resumed hiking and I enlightened my family about the celebration—and challenge—ahead.

"When we get to the parking lot, we need to stop at the Pine Grove Furnace Store," I began. "There's an infamous food challenge for thru-hikers to complete and commemorate finishing half the AT. If you complete it, they reward you with an entry in the year's record book... and a tiny wooden spoon trophy."

"What is it?" my nephews demanded. "What do you have to do?"

I surveyed them with wide eyes to amp up the dramatic effect. "It's called the half-gallon challenge. I get to eat half a gallon of ice cream in one sitting!"

"Get to?!" Devorah's voice came from behind me. "Half a gallon of ice cream? You have to be kidding. You honestly think you can handle that?"

"Oh yeah," I said, patting my stomach. "This thing? It's now a bottomless pit."

Not long later, I sat on a picnic bench outside the general store with a giant metal spoon, a 1.5-quart tub of Hershey's finest raspberry ice cream, and a pint of locally made peach ice cream to cap it off. Together, they made up the required half-gallon. I looked up at the boys, gave them a wink, and dove in while everyone cheered me on. I loved raspberry, my favorite flavor in fact, so it disappeared quickly without much hesitation. But the quart of peach took some mental fortitude. Down it eventually went, and I soon stood victorious with my empty tubs, my tiny spoon trophy, and a very full stomach.

"That really is a bottomless pit!" my youngest nephew exclaimed, pointing at my bloated gut. Pure awe ran across his face, and I had to admit, even I was impressed.

We hopped in their car and made our way to Boiling Springs for the night, staying at the amazing Allenberry Resort and Theater, a gorgeous place that felt far too nice for my hiker chic.

Only one of the backpacks I'd ordered was delivered earlier in the week, so Devorah presented me with the Zpacks Arc Haul to test out on tomorrow's hike. With its small hip belt, it should fit my slimmer waistline much better, providing the even weight distribution I'd lost with my Osprey.

The following morning, I transferred the contents of my old pack over, and after a slow start and huge breakfast, we made it back to the trail. I had the company of Devorah and her family for the first couple of miles, but then they said goodbye and turned back, leaving me to solo hike once again.

I could tell the immediate difference the new pack made. The size was perfect, the fit was snug, and the comfort was incredible. There were no twinges of pain in my shoulders, and I felt like I could comfortably carry fifty pounds, even with the minimalist design. Just five metal rods held the pack's structure intact, and a curvature along the spine allowed air to flow through and cool my torso. It was also waterproof, which meant I didn't need a rain cover or worry about water leaking into the fragile contents. It was perfect. And so with my shiny new backpack, I was in great spirits and ready for the yet-again forecasted week of rain.

Rocks, rain, farm pastures, rain, a trail town with the decrepit but historic Doyle Hotel, more rain, and more rocks characterized the next few days in Pennsylvania. Oh, and a mountain or two. By the time I reached my eighth state, my patience toward rocks, especially wet ones, was growing thin. Another week of storms was ahead, and I had another 60 miles before reaching Port Clinton, where I'd be rewarded with a resupply box from Dana and my next warm bed. The shelters were very spread out in this part of the trail, which meant camping at whatever rain-soaked campsite I could find. It wasn't ideal, but I was trying to let the next town motivate me to push through. *Embrace the suck,* I reminded myself.

Twenty-four hours later, I broke down. And I broke one of the rules I'd set for myself: never walk more than one mile off trail for resupply or lodging. But after another whole day of rain, it was easy to convince myself to walk three miles along the road to a highway rest-stop hotel in Lickdale, Pennsylvania. My conscience was mostly cleared by the fact I'd also put in five extra miles I hadn't planned, which meant tomorrow night's shelter would now be a manageable 26 miles away. I was becoming a bit of a rain wimp, but given the five-day forecast of nonstop precipitation, I decided I was more than okay with it.

The next morning, I tried to look extra sad and pathetic, hoping for a hotel patron to take pity on me in the form of a ride back to the trail, but no dice. So, I donned my rain gear and hiked the three flat miles back to the trail.

Eight miles of the AT behind me, my enthusiasm for reaching even 20 miles was waning. The combination of rocks and trail rivers that had become all too familiar was weighing heavily on my mind (and feet), and the gray gloom surrounding the hilltops didn't add much hope. So when I reached the next shelter a few miles later and it was still raining, I knew I was done. Not a horrible day at 11 miles, but not nearly as much as I'd hoped.

The shelter itself was also a big factor in convincing me to stay. It was actually more of a cabin, fully enclosed with bunk beds, board games, and a giant ten-foot octagonal skylight. It was the 501 Shelter, named after its proximity to Highway 501, a hundred yards away.

I chose my bunk and started laying out my gear when the door swung open in a whoosh of wind and rain. In walked an older man, decked in a heavy trench coat and no discernible backpack. He pulled his hood back and fixed me with an assessing stare. I offered a hesitant smile as he approached.

"I'm the caretaker of this shelter," he advised. "You planning on staying the night?"

"Yes, sir." I added the sir as he clearly looked like a man who expected respect.

He looked me up and down, taking in my rain skirt, sweat-soaked shirt, and orange bandana. "You here to party?"

"Just sleep. I'm hiking out in the morning." I wasn't even sure what a party would mean at an AT shelter, but I guessed he was very familiar by his tone.

"Alright, then. I don't tolerate riff-raff in here, so mind the rules and we'll get on okay. If you see any partiers, I'm in the house next door."

I nodded, thanking him, and with a nod of his own, he pulled his hood up and stepped back out in the pouring rain.

It hit me as funny that I didn't count as riff-raff. In any other setting, my days of unshaven beard, the same ragged clothing worn day in and day out, and general dirt-caked state would have instantly earned me riff-raff status.

Since today had ended up being a nero day of sorts, I decided to spend my extra time researching and planning out the next couple of weeks. Not so much where to start and stop, but what to expect and what to do if I couldn't reach Bear Mountain in time to meet Dad's arriving flight eight days from now. I researched all the major trail towns ahead and mapped out bus routes from each one so I could quickly jump up the trail, if needed, to meet him as planned.

I then updated my blog with the latest adventures, plans, and hopes. At the bottom of each post, I'd been recording some trail data: the starting mile, ending mile, miles hiked, and how many more miles to go. That night, when I finished the calculations, I sat back in astonishment. I was now less than 1,000 miles to Katahdin—996.1 to be precise. It was a good reminder that even though the last few days had felt like a slow and depressing slog, I was still making progress. And that was worth celebrating. But not with another half-gallon of ice cream. Bottomless pit or not, I was never doing that again.

34

BLAME IT ON THE RAIN

I woke to a gray curtain of rain covering the trail outside. My eyes hurt from the large eye roll I gave the darkened skies, but with my new plans in place, I was determined to make it to Port Clinton, 24 miles away. I couldn't avoid walking in the rain unless I stayed put for who knows how many days, and this one could possibly end with a hot meal and a warm bed. The others in the shelter woke early, too, so I ended up hiking with three guys named Reboot, Gandalf, and Traveler, my first company in weeks. It was a nice change to hike alongside a few others, and I was especially grateful for it with each challenge the trail brought.

It alternated between three rock grades all day—small stones that sat like spikes in the trail, medium-sized stones that covered most of the trail, and boulder-sized stones that completely were the trail. In addition, there were swampy areas overrun with water, sometimes up to ten feet on either side of the path. Those stretches required off-trail bushwhacking through the trees. It was frustrating and slow, but the rain eventually let up and the going got a little easier.

The final one-mile descent was an extremely steep and muddy

slip-and-slide into Port Clinton. The trail emptied into a historic railroad station, which I learned from helpful information boards, had been used to support the anthracite mining industry that established this area of Pennsylvania.

The town itself was very small, home to just one boutique hotel, a candy shop, some motorcycle shops, a barbershop, and a restaurant called The Union House. I stopped at the hotel to see about a room, but even at an expensive seventy dollars, it was already full of hikers. Instead, I headed for a giant covered picnic pavilion farther along in town where hikers were allowed to camp for free. Thankfully, it wasn't crowded, and I easily found a spot to set up on the ground for the night. Reboot, Gandalf, and Traveler set up next to me, becoming my camping companions for another night.

The next morning, I woke to the sound of rain drumming along the pavilion roof and falling in streams down its open sides. I groaned, wanting to pull the hood of my quilt over my head and ignore what was inevitably coming. But within thirty minutes, the pavilion filled with the sounds of hikers getting ready, and I begrudgingly admitted it was time to get going too.

Fifteen miles was on the agenda, ending at Eckville Shelter, an enclosed cabin with bunk beds that slept six comfortably. It would be perfect for a rainy night. But first, I needed to make it to Port Clinton's post office to collect my resupply box.

Like everything in town, the post office was a short walk away, so it wasn't long before I was giving the postal worker my name. She searched diligently through the packages, but mine was not to be found. I checked my tracking information and quickly realized this particular box had not been sent. Somehow, I'd gotten mixed up on my resupply routine with Dana again, and this one was still sitting in my spare room back home. Waking up in the rain was the beginning of my sour mood, but this turn of events quickly worsened it.

I pulled out my phone to search for nearby grocery stores and came up with a Walmart a few miles down the highway. It would delay my start time, but I had no choice. I was out of food.

Relying on the amazing community of trail angels mentioned in my guidebook, I was able to bum a ride to the brightly lit aisles of Walmart and fill my food bag for the coming days. As my trail angel returned me to downtown Port Clinton, I tried to get my mind off the day's negative trajectory and again reframe the positive. But it was easier said than done, as the day's hike continued to throw obstacles my way.

The trail was wider than it had been for a while, which usually meant fewer rocks and easier walking. But with all the rain today, it just meant a wide river. Trying to keep my feet dry made it impossible to make any reasonable progress, and my pace slowed to a crawl. The views from Pulpit Rock and The Pinnacle that should have been incredible were nothing but a white cloud of fog, and I couldn't even find a dry rock to sit on and rest. I ate a miserably cold lunch of crackers, salami, and cheese hunched below a tree while the skies continued to drench me.

By the time I reached the shelter at 6:15, I'd worked myself into a frustrated mess. I opened the door, wanting nothing more than to get my dinner cooked and set up my bed. But I stopped, clenching my jaw as I stared at bunks and floor space filled with the sleeping gear of hikers who weren't even there. Sleeping outside wasn't an option either because a group of Cub Scouts had completely filled the surrounding area.

It was the final straw for this camel's back. The day could have been amazing, and it would have been amazing... had it not been for another onslaught of nonstop rain. I could tell I was beginning to lose any romantic feelings toward hiking the AT.

I pulled my phone from its pocket and dialed the trail angel's number again.

"Any chance you're available to take me back to Port Clinton tonight?" I asked, after explaining my pitiful situation.

"Sure, man," the guy answered. "Hike to the road. I'll be there in fifteen minutes."

Despairing thoughts crowded in on me as I trudged back along the trail to the rendezvous point. I knew more of the dreaded Rocksylvania, an apt nickname for this state, still stood between me and New Jersey. Still to come were some of the hardest, sharpest, and steepest rocks the trail had to offer. And given how everyone referred to it, that section would make everything before it look like paved asphalt. If the weather didn't break soon, it seemed very possible that it would break me.

A wonderful conglomeration of smells greeted me in the Port Clinton pavilion the next morning, as the sweet aroma of banana pancakes and freshly brewed coffee wafted through the air. I'd woken to the most cherished of surprises: trail magic! Fresh Ground was the name of the trail angel serving up breakfast out of a van parked nearby.

"More?" he asked me, seeing my plate emptying.

"Mm-hmm," I mumbled through a mouth full of syrupy, fluffy goodness. Fresh Ground smiled and placed a few pancakes on my plate. "So, how long have you been doing this?" I asked.

"Four years now. I start in Georgia, just like you northbound thru-hikers, and keep driving up and down the trail, stopping to feed hikers from donations I collect every couple of days."

"That's so appreciated!" I said, before adding, "You have no idea how badly I needed this. Yesterday almost did me in."

"You'll have those days, don't let it get to ya. And if I'm around, you can count on a meal to lift your spirits back up!" He exclaimed. And I believed him.

I asked him a few more questions about his lifestyle and heard some stories from his adventures this season, but it was soon time to meet my ride back to the trail I'd abandoned the night before. The sun was peeking out from behind the clouds, and my spirits were considerably lifted, just like he'd promised.

The sun continued to shine as the day wore on, and I reached the treacherous rock scramble that gave Rocksylvania its reputation just after lunch. Names like Balance Rocks and The Knife Edge were enough to strike fear into any hiker's heart. But when I got to them, I discovered that it was actually enjoyable maneuvering around the ridgeline of boulders. The Knife Edge was particularly wild, referring to a steep and razor-thin ridge of gigantic stone slabs that barely had enough space between them for a clean footing. But the rocks were dry that day, and I kept my pace slow, so even that death-defying feat didn't dampen my spirits. I couldn't believe I was almost willing to throw in the towel just a day before. And it was refreshing to be out on the trail again, feeling both physically and mentally fit with an eagerness to hike the next day.

Something I recalled from memoirs I'd read in the past flooded my mind, reminding me that you should never quit on a bad day, and to just give it one more. If you still wanted to be done when the sun was shining and the air was warm, so be it. But most likely, you'd realize the ups and downs were worth it, and you'd be ready to keep moving forward. With no rain, it was like the flip of a switch in my mind, and I was ready for whatever challenges came next. It had honestly been days since I felt this good, and I welcomed the change.

The next day brought more sun and warm temperatures, and despite a few miles of clumsy tripping due to bouts of dehydration, the path eventually became easier. The irony did not escape me that I'd just spent days complaining about constant rain, and now I couldn't find enough water to drink.

The nicer trail conditions and sunny weather lasted into the next day, and I finally reached Delaware Water Gap, which signified the end of Pennsylvania. I was not in the least bit sad to leave behind the rocky, rainy mess that crippled my attitude the past week. Pennsylvania had been, by far, my most challenging and least enjoyable state. The weather was brutal, my morale had been low, and my eagerness to hike felt challenged each morning. Most days were spent questioning why I was still hiking while tripping over incessant rocks. But with the Keystone State now behind me, I was eager and ready for the next chapter.

The weather had slowed my progress, and the hike out of Port Clinton nearly had me throwing in the towel. It was clear I was desperately in need of a mental recharge. I'd also run short of time before Dad arrived. My body and feet were beaten up from the trail conditions and constant hiking, and I knew I needed a long rest. It was still 100 miles to Bear Mountain, where I'd meet Dad in a couple of days, but a Greyhound bus also departed from here to White Plains, where my in-laws lived and where I could get two much-needed zero days instead.

I hated the thought of skipping 100 miles and disrupting the trail's natural progression northward, but there was no way I could keep this pace up in my current condition. I needed time for my mind, body, and soul to recover—to get excited to hike again for Dad.

I accepted temporary defeat, but a plan was already forming in my mind to come back later in the year to complete those miles. For now, I'd have to put an asterisk next to New Jersey on the blog. It was unfortunate, but it was the "hike your own hike" mentality that I truly believed in. So, with my bag packed and my mind occupied with images of family meals and fitted sheets, I did what I never thought I'd do... I hopped on the bus and skipped up the trail.

PART 4

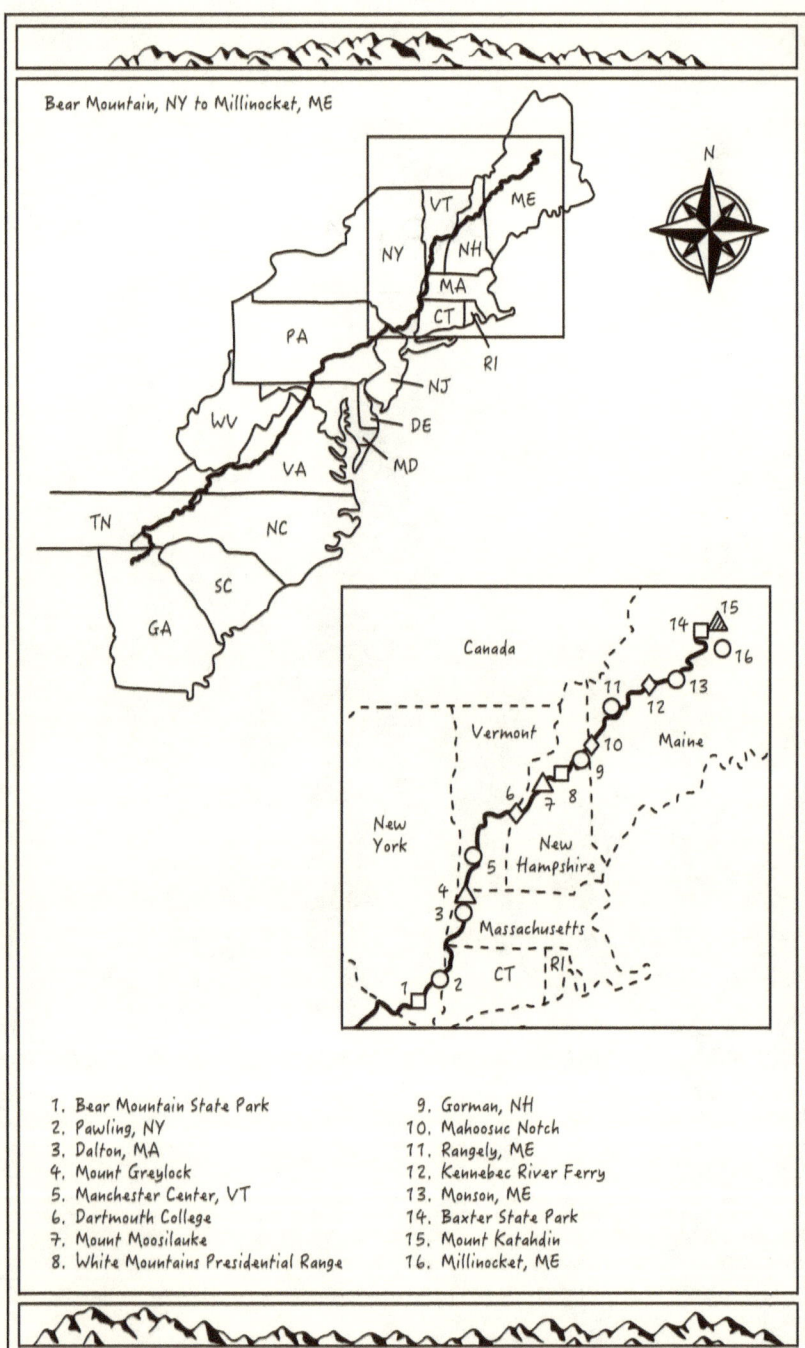

Bear Mountain, NY to Millinocket, ME

1. Bear Mountain State Park
2. Pawling, NY
3. Dalton, MA
4. Mount Greylock
5. Manchester Center, VT
6. Dartmouth College
7. Mount Moosilauke
8. White Mountains Presidential Range
9. Gorman, NH
10. Mahoosuc Notch
11. Rangely, ME
12. Kennebec River Ferry
13. Monson, ME
14. Baxter State Park
15. Mount Katahdin
16. Millinocket, ME

35

HAPPY TOGETHER

It was weird to be back in the real world. I sat at my in-laws' house watching TV, eating takeout, and not walking farther than a quick stroll around the block. While it felt amazing to relax and take a mental break from hiking every day, I was quickly getting anxious to be back out on the trail again.

I spent some time on my second zero day reviewing the itinerary for the next two states I'd hike with Dad. He was excited and ambitious, but it was unrealistic to think he could put in more than eight or ten miles a day. Fortunately, the terrain we'd cover in New York and Connecticut looked moderate compared to how rough I'd just had it. I knew he could handle it, but even if it put up a challenge, I was excited to create some great memories together.

Finally, Friday rolled around, and it was time to meet Dad at the airport.

Dana's parents and I waited outside arrivals, watching the slew of passengers coming through the gate. They mostly pulled carry-on suitcases, heads buried in cell phones as they hurried past. And then Dad came strolling out, his diminutive frame hidden by a huge burlap sack in his arms that was lashed shut with straps and ropes as if just unearthed from a long-dormant burial.

"Pride!" he called out from across the terminal. Several heads swiveled at the name, and I felt the flush of heat to my face that only parent-induced embarrassment can bring.

"Hey, Dad," I replied, reaching him and going in for a hug. The oversized bag impeded the first attempt, and I pulled it away from him, laughing. "Let's get this backpack off your hands." With a grunt, I let the full weight of it fall onto my arms. "What on earth do you have in here?"

"Oh, just the essentials."

Unless the essentials included the majority of REI's online catalog, I knew we were going to have a very tough discussion about leaving some of his items behind.

After a successful second hug, we left the airport and made our way to the Bear Mountain Inn, a beautiful resort along the Hudson River that the AT walked right through. Dad, always a natural storyteller, filled us in on his last few days of preparing and traveling, and it wasn't long before we were waving goodbye to Dana's parents and settling into the hotel.

"Alright, Dad," I said, untying the ropes in our hotel room and removing his backpack from its protective wrapping. "Show me what you've got in here that's so essential."

After quite a few online deliberations with Dad over the past few weeks, his backpack remained the long-trusted Kelty external-frame pack. Outdated by at least 30 years, it was a relic among hikers today, but it had served him well on many Montana trips. In fact, you'd be hard-pressed to find any external frame on the AT, where the aluminum frame sits outside the nylon storage pockets. It was heavier, bulkier, and designed to carry most of its contents as attachments, and I knew from just my brief stint carrying it that it weighed about as much as a pregnant hippopotamus. And when he started pulling out his "essentials," I saw why. Extra shirts, pajamas, aluminum pots, a jacket, and several thousand plastic bags, which he could definitely live two weeks without, were jammed into every inch of available space. We created a substantial "toss" pile, but his pack still dwarfed mine.

While Dad played Tetris with his gear and a box we'd ship back to Mom in Minnesota, I continued rummaging in his pack, pulling out a heavy block of Gouda cheese.

"Dad, do you really need this?" I asked, waving the cheese at him.

"Definitely, son. It will keep fresh in that wax for days, and you know I love it. Do not throw that away."

I reluctantly repacked the three-pound weight, and after organizing, reorganizing, and reorganizing the reorganized organizing, we finally felt good to go.

"It's time to give you a trail name," I informed Dad the next day as we crossed the Hudson River on our way back up the mountains.

"Well, actually," he started, slightly turning his body, "I already have one." He fully turned his body around, the gargantuan size of his pack demanding a full-body maneuver if he wanted to see me. From my vantage point, he looked like a vintage 1980's backpack on legs.

"Oh yeah?" I responded.

"I've been telling everyone back home about the trip," he added, turning back around. I could no longer see his face (or head, neck, and torso), but I knew he was smiling as he continued. "I keep saying how I'm happy to finally get back on the trail with you. Then they'd say they're happy too, and I would reply, 'No, I'M happy. You can be yourself!'"

Dad's burst of laughter echoed across the Bear Mountain Bridge, like it was a joke he'd rehearsed to hundreds of others, landing the punchline perfectly each time. I always enjoyed how he was the loudest laugh to his own jokes.

"Well, thru-hikers don't normally name themselves, but I have to admit that's perfect! Happy it is," I replied. I discovered early in childhood that Dad lived to laugh, sometimes for himself more than others. He'd retell stories to anyone that would listen, knowing full well they'd already heard it... just in case they forgot. But he made the most out of every day and really was happy all the time, and it was infectious to everyone around him. The trail name was a perfect fit.

Little did we both know, though, Happy's trail name was about to be severely tested. As soon as we reached the eastern bank of the Hudson River, the trail shot straight up. We were met with a very steep and strenuous staircase of a path, crowded with day-hikers heading to the popular Anthony's Nose lookout. It was far from the best first experience for a new AT hiker trying to get comfortable in their surroundings. Happy did his best to take it on the chin, cracking sarcastic jokes to casual hikers walking by ("Passports please, need to see your passports!"). His jovial humor received mostly confusion in return, which didn't help the strenuous hike. From time to time, he'd shoot me a look that said in silence what I knew he was thinking. Just that morning, I'd told him the trail conditions would be a "piece of cake," but it was already turning out to be quite the opposite.

"It's not that I mind crawling several miles on my hands and knees while carrying my worldly belongings," he advised to me and a few day-hikers as we neared the top of the mountain, "but why would anyone want to climb this snot-nosed Anthony peak for fun?"

"It's probably not helping that your pack is twice the size of mine," I pointed out.

A grunt was his only response.

Our pace was slow and steady at one mile per hour. But eventually we did summit the mountain and made our way toward Appalachian Market, a combination gas station and deli that would be a common sight throughout New York. Happy dropped his pack and collapsed on a picnic table.

"That settles it. I'm throwing away the Gouda," he announced to everyone in the vicinity.

After some hydration, a snack, and a rest, we were ready to head out again to finish our day's hike. The afternoon was spent on an easier part of the trail, comparatively speaking to the morning's mountain scaling, and we made it to a place to rest around 5 p.m.

The Graymoor Spiritual Life Center we walked past was not the original plan, and it cut our day a little short on miles at just 7.3, but we were both ready to quit and enjoy a quiet and relaxing evening. The center sat a short half-mile off the AT and belonged to a ministry called the Franciscan Friars of the Atonement, who generously allowed thru-hikers to sleep at the old sports field on the edge of their campus. It contained a pavilion with electrical outlets, a water spigot, and even a porta-potty.

Rain was expected the next day, so Happy and I set ourselves up in the pavilion with several other thru-hikers. But just as we were making final adjustments to our camp, a man in a rain jacket, hiking boots, and a long white tunic announced his presence by clearing his throat. Heads turned toward him, and we could see even in the dim light that he wore a pained, apologetic expression. He held his hands up, palms together in a prayer position, and bowed his head to his fingertips.

"I'm so sorry to have to be the bearer of bad news, but this pavilion is reserved tonight. We have a bonfire party planned until midnight for fifty or so people," he announced in heavily accented English.

Fifty people? Midnight?! As I was trying to interpret what that would mean for our night's rest, the despair in Happy's eyes was impossible to miss. The pavilion, fire pit, and picnic table were all forfeited, and the group of dejected thru-hikers gathered their belongings, moving to the far side of the field. We still had a place to camp at least, but it became quickly apparent that peace and quiet were going to be forfeited for the night.

Happy snuggled into his new tent and I slid into the confines of my hammock. I was hoping to get 12 miles in tomorrow so we could make it to Clarence Fahnestock State Park, but that looked less likely after the difficulties of today's hike and the reality of an all-night party within earshot.

I'd known it would be slower hiking together, but I couldn't help wondering as I listened to the intensifying sounds of the party preparation if the reality of this trail was too much for Dad to take. Had I failed to prepare him appropriately? Was he in worse physical shape than we both anticipated? And was the constant string of disappointments too much for his usual optimistic self?

But as if he could hear my thoughts, Happy called out into the darkness, "I want you to know, I'm having a great time."

I smiled and whispered back, "Me too, Happy." And hoped sleep would soon take us.

About an hour later, the real fun began. At first, we only heard it—the thundering of footsteps, drums, and voices snaking their way up the path and toward the pavilion's fire pit. The darkness of my hammock blinded me, but the image in my head that accompanied the procession was unmistakable. In vivid technicolor, J.R.R. Tolkien's famous scene from *The Lord of the Rings* formed, where Frodo and friends waited in the Mines of Moria for the impending assault of thousands of orcs. Tolkien's words echoed in my mind: "The ground shakes. Drums, drums in the deep. We cannot get out. They are coming..."

When it felt like the parade of orcs would surround our campsite, I peeked out to see a marching line of adults, similarly dressed in various white tunics and carrying fiery torches—not too different from my vision. They arrived at the fire pit, where wood had been piled ten feet high. Cheers, chants, and various songs clanged together as the torches were lowered to the wood pyre. Twenty-foot flames soon leapt into the air, and the group responded with an eruption of sound.

The celebration continued for the next two hours, making any chance of rest a distant prayer. I finally knew it was coming to an end when my body stopped absorbing the loudness of thumping feet and discordant drumming that reverberated across the field and rang through the trees. It was now midnight, which in hiker terms meant half the night was gone.

At last, I readied myself for sleep, but while the people had made their exit, intermittent banging continued. I looked out of my hammock again toward the pavilion to see a family of raccoons carrying on the party, tipping over trash cans and enjoying a garbage feast. I sighed, not only irritated that I was having a rough night of sleep, but that Happy was having a rougher first night on the trail.

Sipping my coffee the next morning, I watched in amusement as Happy emerged from his tent. Or should I say, was birthed from it. His exit from the petite structure brought another movie scene to mind, this time Jim Carrey's hilarious exit from the mechanical rhino's rear end in *Ace Ventura: When Nature Calls.*

"You alright?" I asked as he grappled for leverage with his feet, body halfway in and halfway out.

"Oh yeah. Just grand," he grunted. Doing a final push up and out, he stood on his feet and grinned at me. "I don't know what the heck that was last night, but I didn't get any sleep!"

"Oh, you heard that too? I guess this life center can get quite spirited." I almost couldn't keep in the laugh as I laid on the thick sarcasm.

"Spirited? I was spirited alright! I woke up to my whole body shaking like the friars were using me as a marionette doll. This place should be renamed Happy's Spiritual Awakening!"

It was a rough night, but I knew this was a legendary Tom Neiman story in the making, and that he'd tell everyone for years to come of the day he climbed up Anthony's snot nose to receive his spiritual awakening.

Happy shook his head as he pulled granola and powdered milk out of his food bag. Over thirty years had passed, but he still packed the same breakfast from our first camping trips together. And as he filled his pot with ingredients and water, the sight of his reconstituted meal brought back a flood of nostalgia for my childhood.

"Okay, so what's the plan today?" Happy asked as we packed up our gear a few minutes later.

"I thought we might see the sights. You know, trees, rocks, a winding path that endlessly goes up and down. And if we're lucky, maybe some rain."

"Perfect," Happy replied, a genuine smile on his face.

There was one thing that could be said of Dad: he could shake off a horrible night, and just like the familiar breakfast, he could still fill his pot with optimism the next day.

After convincing Happy to let me carry his birthing tent, more to appease my concerns than his, we agreed to play it safe for the day and aim for just six miles. The terrain was much kinder, but there were still some heftier boulder scrambles to navigate. And I had to hand it to Happy, he did exceptionally well. I was impressed that a 71-year-old man carrying forty pounds on his back could traverse the trail so smoothly and with such a joyful attitude.

We ended our day around 3 p.m. at a small stealth campsite on the far bank of a stream. It was everything the night before had not been—peaceful, empty, and quiet. We cooked an early dinner and then relaxed by the embers of our fire pit, discussing plans for another easy day tomorrow. Happy tried to stay focused, but exhaustion overtook him, and he retired to his tent at 6 p.m. I stayed up a little longer to enjoy the fire's warmth in the chill of the night air, thinking how much better Happy's second day on the trail had been. I finally smothered the remaining coals and retreated to my hammock, just as the moon began to brighten the dark sky. It was a perfect end to the day.

36

FATHER AND SON

"Can't we walk down there instead?" Happy pointed his hiking pole down at the beautiful Canopus Lake that we were not walking around. He flipped off his baseball cap and pulled up the bandana tied around his neck to wipe the sweat from his face.

"I thought we would. We really should have been there by now," I replied, stopping to breathe and swig some much-needed water.

Instead of walking along the picturesque lake, the white blazes of the Appalachian Trail had taken us arduously up and over some serious boulders. It was further compounded by the fact that Mother Nature decided to drop a tornado in the area the week before, which had created many strenuous and frustrating detours around and through fallen trees that we'd been navigating all morning.

Happy now lifted his 5-foot-3-inch frame over the top of one such tree in silent acceptance of his fate. In a combined maneuver of a seated twist and a barrel roll, he made it over. It was impressive to watch. I checked our location against the Guthook app trail map, and a sinking feeling settled in my stomach.

"Uh... Dad?" I began.

"Yes, son?"

"It looks like the AT has been temporarily rerouted up to the left. Maybe because of the storms. So we aren't going to walk around the lake after all, and it's going to add another four miles to our day."

Happy paused in front of the next fallen tree he was eyeing up. His look back at me could only be described as despairing. "So, not almost done?"

I shook my head, and Happy took a deep breath in. This unexpected detour above the lake doubled our mileage for the day, so I could understand his need to take a moment.

"Okay, that's fine," he eventually said. "Could be worse, you know. Could be raining. Nothing we can't handle."

He delivered it with a slight twinkle in his eye, knowing his catch phrase would motivate both of us. And it did. Happy's positive outlook on the day returned. And with visions of finding teriyaki grilled salmon or a Wagyu filet mignon at Clarence Fahnestock State Park leading him on, we made it to the park's Acorn Cafe in time for a hot dinner.

We were perhaps a bit overzealous about what this concession stand would hold, as we sat down a few minutes later with breaded chicken patties covered in American cheese and encased in a flimsy white bun. Even so, Happy devoured his in record time, licking the final grease off his fingers.

"Well, that was an epicurean experience I will never forget," he sighed.

The sun heated the air temperature to a sticky 90 degrees over the next two days. Thankfully, it was pleasantly cool under our canopy of trees, and despite a few challenging sections that let us know we were still in fact on the AT, the trail conditions were much less rocky and arduous. We even increased our pace to a speedy 1.5 miles per hour. This really helped us cover more miles, but unfortunately, it couldn't completely make up for the ones we'd already missed.

Our aim for the day was the town of Pawling and to see Dana's aunt and uncle, who'd promised us some trail magic while we were there. We walked around Nuclear Lake, which provided the perfect lunch and rest stop, before continuing on to reach our hike's end point. And I was so preoccupied with the lack of progress on our mileage that I'd completely forgotten what was waiting for us at the road crossing to Pawling—Dover Oak, the largest tree on the Appalachian Trail.

Unlike the Keffer Oak I'd seen in Virginia, this one stood like a massive monolith blocking the path of any would-be hikers. It was over six feet wide, and estimated to be well over 300 years old, but something about this tree was even more awe-inspiring to behold as we stood under its mammoth branches, imagining the centuries of history it had seen.

After a delicious dinner at Big W's Roadside BBQ with Dana's family, Happy and I settled down for the night at a B&B called the Station Inn. The owner offered us a hiker rate of one-third their usual price because they were still undergoing renovations, and although it was still pricy compared to most thru-hiker accommodations, we couldn't pass up the opportunity.

From the luxury of our bedroom, I loaded up my phone's weather app to see what the next day would bring us. We'd been fortunate so far, and the 50 percent chance of showers predicted every day hadn't reached us, but the radar showed that more imminent rain would finally arrive tomorrow. I showed Happy the outlook, and he wisely recommended that this would be a good day for him to take a zero while I slackpacked the miles out of town. It was clear these rain-slicked rocks weren't the ideal walking environment for him, especially as his knee began showing signs of pain from the difficult terrain.

So we decided to stay another night at the Station Inn, which was no great hardship to either of us. And when Happy woke up on the second morning with a knee that still wasn't 100 percent, it cemented our new plan. I wanted to hike 11 miles to Kent, Connecticut, by the end of the day because Devorah was driving up to meet us there for the weekend. So, it was decided that I'd walk those miles, and Happy would take a cab directly there to day-hike back to meet me.

It was a plan we both felt good about, and the 11 miles should have been a breeze if it weren't for two factors: intense humidity and even more intense bugs. The humidity made every step feel like I was wading through the swamps of the Everglades, while the summer insects of the Northeast made their presence very well known. Up to this point, bugs hadn't really been a concern, and although I packed a tiny one-ounce head net, I hadn't seen a need to don it yet. But the two months of absent pests made up for lost time all day, and before I was done with those 11 miles, I vowed not to go out on the trail again without the bug net securely fitted over my head.

Around 2 p.m., after my fourth arm-flailing and screaming fit at the black flies that were constantly buzzing my eyes and ears, I called Happy to check in. He informed me that he'd been hiking south for some time and was only half a mile ahead of me atop a small summit.

"Great!" I replied. "Wait there. I'll meet you in a few minutes."

But when I got to the top, Happy was nowhere to be found. Trying his phone again sent me straight to voicemail, so I hiked on for another half a mile, but there was still no sign of him. Did I pass him somehow? Did he accidentally hike north? Was he even on the Appalachian Trail? Visions of Happy wandering aimlessly through the forest, delirious from dehydration, and desperately pleading with chipmunks to point him in the direction of the nearest white blaze chased these questions.

Then, just as worry was turning into the heart-pounding rush of fear, I heard a yell: "Yoooooooooo, Sharkbaaaaaait!"

"Yooooooooo!" I called back, hurrying forward to the location his voice had come from. And there he was, casually resting on a log about halfway up the mountain.

"I was starting to get worried back there when I didn't find you at the top," I said.

"Huh," Happy replied, a little sheepishly. "I thought this was the top."

The false summits of the AT had claimed their next victim. I'd become accustomed to the concept by now, where you think you're at the top, only to then realize the trees keep going up. Happy was less familiar with the trail's trickery, but I doubted he'd fall for it again.

We hiked the final two miles back to Kent together, where a surprise waited for us: trail magic! Happy got to meet his first trail angel at the Schaghticoke Road intersection, a 2017 thru-hiker named Tumbleweed. She sat in the shade with a friend and a cooler filled with cold water, sodas, donuts, and beer. I quickly took up Tumbleweed on her offer of the latter, taking a sip of the most incredible-tasting ale. It was a great end to a humid, bug-ridden day.

After a wonderful dinner with Happy and Devorah, I woke the next morning to realize it was my birthday. With all the trials and tribulations of hiking with Happy, I'd completely lost track of the date. And what better way to spend my birthday than to do the same thing I'd done on the ninety-four days before it... hit the trail. Happy and Devorah joined me for the first half of the day, which was a very steep and treacherous path. Halfway up, a fallen oak lay along the edge of the path. Happy spotted it and stopped, staring at its sizable girth.

"You okay, Dad?" Devorah asked, stopping alongside him.

"Michael," he addressed me. "Do you remember the photo hanging above my desk at home? The one from your first camping trip when you were a kid? You were sitting on a log that looked just like this, and I stood next to you. It's still one of my favorite pictures."

I remembered the specific photo he was referring to. It was one of my favorites too. Then a great idea came to me. "Let's re-create it."

I handed Devorah my phone, and Happy directed us into the proper pose from memory to ensure accurate re-creation. We snapped the picture, and I looked up at Happy to see a proud smile illuminating his face.

"I am so glad I agreed to come out here and hike some of this with you," he said, gripping my shoulder. "Even though you gave me a spiritual awakening while making me do death marches up crazy boulder-ridden mountains and trapeze acrobatics through tornado war zones, I wouldn't have missed this opportunity to adventure together for anything."

A lump moved into my throat, and all I could do for a moment was look back at him as he continued to watch me.

"Same, Dad," I finally managed to say. "Do you want to hike another week together?"

"No way in hell!" came his fast response, and we all burst into laughter.

We continued on, reaching the summit and Happy and Devorah's exit point. I had to laugh because the second half of the day was an easy hike along flat and beautiful terrain, following the Housatonic River. Happy had failed to walk the best this section of the trail could offer.

Later that day, back at the Fife 'n Drum Inn with Happy and Devorah, I informed them of my good fortune, thinking of the joy they'd find in my birthday gift of a leisurely afternoon hike. Instead, I learned a few new swear words.

The time had come to say goodbye to Dad. He'd been with me for nine great days but now needed to get back home to Mrs. Happy. I was both sad to see him go and grateful for the time we'd spent together doing something we both loved. My pace had been slower than usual, and conditions near brutal, but the company I kept was better, and had the jokes and stories to prove it. I still had over 700 miles to hike before the journey was done, so there was no time to waste. I was two days behind schedule, and unless I wanted to skip more miles, which I didn't, I needed to hit the trail again in earnest. It was time to get back to the serious business of thru-hiking.

Re-creating the childhood photo with Happy on Day 95.

37

ALL HAIL TO MASSACHUSETTS

Nomad trail life quickly set back in. Within five minutes of stepping onto the trail alone, I was back in my familiar routine. And with the slow pace of the last few days, I started seeing familiar faces that had caught up to me. One of these was Starman, the friend of Tarzan and Happy Feet that I'd last seen in North Carolina. Starman's dad was still following the blog and commenting from time to time on his whereabouts, but this was a surprise reunion.

We caught up on adventures over the last few weeks, and then, eager to hear news of other familiar people, I asked, "So are you solo now? Where are Happy Feet and Tarzan?"

"Nah, not really. Happy Feet is only a day behind, trying to catch up," Starman replied. "Pennsylvania hit Tarzan hard, physically and emotionally. He decided to go off-trail a bit and visit a friend. He's back but pretty far behind now."

I nodded my understanding. Pennsylvania could do that to a person.

We hiked the next few miles together, walking Connecticut's continuous ups and downs. As he checked Facebook at lunchtime,

Starman informed me that Fresh Ground's van was stationed just a few miles ahead with trail magic. At the mention of his name, I could instantly taste the banana pancakes he'd provided me back in Pennsylvania.

"If we hurry, we can make it for dinner before he packs up," he added, slapping me on the back as he sped past.

"That's a no-brainer," I said. "I haven't seen him since Port Clinton, but he was a gift from heaven after an absolutely awful day."

We increased our pace to a brisk 3.5 miles per hour, arriving just in time for burgers, baked beans, watermelon, hard-boiled eggs, grilled cheese sandwiches, and a giant cooler of pink lemonade. Fresh Ground had worked his magic once again.

Our bellies full, Starman and I sluggishly made our way back onto the trail. I hoped to start catching up on the plan I'd fallen behind on this last week, putting in 20-plus miles for the day, but my feet began to beg for rest somewhere around mile sixteen. Then they started to scream for it. My brain wanted to do more, but my feet, back, and shoulders told my brain to quit being an asshole and just stop. This was the reality of not having hiked hardcore miles the past two weeks. I wanted to go on, but I needed to stop if I didn't want a full-body mutiny.

"I'm going to stealth camp at Giant's Thumb," I advised Starman after checking the Guthook app. "My legs are done for today."

"I'll join you," Starman replied. "I could use a lighter day."

Giant's Thumb was a huge ten-foot-tall glacial erratic that stuck out of the ground on top of a wooded hill. The dirt sitting area gave Starman the perfect space to set up his tent, and the surrounding trees provided me with great options for my hammock. It was hard to tell what could have caused this massive stone monolith and calm clearing around, but it made the perfect setting for a relaxing night.

I woke the next morning to complete silence. Starman's tent was gone, and I was alone in the woods once again. It may be odd to abandon a friend in the wilderness in real life, but on the AT, that was just the natural way of things. So I set off with just me, myself, and I for company. And it was good. There was a mental shift I'd noticed since Dad joined up with me and took me out of my usual routine. Through Pennsylvania, I'd been struggling against the challenges of the weather and trail. But even with the strenuous terrain of New York and Connecticut, I was honestly back to loving it again. Having him out here with me had really lifted my spirits and rekindled my passion for tackling whatever the trail threw at me. And throw it did.

The day ended up presenting me with four massive peaks to climb, peaks I slipped and slid my way along through cold and wet conditions. But even with those challenges, I was still loving it. Lion's Head provided me with views of last week's journey, and (another) Bear Mountain showed me everything coming up in Massachusetts. It was the most challenging climb I'd done in weeks, but the views were well worth the effort. As I surveyed the vistas ahead, I felt a sense of peace and contentment wash over me. I would cross the line into Massachusetts that afternoon, reaching my eleventh state since Georgia. The state line was also the marker for 1,500 miles hiked. With those two huge milestones achieved, it felt like the end was truly within reach.

I rolled into Glen Brook Shelter around 4 p.m., deciding to have an early night to make a big dinner, call Dana, and write the day's blog entry. I saw Dad had left a comment on the post from the day before, noting that he was once again in the lap of luxury. *"I've got my bathroom, refrigerator, and AC, but strangely enough, I miss being on the trail with you."*

"Miss you too, Happy," I commented back.

I checked the Guthook app next to plan out the coming week, which showed I was only a few days away from Dalton, Massachusetts. My memory jolted back to the first day on the trail when I met Huevos and he told me it was his hometown. I pulled up my messages app and texted him, and within minutes, an incoming video call appeared.

"Huevos!" I said, answering the call. His face broke into the same wide grin, but his look had changed. At first, I thought it was just the patchy beard that had set in, but then I realized a calmer demeanor now rested on his face.

"Hey, Sharkbait! Mass already? You must be flying," Huevos replied.

"Haha, I sure am. Where are you at?"

"Relaxing in Harpers Ferry. This place is awesome!"

I did a quick mental calculation. That meant he was nearly a month behind me.

"Are you still hiking the trail?" I asked, not sure what answer it would produce.

"Still hiking strong," came his fast response. "Just taking it at my own pace. Honestly, I really feel like I've finally found happiness out here. All that stuff with my ex had me in a weird place, but I'm good now. Really good."

"That's awesome, man. I'm happy for you." And I was. Huevos was in a sad state when Keg, The Captain, and I found him bedraggled and ill-prepared for life on the trail that first day in Georgia. To hear he'd found his own peace on this journey warmed my heart. We caught up for a few more minutes before hanging up to prepare for hiker bedtime. Tomorrow, I was determined to get in more than 20 miles, so I knew I needed a good rest.

The next day ended up being perfect for a nice long hike. Temperatures in the high sixties greeted us, with partly cloudy skies void of wind and rain, and a mostly soft trail of pine needles to walk on. There were steep climbs to remind me I was still walking the AT, but the views were well worth the effort. There was also plenty of water everywhere. I passed a dozen gentle streams, five ponds, and even walked along the gentle Housatonic River for nearly a mile.

And around one of the ponds, I finally—after fourteen weeks of hiking—saw my first bear on the AT. I'd all but given up hope, but as I hiked along the shoreline, I spotted a black shape moving along the opposite side. Then two more tiny figures appeared bouncing behind. I watched the two cubs follow their mother along the pond's edge and bounce into the woods. I had a full minute to watch from the safety of my side of the water. It was a beautiful addition to what would have been a perfect day, if not for one thing. One damn thing. Actually, one million of one damn thing. Mosquitos.

All those peacefully serene ponds and streams were also breeding grounds for tiny blood-sucking demons of Satan, and just like the black flies from the week before, they all carried a torturous will to suck my body dry. They attacked my arms, legs, hands, neck, ears, and face. Every inch of exposed skin was a feast for their feeding frenzy.

I, of course, hadn't put my head net on after swearing I would never walk without it, so after trying in vain to swat them away for the first nine miles, I gave in and pulled out my 99 percent DEET bug spray. I wanted to take a *Flashdance*-inspired shower in it right there, but bathing one's body in a layer of DEET is generally frowned upon. Hoping to avoid any neurological or cardiovascular issues on the bottle's warning label, I only sprayed a tiny bit instead. Fortunately, that was all I needed. At least it was, until it wore off a couple hours later and the tiny demons returned.

I pulled my bandana over my neck, face, and ears, resigned to swatting away the beasts for the rest of the day and made myself a renewed promise to hike with my head net on tomorrow.

I eventually made it, several ounces of blood lighter, to Shaker Campsite. The site took its name from the remnants of a nearby pre-Civil War religious community, known for breaking into spontaneous convulsions, or shakes, during prayer. At 25.5 miles, it had been a successful day. My body was feeling the extra miles, but it was nothing I couldn't handle. It was only 25 miles from here to Dalton. I could maybe do that in one day. Maybe.

One consequence of setting a one-day hike to Dalton was that I would miss camping at the Upper Goose Pond Cabin, supposedly one of the best places to stay on the trail. The large red cabin was maintained and staffed by the Appalachian Mountain Club, or

AMC, a conservation group that worked to protect the mountains and trails of the Northeast. It held fourteen bunks and was overseen by a caretaker during the summer. Due to its location on a large pond, I'd heard there was even a beach with swimming and canoes. And best of all, the caretaker was known to make pancake breakfasts. But it was only ten miles into the day's hike, so too early to stop. It hurt to pass up, but I knew I couldn't do everything on the AT and still finish in time.

I also soon discovered that for every missed cabin there was another treasure to find. The first came very early in the day. A red shed no larger than a shelter privy sat on the side of a farm, stocked with cold sodas, candy bars, fresh eggs for sale, and a power cord to charge electronics. I selected a Mountain Dew and a Clif Bar from the aptly named "Trail Stand" for my second breakfast before heading up Baldy Mountain.

Eight hours later, I stopped at another farm and found my second treasure of the day. This one home to the famed Cookie Lady, a trail angel who ran a blueberry farm and spent her free time giving fresh-baked cookies to hikers who knocked on her door. Both discoveries were great consolation prizes for missing out on caretaker pancakes.

By the time I'd finished devouring my cookie, I knew I was pushing it to go much farther. My feet were tripping dangerously, and my back was protesting the weight of another uphill climb. I was at 25 miles, and I knew Kay Wood Shelter was only another two miles ahead, just three shy of Dalton. Getting to the shelter would make tomorrow morning an easy hike to town, where I could get breakfast, do laundry, and pick up a resupply. If I did all that fast enough, I could also hike to the next town of Cheshire for lunch. I could still put in 18 miles but also get two town stops in, and as I was pretty much out of food, that was a necessity. With visions of Samuel Adams beer and New England clam chowder in mind, I made my drunk feet continue down the trail again.

38

RUNNING UP THAT HILL

Dalton was exactly what I thought a Massachusetts trail town would look like—small, quaint, and surrounded by trees and farmland. But it was also packed with thru-hikers. I'd hit a bubble of people again since my slower days with Dad, and they all seemed intent on also spending the day at Dalton's few amenities.

After a double breakfast at the Dalton Restaurant, I waited in line at the Post Office for my resupply box. After Cheshire, I would need food for six or seven days, my longest stretch between town stops so far. But all my resupply boxes were packed for just four days, so I'd also need to stop at the Dollar General store in Cheshire for a few extra items when I passed through later that day.

The next errand was laundry. The laundromat was a mile away, so I set off at a brisk pace. Fifteen minutes later, a closed sign greeted me. Swallowing down my frustration at the wasted hour that would have been a few minutes in my non-trail life, I walked back to town and the Shamrock Inn, where I'd seen a sign advising they'd do hiker laundry for five dollars.

Lunch was a quick sandwich at a sub shop and then back to the

Shamrock Inn for my clothes. But upon return, I discovered my laundry still sat in a dirty pile next to the washer. A matronly woman, seeing me rooting around, came over from the office. "Is that yours, dear?"

"Oh, yeah. I was hoping to get back on the trail by now, but it doesn't look like it's been through the wash yet."

She sighed, giving me an apologetic smile. "Sorry, hon. Seems it's a popular day for laundry. We just got backed up." She gestured toward the living room area attached to the office. "Would you like to sit in here while you wait?"

With nowhere else to go and nothing more to occupy my time, I accepted and spent the time texting with Dana on the latest news from home. Two hours later, my laundry finally completed and I was ready to get back on the trail. It was 2:30 p.m., later than I'd hoped, and I still needed to hike 14 miles to keep to the day's plan.

The trail to Cheshire was a casual nine-mile stroll up and then back down one huge mountain. It was a soft and pleasant pine-needle-covered path, and although I used this to hike more briskly than usual, I still didn't make it into town until 5:30. I also couldn't avoid going to that Dollar General if I was going to make my resupply box stretch two extra days.

As the sun got lower, I walked the trail through town to Dollar General, blinking against the brilliantly white lights illuminating the aisles. A sign proclaimed the store carried a "wide array of items at discount prices."

I wandered the aisles, scanning the yellow price stickers eagerly displaying goods for one, two, or three dollars. The numbers were large and the descriptions small because in the world of Dollar General, it didn't matter what you were buying, just that it was cheap. I felt tempted to start throwing things at random in my cart, imagining my slightly hysterical laughter when I approached the checkout lady to be informed that my truck-load of goods would cost roughly eighty-seven dollars but provide enough shelf-stable food to stock me through the end times. A short laugh escaped my lips at the thought of lashing dozens of plastic grocery bags to the outside of my pack. I eventually put the daydream aside and walked up to the register, dropping my meager five items and a much more reasonable total of nine bucks.

Back outside, I assessed my options. It was now 6 p.m., and although the sun was still high, it was edging toward my typical bedtime. I could either use my hiking poles and hammock tarp to set up a makeshift tent behind a local hiker-friendly church in Cheshire, or I could try to get to the next shelter 4.5 miles away in the waning hours of daylight. That shelter was also 1,700 feet straight up Mount Greylock—the tallest peak in Massachusetts. And I'd be carrying at least five pounds more food than usual.

For some reason unknown to the saner part of my brain, the idea of going on seemed a challenge that had to be overcome. The thought ignited me and I ran back into Dollar General, emerging five minutes later with a power dinner of Mountain Dew, Grandma's Peanut Butter Cookies, and a king-sized Snickers bar. I chugged the Mountain Dew, washing down the cookies with the final dregs, and walk-jogged into the woods.

Fueled only by sugar and stubbornness, I began what my later blog entry would coin the "Climb of Insanity." With the first mile down, I'd already climbed what felt like three miles. The Mountain Dew and cookie rush continued to aid me until I made it halfway up the mountain. At which point, my body started to protest the increased pace and incline. But I had one more trick up my sleeve... the Snickers bar. I munched as I power walked, literally feeling the carbohydrates surge through my veins.

After 100 days hiking this trail, that's how it was now. My body had become a well-oiled machine, able to hike miles upon miles of trail. And as if I'd built that machine from scratch, I knew every component like the back of my hand. If something was out of place, I knew exactly what to do to fix it. Although food, water, or rest were really the only tools available, I could tell the second my body needed one to recharge. So when I ate that Snickers bar, I physically felt the chocolate's sugars absorb into my bloodstream, instantly taking my battery to 100 percent.

Ninety minutes of insanely fast hiking later, I reached Mark Noepel Shelter. I was now two-thirds of the way up Mount Greylock, leaving me with only a short hike to the top tomorrow. I gave a whoop of achievement (quietly so as not to wake my fellow hikers) and started to settle down for the night, adrenaline still pumping through my veins long after I curled up in my hammock.

Making it the rest of the way up Mount Greylock the next morning was a breeze after the antics of the night before. I took it slow and hiked the last couple miles in the same time I'd hiked the first four and a half. At the top was quite the setup. A lodge and café were set off to the side, but the dominant feature was the veterans war memorial tower. Looking like a giant white lighthouse in the sky, it stood at the very peak of the mountain. I climbed its 100 stairs to the top and was rewarded with a view of hundreds of miles in every direction. It felt rewarding to have such an awe-inspiring view up here, as if making up for the lack of one atop Clingmans Dome in the Smokies three months before.

"Incredible," came a voice from behind me. I whirled around to see a young hiker with a large backpack smiling at me. "Hey, man, can you take a picture of me with this view?"

"Sure." I smiled back, taking his phone and waiting while he took off his hat and sunglasses to pass a hand through his straight black hair.

"How do I look?" he asked.

"Like a ragged hiker," I replied coyly.

I snapped a couple of pictures before asking him to do the same for me. I thought that encounter might have been it, but the young guy stayed next to me after he handed my phone back, observing the view in the same quiet reflection I felt.

"Well," he said, "better get started on this trail."

"Started?" I couldn't help asking, having assumed he was a thru-hiker like me. Was he starting a flip-flop from up here? I eyed his large backpack again. "Are you day hiking?"

"I'm thru-hiking The Long Trail, but the guidebook said to take my time and enjoy it by starting at Mount Greylock." He shrugged. "I thought I would try it out. Turns out, it's pretty cool."

"Oh, nice," I replied. As the oldest long-distance hiking trail in America, the Long Trail of Vermont held some infamy in the hiking community. Most trail journals I read commented on it, noting that its completion before the AT in 1930 had provided some of the inspiration for the Appalachian Trail I was walking. At 272 miles, it was short compared to the AT, but for about 100 miles of that distance, they shared the same path.

"I'm thru-hiking the AT," I added.

His face lit up. "Damn, now that's awesome. We'll be on the same trail for a while. Want to hike together? I'd love to hear more about the AT... maybe I'll do that next!"

I liked this kid. He was eager, fresh, and passionate... everything I recalled about myself all those weeks ago. I readily agreed, and we started back down the tower. We talked as we walked, getting to know each other and our reasons for being out in the woods. He told me his name was Paul, but he was hoping to get a trail name. He was a 22-year-old college graduate, and it was his first time getting out on a serious hike. Looking him over more closely reminded me of my earlier self once again. His slightly hunched-over shoulders showed he was carrying a good amount of weight in his pack. He favored one leg in his stride, and he didn't have any hiking poles.

One fact I'd read about The Long Trail was that it was strenuous. Lots of elevation and lots of rocks, and with the Northeast's reputation for rain, that meant lots of opportunity for slipping. I encouraged him to stop and get some poles at his first opportunity, and while he nodded along, it felt like I was looking at Dad talking to my teenage self, hoping some advice would register before it was too late.

We quickly reached the majestic Green Mountains of Vermont,

and within a couple miles, I officially crossed into my twelfth state. We swapped turns taking pictures of each other with a sign that listed the AT and the Long Trail, and continued on. I was impressed with Paul's hiking speed. We were making good time, and I felt pretty confident we'd make it into that night's shelter early. But I'd forgotten about Vermont's nickname. Ver-mud.

Almost immediately, the trail became a mess of rock and sludge, and I started to mourn the loss of the nice pine-needle-covered paths of Massachusetts. Even though it hadn't rained in days, I was slipping and squelching through thick, wet mud, which slowed our pace significantly. Fortunately, my poles helped give me leverage, a fact I pointed out to Paul as he stumbled his way along the path.

We eventually reached the blue blazes to Congdon Shelter around 5 p.m., putting me at over 23 miles for the day. As I reviewed the Guthook app over dinner that night, I realized the next day could either be shorter at 18 miles or a bit longer at 23. I was leaning towards the latter, nervous about stretching my food to last the next six days, but I needed to see how my feet were feeling in the morning. The extra friction from Vermont's infamous mud had worn them out more than I expected for such a manageable day of miles.

When I woke the next morning, I discovered Paul had already left. I was impressed that he was such an early riser after just one day of thru-hiking, but he seemed in good shape, and I was confident my seasoned trail legs would catch him quickly. I hit the trail after a leisurely breakfast of oatmeal, walnuts, and coffee, and was immediately hit with a steep ascent up Harmon Hill. After that, the next 15 miles climbed up, up, and more up. One hill after another. There weren't many views through the trees, and I was chased away from any potentials by the relentless bugs that were still attempting to eat me alive. After 18 miles, the side trail to Kid Gore Shelter came into view, and given it was already late in the afternoon, I made an immediate decision to stay. Turning towards the shelter area, I realized I'd made the right choice.

"Hey Paul," I said, seeing a familiar mop of black hair sitting on a picnic bench in front of the shelter.

He turned and gave me a half-grin, his forehead creased in visible pain. I noticed his right leg was up on the bench. A couple other hikers were seated around him, expressions of concern across their faces. I circled the table until I stood facing him. "What happened?"

39

WITH A LITTLE HELP
FROM MY FRIENDS

P aul gestured at his leg, which I now noticed had ballooned in size around his knee.

"I fell earlier today," he began. "I was trying to keep up with yesterday's pace, but that cursed mud got me." He looked down at the walking poles I still had clutched in my hands. "Guess I should have packed those."

His dejected expression pulled at my heart, and I wanted to ease his sorrow. Putting my backpack and poles to the side, I knelt to inspect his knee more closely. "Maybe we can wrap it up and get you to town for a couple zero days? You might be able to come back out once the swelling goes down." But even as I said the words, I knew it wasn't going to happen. I had an ACL repair done in my twenties, and I knew what a torn ligament looked like. His knee was the size of his upper thigh, which meant serious damage had been done, and the nearest town was at least 15 miles in either direction. There weren't even any nearby highways.

Paul shook his head, swallowing thickly. "Nah, man. I appreciate it, but I could barely hobble the last two miles to get here.

I can't believe I'm saying it, but I think my hike's over. I already called 911 and asked them what to do about getting off the trail."

"What did they say?"

"Just to wait here and that they'll send a rescue team to come and get me."

My eyebrows raised slightly, even as I tried to control my reactions, not wanting to put any extra stress on Paul. How were emergency services going to get in here without road access? It seemed impossible, or would take many hours and cost him a lot of money in the process. Years ago, Dad had gotten food poisoning in Glacier and needed a helicopter medevac to a nearby hospital. Even with insurance, it was not an inexpensive trip.

About three hours after Paul's call, just as we were both finishing the dinner I'd pulled together for us, we heard distinctly human sounds coming from behind the shelter's privy. A few moments later, ten men and women, a dog, and a stretcher pulled on two off-road wheels like a wheelbarrow all rolled into view. Two EMTs immediately began taking Paul's vitals and wrapping his knee while the others, all firefighters, discussed an exit strategy.

"Where did you guys come from?" I asked one of the men, who I'd learned was fire chief of the attending crew.

"That path we came up," he said, pointing back toward the privy, "is an unmarked trail. It's only used for site maintenance and rescue purposes. Almost every shelter has one for situations like this. It's about a mile straight down to a wider dirt path, where we've got some ATVs waiting to take us back to the main service road."

"Wow," I said, genuinely impressed by the thought that went into planning the AT's support structures. At Dana's insistence, I always had a personal locator beacon in my gear. A small satellite-enabled device I could activate anywhere to alert emergency services of my location, but it was reassuring to know that easy rescue was possible on the AT with just a phone call.

Less than twenty minutes later, the firefighters had Paul secured in the stretcher they'd take turns rolling down to the ATVs. I leaned over to where he waited midair and clasped his left hand in mine.

"It was great to meet you," I said.

"You too," he replied, raising a half-hearted smile.

"Maybe you can try again next year. The trail will always be here," I said, wanting to offer some hope to contrast the disappointment.

"Yeah, maybe." His smile widened slightly. "But with some poles next time."

I laughed. "I started off thinking the same as you, but we're all learning new things out here, man. Nothing to be ashamed of."

Then, just before turning to leave, an idea hit me. "You know, that's not a bad trail name."

"What? Ashamed?" He replied, cringing.

I laughed again, realizing my mistake. "No no, that would be cruel. I was thinking something a bit more optimistic... Next Time."

And with that, four of the men hoisted the stretcher up and the group exited the way they'd come in. But as he left, I could tell from the smile on his face that the trail name was a winner.

It wasn't until later, as I lay in my hammock, that I realized I didn't have any contact information for Paul. I wouldn't be able to follow up to find out how he was doing. It was one of the sad realities of my time on the trail—the amazing people I was meeting would only be featured in a small section of my life's longer path.

I woke the next morning to a strong desire for real food, as in not the kind that could be carried on my back. Burgers, pizza, mozzarella sticks... the protein and grease combo I was only going to find in a town. The only problem was that most trail towns around here were more than a mile off-trail, so stopping for food probably meant stopping for the night. And hotels in the Northeast were far more expensive than down south, so I did some searching on Guthook and found a trail angel in a town nearby named Jen who rented out her kids' empty bedrooms in the summer to thru-hikers.

At thirty-five dollars, it was the most economical option I could find within a day's walk. She lived in Manchester Center, and there was a road crossing to the town about 25 miles away. Very doable, especially with the reward of a hot meal and real bed at the end. But it was five miles away from the trailhead. I brought this up to Jen, hoping she had a shuttle option.

"You can just hitch a ride from the locals to town, get some dinner, and I'll pick you up from there," she replied in the same cheery voice she'd used throughout the conversation.

"Oh, ok," I responded hesitantly. Before coming out on the trail, I knew hitchhiking was common among hikers, but I didn't really expect to do it, as my plan had me never visiting a town more than a mile off-trail. I'd already broken that plan once back in Pennsylvania, but still wasn't comfortable with the awkward feeling of hitching rides from the side of a highway.

Jen must have heard my hesitation because she added, "Don't worry, you'll get picked up quickly. This is a very hiker-friendly town."

So there I stood at the trailhead, with my thumb out, feeling dirty, somewhat criminal, and vulnerable to the whims of strangers racing by. But it turned out Jen was right. Within minutes, a car stopped.

"You heading to Manchester Center?" the middle-aged woman in the front seat asked, peering around a teenage girl in the passenger seat who resembled a miniature version of her.

"I sure am." I gave her the address of Mulligan's Pub, a trendy rustic bar that looked like it would fulfill all my fried-food needs.

"Throw your bag in the back and jump in. We're heading right past there."

Instantly, all nervousness faded away. What seemed so offensive moments ago was now as natural as asking for directions. During the short drive, the woman introduced herself as Sarah and informed me that her husband and their other daughter were out thru-hiking the AT as well. They'd just started a couple weeks earlier, heading southbound from Maine. As we drove, it occurred to me how rare it must be to randomly hitch a ride and have it turn out to be the family of more thru-hikers! Sometimes the world could be a small and fascinating place.

"We've lived out here along the trail our whole lives, and always happy to help a fellow thru-hiker out," she smiled as she looked at me through the rearview mirror. "Oh, and here we are. This is your stop."

I jumped out, retrieving my bag and thanking them profusely. "I'll keep an eye out for your family," I said before waving goodbye.

The dinner was everything I'd dreamed of. Chicken wings, beer, burger, and a basket of fries were all inhaled rapidly. I sat back to stretch my stomach, astonished at how much food I'd just engulfed.

Jen picked me up a few minutes later and we headed to her home for the night. After a much-needed shower, I crawled into her spare bed and re-evaluated the next few days. Thanks to this side trip, I had enough food now to make it to the next big town, Killington, in three days. The original plan was to stay there for the night, but two expensive stops in three days would strain the week's budget, and I still needed 15 more miles to catch up to my schedule. I had a hard deadline coming up, as I planned to get off trail in a few days to meet Dana for the wedding. I needed to make it to New Hampshire, where I had a rental car waiting, to avoid a second asterisk for more missed miles. I had to stay on track.

The weather forecasts also showed rain on the horizon for the next few days. By now, I knew that would likely bring my attitude down a few notches and slow my hiking pace to match, so I needed to get more miles behind me while the sun was shining.

The next day was just that—24.6 miles of sun-drenched path interspersed with some of the most breathtaking views I'd yet encountered. There were still rocks, roots, and steep climbs to contend with, because it was still the AT, but with the day so full of natural wonder and beauty, I almost didn't mind. Almost. After standing at the top of Bromley Mountain Ski Resort, ridge-walking Baker Peak, walking the edge of Little Rock Pond, following the winding banks of Big Branch River, and hiking through Rock Cairn Garden, I finally stopped at the seventh shelter I'd passed that day.

Dinner and camp setup were quick, so I could go to bed early and get going early. The rain was forecast to start around 11 a.m., with a chance of thunderstorms lasting throughout the night. It was not the most encouraging news because I was also going to summit Killington Peak, a 4,235-foot giant, something I didn't really want to do in inclement weather.

Fortunately, luck was on my side. At least at first. The sky remained clear and blue all morning, and I wondered whether it might stay that way all day. But by 1 p.m., the clouds had moved in, and the wind was getting a little, well, windy. I continued to follow the white blazes down the path, glancing along the tree line for each next one.

I spotted one a few trees ahead and did a double take. Something was tacked below it. Walking closer, I saw it was a small, oval sign that stated in bold, black letters: "Katahdin 500 miles." I paused in front of the tree, reading and rereading the sign. So far, I'd been counting my journey in miles since Springer Mountain, and I'd missed how close I actually was to the finish line. Even though I was alone in the woods, I let out a loud, excited holler, followed by celebratory selfies to share on my blog later. It felt good to count the miles left, rather than those behind me.

A few minutes later, just as I reached Governor Clement Shelter at Mount Killington's base, the first gentle sprinkling of rain began. I hopped into the shelter and checked my cell phone for the radar, but found service was nonexistent this deep into the woods. I was going to need to rely on my ears and what was between them to evaluate any threat of danger ahead.

I rested and ate lunch, watching, listening, and contemplating the weather for thirty minutes. I hadn't heard any thunder, and I'd seen four other hikers pass through en route to the summit. Staying longer felt silly and cowardly, so I stepped back onto the trail. As if rewarding me for my courage, the rain stopped immediately, and the next five miles to the top were surprisingly dry and pleasant.

I was now 20 miles into the day, and although an old, ugly shelter stood at the top of Killington Peak, I felt like I could make it the 11 miles farther into town if I wanted to. So, emboldened by the day's success and telling myself it was the most sensible decision not to get stuck on top of a mountain in a thunderstorm, I pressed onward down to Killington.

40

BACK IN TIME

After 105 days on the trail, I should have known better. It was never just downhill, and it was never as simple as I thought it might be. The first seven miles were okay. The trail on that side of the peak had received more rain and was slick and dangerous to descend, but as long as I took it slowly, it wasn't too bad. It was at the bottom, though, that things turned from bad to worse.

It was now 6 p.m., and although I only had four miles left to reach Killington, those miles consisted of going up and down another mountain. It had also started raining again. Hard. To add to the drama, a peal of rolling thunder erupted in the not-too-distant hills. I reached a highway crossing and contemplated whether to hitchhike to town and miss the remaining miles for the day. But heading to town from here would mean having to backtrack to the same spot tomorrow, and I really didn't want to go backwards, so I stubbornly hiked on.

For the next two hours, Mother Nature tried her best to break me. The AT had split from the nicely maintained Long Trail, and I was back to huge rocks, fallen trees, and unnecessarily steep walkways. The rain got heavier and heavier, immediately liquefying the muddy ground with an oily slick on the path of rocks.

And if this wasn't enough, the mosquitoes decided to join in on the fun. Somehow undeterred by the cold wind and rain, they began their usual kamikaze attack, this time on my exposed calves. Bug spray was pointless in the rain, so I settled into a rhythm of half-walking and half-crouching to slap and scrape the vile creatures off my legs with each step. By the time I reached Killington, I was convinced that this suicidal strain of skeeter must have some insect version of rabies—delusional in their pursuit for blood with no regard for self-preservation.

It was after 8 p.m. when I finally reached Mountain Meadows Lodge on the edge of town, and darkness settled thickly around me. The lodge rested in a beautiful resort beside a lake, whose levels were currently being filled by the continuing downpour. The owner met me in the lobby, eyed up my disheveled state, and immediately offered me leftovers from the wedding reception they'd just hosted. I gratefully received the delicious meal, and in return, tried not to drip too much on the lobby's beautiful wooden flooring.

My bedroom was as lavish as the rest of the lodge. After a quick shower and hanging of all my wet gear, I fell into the queen-sized bed with a sigh of pure elation. Even the loud cracks of thunder outside the windows couldn't keep my eyes open.

I awoke the next morning feeling rested. Not surprising after another 30-mile day in the mountains. In my planning, I must have known I'd want to give my feet a break on day 106 because my original plan called for only 16 miles today. I smiled as I realized this would have been an extreme mileage day in the first couple of weeks on the trail, but now it was just a relaxing nero.

When I finally got started around noon, the temperature was still in the low 60s. The air was damp, keeping me just shy of dry but pleasantly cool. The higher elevation I'd attained over the last couple days reminded me that I needed to ask Dana to pack my winter gear in her suitcase that I had shipped back in Maryland. I was going to want my puff jacket, long underwear, fleece hat, and gloves again in New Hampshire's White Mountains, especially at night.

The going was easy for the day, although still muddy, and I could have made 16 miles without breaking much of a sweat. That is, if it not for the amazing hideaway I stumbled upon two miles before the end. It was a private and empty cabin that sat high atop a hill. Built by the owners of Lookout Farm, a few hundred feet away, this Lookout Cabin allowed hikers to stay for free if they respected the property. The wooden siding and green aluminum roof gave it a modernized barn feel, but what was perched atop the metal roof gave the cabin its name. Wooden stairs climbed steeply up the side of the building to a peaked roof in a widow's walk, a platform with views for miles to the north and east.

The decision to stop here was made easily. Sleep on a cold, dirty, wet, exposed shelter floor or in a clean, dry, warm, enclosed cabin? No-brainer. After hiking past Upper Goose Pond cabin earlier in the week, I wasn't about to pass up this opportunity for luxury trail accommodations. The only other hiker here was a friendly girl my age named Ultra, but she took the upstairs loft, allowing me to hang my hammock from the loft's rafters below guilt-free.

Ultra and I exchanged thru-hike stories over dinner, which although had run in parallel for months, had barely crossed paths. It turned out, the only time we'd stopped at the same place before was my miserable second night at the Port Clinton pavilion, after walking all day in the rain and getting shuttled back to where I started. I learned we had very similar hiking timelines and styles, and it amazed me that it had taken 106 days to meet. It was a pleasant dinner, but then we cleaned up quickly and quietly retreated to our beds. As sleep started to take me, I reflected on the many like-minded people out here with me. Ultra and I were living such a unique life, almost in unison, but I'd probably never see her again. It was a sad thought, which made me appreciate just how precious this adventure was.

The night passed quickly, as excellent nights of sleep often do.

The rain plinked gently against the metal roof, continuing through the early morning. I dressed warmly after the cooler temperatures of the day before, but about an hour into the day, I arrived at Winturri Shelter and shed a layer. Even though it was cold and wet, my rain gear still trapped the moisture I produced inside my fleece sweater— a very uncomfortable feeling.

After a snack and a few minutes of rest, I turned out of the shelter and back onto the mud-laced trail that remained untouched by the sun's rays. I hopped and side-stepped my way along, trying to avoid the deeper imprints made by the feet of hikers who'd come before me.

In fact, there were a lot more southbound footprints than I recalled seeing on any day before this. I waved it off as the result of a hiker bubble passing by or because there was more mud, giving more opportunity for footprints to stick around.

Almost an hour of trail hopscotch later, I came to a sign. Checking signs on the trail was a habit now because there were many crisscrossing paths and historical markers, so I never knew what information I would learn from them. This one, though, was very familiar. Almost as if I'd read it before.

Realization dawned on me as my brain put the pieces together. Anger rose swiftly with it, leaping out all at once in a feral scream of frustration that every human and animal within a ten-mile radius was sure to have heard. I'd been hiking the wrong way. I must have turned the wrong way out of the shelter and been so focused on keeping my feet dry that I hadn't looked up to see which direction I was walking! I'd hiked 2.6 negative miles, as they were lovingly called in the thru-hiker community, and wasted an hour of daylight in the process. That meant I now had 28 miles to cover instead of 23 and would be hiking miserably late into the night.

Muttering obscenities that would have left my nephews wide-eyed in alarm, I turned back to start the demoralizing deed of reversing the negative miles to Winturri Shelter again. It was time to reevaluate my day. West Hartford was a town near the trail, about

21 miles from my current location. I saw in AWOL's guide that a trail angel called Linda lived right on the trail in that area. She rented her barn to hikers for the night, so I could stop there instead of trying to go the whole way. And as if Mother Nature had heard the inner workings of my mind, the rain suddenly stopped, and the sun came out. Today, it seemed, she thought I could use a break.

Five miles later was a road crossing and my first stop at On the Edge Farmstand. It wasn't in any of the guidebooks and was only mentioned in a few comments on the Guthook app. As soon as I saw it, I wondered why the guidebooks missed it because it was hiker heaven. Fresh pies and muffins, Hershey's ice cream, candy bars, sodas, dried meats and cheeses, eggs, frozen burritos, and more filled the shelves of the warm-honey wooden barn. Picnic tables, a porta-potty, and a water spigot all sat out front. I healed my emotional wounds with some junk food and lemonade and basked in the warmth of the sun. A real treat after the last two rainy days and the thick shade of the trail.

As I munched my way through a bag of Lay's potato chips, I saw a dark shadow moving across the road I was picnicking alongside. It was moving swiftly, and I glanced over just as a midsize black bear reached my side of the road. Hand and chip halfway to my mouth, I froze as it bounded along the grass ten feet in front of me and jumped back into the woods. It was so surreal that I spent the next few minutes convincing myself that I'd truly seen something, and not some ghost bear or hallucinogenic vision.

Still bewildered, but now much more alert, I too crossed the road and headed back to the trail. Seven miles later, I came to another farm with goods for sale. It was the much more well-known Cloudland Farm Market, mentioned often in all the guidebooks. But it was unimpressive compared to On the Edge, selling only a few random items.

I bought a homemade raspberry soda and sat on the porch while I ate my boring tortilla-and-tuna-packet lunch. It was a relaxing break at least, with a beautiful view on the still sunny day.

It was now 3:30, and I was still seven miles from West Hartford. It was time to make the call to stop at Linda's rather than hike on through the night. I turned up to her big blue barn at 6 p.m., spotting a giant AT symbol emblazoned in silver metal where the wooden siding met the roof. Linda and her five-year-old daughter, Alice, came out to greet me with all sorts of delicious treats. I devoured pasta salad, coffee, cupcakes, dried fruit, and soda while she filled me in on the setup.

The barn accommodation turned out to be a room above the garage, containing worn-out mattresses, a TV set, and an extensive collection of VHS tapes from a lost era in time. It reminded me of a clubhouse where kids might hang out and learn about human anatomy together. It wasn't the cleanest setup, but it was quiet and comfortable. I laid out some gear to dry, pushed thoughts out of my mind of what memories the mattress on the floor was hiding, and surveyed the collection of movies. With *Field of Dreams* playing in the background, I laid my underquilt below my top quilt, hoping it would keep any skin from encountering bedbugs or fossilized bodily fluids during the night. Dana, and most sane people back home, would be disgusted by the thought of this bedtime setup, so I decided it best to leave those details out of the night's blog entry.

41

I DON'T WANT TO MISS A THING

I woke the next morning to a text from Leap Frog. I'd messaged her the night before, feeling a parental urge to check in after seeing Next Time get taken off trail from injury. I hadn't heard from her in so long, and unfortunately, her reply confirmed my suspicions.

Hey, Sharkbait! I'm actually not hiking anymore. I got to the end of PA and knew my time on the trail was done. I was really happy with what I got out of it, though. Where are you now?

I replied, updating her with my location and plans. It was sad knowing I wouldn't come across her on the trail again, but I was happy she'd found a sense of fulfillment before it ended.

As for my own journey, a 20-mile jaunt through Dartmouth College and neighboring towns lay ahead. After looking over the mileage left to Franconia Notch—the gateway to the White Mountains and where my path would temporarily turn south for the wedding with Dana—I knew the next week would be lenient. There were some tough climbs ahead before I even got to the Whites, but after working out the number-of-miles-divided-by-number-of-days equation all thru-hikers kept a constant check on, I knew it was possible to keep to a breezy 20 miles a day. The thought didn't escape me that what would normally be twice the length of a difficult day at the start was now breezy. But 20-mile breezy is who I was now, and it would make the next few days very manageable.

First up were the three towns of West Hartford, Norwich, and Hanover. Easy hiking along sidewalks, side-stepping tourists and students, set me up for the next ten miles of equally easy trail walking. I stopped for lunch in Hanover, the bustling Dartmouth College town, and took advantage of its many hiker-friendly amenities. Most notably, lots of free food! Three different locations were advertising trail magic for thru-hikers, so I had a donut, slice of pizza, and cup of coffee as gifts before hiking back up into the mountains. Bright orange signs posted by the Dartmouth Outdoor Club on tree trunks indicated the correct trail for the AT, among the many crisscrossing day-hike trails. I especially appreciated the helpful arrows labeled north and south... markings I might have laughed at before but now humbly checked after every rest break. I ended at Moose Mountain Shelter, which featured its own orange sign, complete with a drawing of a moose and a map of the shelter amenities.

The day's hike had also taken me into New Hampshire, and with its soft trails, switchbacks, and great views, I was happy for the change. I still had 400 miles left before reaching the base of Katahdin, but with New England states being rapidly checked off, it really started to feel like I was nearing the finish line.

The next day was a scorcher. The humidity rose with the temperature, and even at the 3,200-foot summit of Smarts

Mountain, there was no break. It made the climbs tough, especially since Smarts Mountain steadily climbed from sea level over four grueling miles. And that was after climbing two earlier mountains. But with my breezy daily distance now, I had lots of time for breaks.

Following my brush-ups against dehydration in North Carolina and Pennsylvania, I was extra vigilant to stop at every available water source, which were only every five miles or so. Each time, I downed a full liter before filling back up. One liter in me one liter on me, that was my new mantra. But even with that plan, trips off trail to suitably secluded trees to relieve myself weren't as frequent as they should be.

After a quick thirty-minute nap at an old ranger station gracing the top of Smarts Mountain, I woke feeling refreshed and began the long march down again to Hexacuba Shelter. It was aptly named for its six-sided shape, which easily would have fit eight or ten people. But only two others showed up and, forgoing the usual thru-hiker thoughtfulness of not setting up tents inside shelters, they did just that.

Georgia Sharkbait would have scoffed and grumbled about trail etiquette or politely recommended consideration for others that may still come. New Hampshire Sharkbait thought nothing of it, choosing comfort over considerate, and I hung my hammock from metal hooks on the wall to join them. Clearly having no care for Georgia Sharkbait, I then strung up a line of rope next to my bed to hang socks and shoes that were damp with sweat. Two gear sacks also hung from the hook at the other end of my hammock, and my backpack hung from the ceiling. It was a functional and neat setup, and I forgave myself by acknowledging that, even with my hammock and the two tents, five more people could still easily fit inside. But as no one else arrived, the three of us gave each other silent nods of acceptance and turned in for the night under protection of the shelter roof.

The next morning, the two other hikers began moving around 4:30. One had shared his plan the night before to get up early and make for Hikers Welcome Hostel in Glencliff because a thunderstorm was on the horizon. I wasn't quite ready to jump out of bed in the pre-dawn darkness, so I decided to scroll through the AT thru-hiker Facebook group instead. What I saw motivated my feet quickly. Other thru-hikers a day or two ahead of me had left comments about a very famous trail angel on the far side of Mount Cube just ahead of me... The Omelet Man. This trail angel waited all summer long on a dirt path at its base to serve ready-to-order omelets of any size to hungry hikers, along with a large selection of drinks and snacks.

Mount Cube wasn't too arduous, but the humidity made the rocks slick, considerably slowing my progress. At the top was a large rock scramble, including one impressive boulder containing a two-foot-wide strip of white quartzite running through the middle. I laughed heartily as I got my phone's camera out. Pointing in the direction of the trail for another thirty feet, this was the single largest white blaze on the AT.

At the bottom of Mount Cube, my excitement started to ramp up, and by the time I reached the dirt road at 9 a.m., a cheesy vegetable omelet was the only thing on my mind. But when I rounded the corner to find the patch of grass where his feast should be set up, there was only bare ground and a host of mosquitoes eager to feast on me instead.

The disappointment piled on when I pulled out trail mix to snack on instead. I looked at every handful with painful sorrow, and every swallow was completed with reluctant force. It was a sad snack, solely eaten to fuel the journey onward.

Once I'd completed my pity party, the last eight miles were relatively flat and manageable. The thunderstorm continued to build on the horizon, but the blue sky above my head let me know I wasn't in any danger of it hitting before I reached Glencliff.

Weary and hungry, I finally arrived, and the sight of the hostel quickly helped to unsour my eggless mood. The main house consisted of a large common room, kitchenette, and tons of junk food. Brooklyn and Bisquick, the caretakers who'd completed their own thru-hike the year prior, showed me around the building, calling out the various amenities for hikers. Just then, a man walked in and dumped two large bags of potato chips and a dozen cupcakes on the counter. Then turning, headed back out with a quick wave of his hand.

I glanced over at Brooklyn. "Is that common around here?"

"Oh yeah." He gestured to the pile of food. "Some of it's for sale, but most is just donated by the locals. Glencliff is a very generous community to thru-hikers."

I surveyed the range of shelf-stable goodies, amazed once again at the generosity of the people living along the AT for nomads like me just passing through.

Our tour took us out back to a rudimentary canvas and wooden structure containing everything a hiker needed to clean up—a shower, laundry, and bathroom. Next to the main house, a new barn had been built as a hiker bunkhouse. It could sleep twenty people in comfortable beds and held the gentle pine fragrance of freshly cut timber.

Brooklyn and Bisquick left me to get settled into the bunkhouse. It didn't take long, and I was soon back in the main house relaxing and snacking. I was glad I made it early because at 4 p.m., the thunderstorm that had been building all day hit in earnest. Heavy rain, strong winds, and even a tornado siren filled the air. It made me exceedingly grateful not to be out on the trail and to respect this precious and generous Glencliff community.

One intense hour later, it moved on, and I decided to join other hikers in a passenger van supplied by the hostel to the one convenience store in town for dinner and resupply. I gazed out the window as the highway sped by, only half tuning in to the conversation flowing around me. It was at the mention of "omelet" that I turned my attention to the guy sitting next to me.

"Did you see The Omelet Man?" I asked.

"I sure did," he replied, a smile appearing through his shaggy brown beard. "Got to eat the most delicious breakfast of my life yesterday. He just asked how many, and so I told him to make a dozen. Ate the whole thing in one sitting, and it totally set me up well for that insane hike over Moosilauke today."

"Huh," I responded. "He wasn't there when I pulled up today."

"Oh yeah? What time was that?"

"Around nine."

He tilted his head back before giving a knowing nod. "Damn, that explains it. He mentioned something about reducing his hours this season on non-peak days."

"Really? So what does he determine to be non-peak days?"

The man shrugged. "I didn't ask. Too busy stuffing my face." He chortled, and the others around us joined him.

I smiled, but my brain was too busy whirring. "Did you say you hiked up Moosilauke already?"

"I did." His eyes widened. "I slackpacked it, and I'm glad I did. That's a beast!"

Another voice came from behind us, and I swiveled to see a younger guy in a black baseball cap. "Man, if someone charged $1,000 to take my pack for the day, I'd pay it. That mountain is pure insanity."

This was a conversation I needed to have because tomorrow, I was hiking the so-called beast of Mount Moosilauke. At nearly 5,000 feet, it was the tallest mountain since Virginia. The climb up was almost six miles of steep and rocky terrain. The climb down was said to be near suicidal—twice as steep with body and pack weight aiding gravity's desire to toss you down like a haphazard rockslide. I knew too well from 110 days of thru-hiking the AT that steep downhill elevation felt tenfold worse on my body than the uphill equivalent.

For this reason, many hikers decided to do the mountain in reverse, keeping the steeper section on the uphill. The hostel offered a shuttle around the mountain for those who wanted to slackpack it and stay with them both the night before and after. But it was a costly option, with two shuttle rides and two nights' accommodation.

I also knew I had plenty of time to go slowly, if that's what the beast required. Even if I only did the mountain's eight miles tomorrow, I'd still be on schedule for the wedding. It seemed wise to continue on with my full pack, but as the conversation lingered on the difficulties Mount Moosilauke presented, I felt that wiggling anxious voice asking if I was being reckless.

42

HERE COMES THE SUN

I clamped a hand over my mouth to stop the snort of laughter that threatened to wake the late sleepers in the Hikers Welcome bunkhouse. Dad's comment on yesterday's blog post was the reason for such extreme measures. I read it again, making the bed beneath me creak with my full-body shakes.

"*Well,*" he began, "*I wish I could say that I am envious of your endeavor, but Mount Moosilauke would be the spot where I burn my pack and gear, strip naked, and run screaming down the mountain to the nearest insane asylum. I admire your tenacity but just be careful.*"

Eventually, I managed to type back, "*Thanks for the laugh, Dad. That visual though, no thanks.*"

I tapped over to my weather app, which showed mid-seventies with clear blue skies. It felt like a good sign, one that said, "Go ahead, conquer the mountain. You've got this."

So, as had become a pattern, I decided to go against common sense and take on Mount Moosilauke headfirst, hiking northward as planned.

Climbing up was not so bad. A slow and steady ascent with a few sections of rocky stairs and scrambles. Nothing out of the ordinary these days. The trail was covered with a canopy of trees until I hit about a mile from the top. At that point, it opened up onto a grassy bald, and I discovered that what those trees had been covering was not a clear-blue sky as promised, but a gray fog of swirling cloud. Out from under the tree cover, the temperature instantly dropped 20 degrees, and with nothing to block the wind, it came barreling over the top of the mountain at speeds of at least 30 miles per hour.

I shrugged off my pack, rummaging around for the rain jacket that seemed as reluctant as I was to be out in these gale winds. Eventually, I pulled it out, only for the sky to attempt to claim it as its own, the wind ripping it out of my hand like Pippa with a new chew toy. Catching the end just before it took flight, I stuffed my arms through the sleeves as the wind came back for a second round. With rain gear firmly secured as a windbreaker and the hood of my fleece cinched tight around my face, I got back to the business of summiting Moosilauke.

The visibility was down to the end of my nose, but the tree-sized rock cairns built to show the way for a snow-covered summit worked just as well in the thick fog. The bitterly cold wind tried its best to fling me off the summit, but a few minutes later, I stood victorious at a small orange signpost indicating the top. As I clutched the sign so I wouldn't end up rolling back down the mountain I'd just climbed, I managed to take a quick selfie to send to Dad. *Save me a bed at the asylum*, I wrote in the message.

Needless to say, I didn't linger at the top, and a couple hundred feet past the summit, I entered the cover of the tree line again. The wind immediately stopped. I unwrapped my frozen face, letting the warmer air under the trees defrost it until I could feel my jaw relax and the icicles on the end of my nose melt.

I squinted in the shaft of sunlight that pierced through the tree canopy. It took a moment to understand what I was seeing, but then I realized that the promised sun had finally appeared. I shook my fist at the sky, crying out, "Where the hell were you ten minutes ago?!"

With no reply forthcoming, I started my descent. It was steep. Very steep. And slick from rain. Everything I'd been warned of immediately came into sight. But I was confident I could handle it as long as I took it slow. Real slow.

"Oomph." The air left my body as my hands hit rock that a second before had been beneath my feet. What was that old saying about pride coming before a fall? Thankfully, my hands caught me, saving me from a bruised and painful tailbone, but my confidence took a beating, and I slowed down even more.

The rest of the way down was completed in slow and meticulous steps, and even with that, I still experienced a few more close calls as my feet skated across wet rock.

It was with relief that I reached Kinsman Notch at the bottom. But even with the challenges of the weather and terrain, I found myself smiling as I looked back up the way I'd come. Up and down Mount Moosilauke had taken me five hours, so while that put me at a very slow 1.5 miles per hour pace, I'd still completed it much faster than expected. I really needed to stop letting other hikers intimidate me with their anxieties. It wasn't an easy mountain, but it wasn't the unscalable mammoth I'd pictured from last night's stories.

It was now only 1 p.m., and I knew there were more miles in me. So after a quick consult of the Guthook app, I decided to hike on and officially enter the White Mountain National Forest. The next 7.6 miles were a tough climb up and down Mount Wolf to Eliza Brook Shelter. I navigated rock boulders the size of Volkswagens, countless fallen trees, and puddles that turned out to be giant mud pits waiting to suck unsuspecting hikers into their depths. It felt like I'd entered a new level on some crazy thru-hiker video game. The first level being steep climbs, the second rocky terrain, the third muddy trails, and now the final level—all three at once.

Eliza Brook was a basic rectangular shelter with the front side open to the elements and no porch, but it was dry and, most importantly, free of mud. Two other hikers were already setting up, leaving me with a corner to lay out my own gear.

The younger female hiker looked up at me and smiled, and I did a double-take. She must have registered the look of shock on my face because she blushed and looked away.

"I'm sorry," I said, hoping to dispel any weirdness my reaction had caused. "It's just that you look exactly like a lady who picked me up off the highway in Vermont."

The other hiker, an older man, straightened from his crouched position and looked me over. "Was that Manchester Center? Was her name Sarah, by any chance?"

"It was!" I replied, instantly seeing the family resemblance.

"That's my wife," he laughed, "and Rose's mom." He indicated the girl next to him. "She told us to keep a lookout for a thru-hiker clad in orange headed north."

"Oh," I exclaimed. "I'd almost forgotten she told me to look out for you thru-hiking south too! What a crazy coincidence." I switched my gaze back to Rose, who I could now see was somewhere in her high school years. "Does everyone tell you that you look just like your mom?"

She grinned and rolled her eyes. "All the time."

Her dad and I chuckled, and he reached out his hand. "I'm Ben."

"Sharkbait," I replied while my hand was gripped in a firm handshake.

"Ha, like the cartoon fish caught far from home," Ben said with a smile. "You're getting close now."

"Yeah. When I started in March, I thought I knew what to expect, but this trail is full of surprises. You guys have quite the adventure ahead of you."

"And you have some incredible mountains ahead of you to close it out. The Presidential Range is breathtaking. And Maine was difficult, but those summits are worth it."

I nodded. The Presidentials were coming up after the wedding break, and I was admittedly pretty excited. From what I'd researched, the hiking and views off that range would rival even those of the Rocky Mountains.

After a quiet minute, he added, "So, want to fill us in on what's ahead? I've heard we've got a heck of a mountain coming."

"Mount Moosilauke?"

Ben nodded, and I huffed a quick laugh. "It's nothing to take lightly, but don't let the rumors scare you. And coming from the north will be much easier than the reverse, I can promise you that."

It was great connecting with Ben and Rose, and we spent a pleasant dinner gathering information for our days ahead from each other's past. It felt truly providential that the first southbound hikers I met would be the very ones I'd promised to look out for. Sometimes, life throws out a reminder that we really are one big family offering a helping hand. Or in this case, a ride for an outstretched thumb.

I left Ben and Rose sleeping the next morning and headed out to Franconia Notch, just under nine miles away. It was a quick hike, but my journey for the day was just beginning. Another one-mile walk up a quiet highway brought me to The Flume Visitor Center, where I met a shuttle to the town of Lincoln, five miles away. There I bought a ticket on a coach bus to Plymouth, 20 more miles south. And once in Plymouth, I hopped in my rental car and drove to New York City, where The Captain was waiting to bear hug me. Work had brought him to Manhattan that week, and the timing worked out to arrive a day early and fit in a day-hike with me. I was looking to recover some of the miles I'd skipped to meet Happy on time, and The Captain was eager to rejoin.

Over dinner and beers that night, we made our plan for the next day. Several options were available so close to New York City, but eventually we decided on a 12-mile hike that would end at Bear Mountain where Dad and I started. This section of the trail covered three big mountains, but it was a well-groomed path, so we figured it wouldn't be too hard.

The morning bloomed in blues and soft whites, and when we reached the trail, the fresh scent of tree foliage and early-summer flowers greeted us. The Captain and I fell into a familiar rhythm that seemed to spring up naturally from all those months ago when we hiked Georgia together. Impressively, he stayed in step with me over Black Mountain, West Mountain, and finally up Bear Mountain. It was so refreshing to have someone from home on the trail with me again who also knew this journey firsthand, and the miles sped by. It also felt really good to chip away at that missed section. By the end of the day, all that remained was 97.1 miles from Delaware Gap to Harriman State Park, where we'd parked the car that morning. Which, strangely, didn't seem like that many now that I'd hiked nearly 1,500 miles.

Later that evening, as we stretched our full stomachs and tired feet in the hotel, the realization fully hit me that I'd be seeing Dana tomorrow. After 114 days of brief texts and quick phone calls wedged between her busy schedule and my intermittent cell service, we'd finally have some time together, face-to-face. It was such a separate world out on the trail that it was easier to feel the gap between us than the ties that bound us. I was looking forward to strengthening those ties with her again while we celebrated our friends at the wedding.

The break would also be good timing for the last chapter of my journey to Katahdin, one that I was eager and, at the same time, in no hurry to complete. The end was in reach, but I'd grown to love my vagabond lifestyle. Who would I be when it was all over? I couldn't say yet, but I did know a few days with Dana would remind me of the life waiting for me after.

43

HAIL TO THE CHIEF

I breathed an audible sigh as I headed back to trail life four days later. My weekend off had truly been relaxing and enjoyable, but also restless. Spending time with Dana and our friends was wonderful... but the whole time away had me feeling uneasy, yearning to be walking freely. There was a peace of mind I experienced on the trail that was instantly gone the moment I sat in traffic or stood in long coffee shop lines.

But now, I was back in New Hampshire. And tomorrow, Devorah and her family were rejoining me to hike through the famous White Mountains Presidential Range. I couldn't wait to see them again but still had another zero day to kill.

After dropping off the rental car and bussing back up to Lincoln, I checked into a hostel called Chet's Place. It wasn't in any of the guidebooks, but someone on Facebook recommended it for people looking to stay in Lincoln. It would also be my first time doing work-for-stay, as this hostel refused to charge a typical rate for guests. After Ground Score's dramatic escape from Zen and Gooder Grover Hostel in North Carolina, I'd been hesitant to try. But the next section would offer many more work-for-stay opportunities at the

AMC-run alpine huts, highlighting New Hampshire. So I figured now was as good a time as any to get comfortable with the concept.

Tent camping was only allowed at official campsites below the tree line, requiring you to hike down the mountain at night. And unfortunately, the popular AMC huts charged a hefty price at over $100 per night. So work-for-stay was both popular and competitive among thru-hikers passing through as quickly as possible. It was first-come, first-served on the two or three spots typically offered at each hut.

The directions to Chet's Place took me to a one-story ranch-style house set down a curving driveway in a suburban neighborhood. A hanging wooden sign with an arrow and the AT logo pointed toward the house, confirming it as the hostel. Another sign attached to the front door told me to let myself in. I cautiously opened the door, yelling out "Hello" as I did. A thin man with long, dark hair and a big grin approached me from a wheelchair across the room.

"Hey, man," he called out. "You looking for a place to stay?"

"I sure am," I replied, unable to keep from staring at the chair. "Are you Chet?"

"That's me." He wheeled over the last couple feet and reached up to shake my hand.

"The garage is actually where the bunkhouse and lounge are at." He spun his chair around with impressive dexterity. "Come on, I'll show you." He swung the door open wide to reveal a large garage filled with bunk beds and comfortable seating.

"Wow. This is amazing," I said, taking in the room. And it really was. From the outside, you'd easily mistake this as the garage to a typical single-family home, but within the walls was a whole secret hiker commune.

"Thanks," Chet said, beaming. "It took me a few years to get it finished, but I couldn't hike after the accident, so I decided to stay involved in trail life in a different way."

"You were a hiker?" I asked, turning back to him, wanting to gather more pieces of the puzzle that was Chet's life.

"Oh yeah." He smiled, and his dark eyes shone brightly in the light coming through a set of French doors at the back of the garage. "I love all things outdoors. I was always outside somewhere getting into something. One night, a few years back, I was out camping and my gas stove exploded right next to me. Burned me pretty bad. Nearly killed me, actually. I spent nine months in an induced coma while the doctors tried to save me. No one expected me to get to where I am today. I still have a lot of problems, and my legs don't work anymore, but at least I can still be a part of the AT in my own way. Makes me feel like I'm not just surviving but living, you know?"

I was stunned into silence by his story, so I just nodded, even though I didn't know. Not really. I hadn't experienced even a sliver of what Chet had just described, and to still be as positive and happy as he was made me realize how many choices he must have made the last several years to live in such an optimistic way.

"Anyway, enough from me." He laughed, pulling his long black hair back into a hair tie he pulled off his wrist. "You're welcome to stay for free. This isn't a business. All I ask is for some help around the house. Why don't you get settled in and come find me. I'll show you where the laundry room is. It could really use a good cleaning."

I agreed without hesitation, eager to help in any way Chet needed. It was people like him that made thru-hiking the AT the amazing experience that it was. He clearly loved the community, and looking around at the handwritten messages of support and admiration posted on every available surface in the garage, it was clear that the AT community loved him too.

Chet's laundry room turned out to be a quick job, so with some time to kill, I visited the town's movie theater and a local brewery. It was a fun zero day and a great interlude between the city life I'd been living the past weekend and the trail life I was getting back to.

Devorah, Kevin, and the boys arrived the next day in a raucous whirlwind of noise, storytelling, and back-pounding hugs. The next section would traverse the White Mountains, where the AT walked along the range's highest ridgelines. Devorah and her family would join me for parts of each day's miles, planned around the terrain's severity and the distance between road access points.

After dinner and a run to the grocery store, we headed to the Highland Center, one of several larger lodges maintained by the AMC. The rooms were tight quarters, but the center was nestled in a gorgeous mountain valley and full of amenities. We got settled into our family room, a 15-by-15-foot space with a queen and two bunk beds, then walked to the main hall to hang out before bed.

The room was full of laughter and conversation, and as I scanned the setup, I spotted an unruly mop of hair in the corner, the man's loud gust of laughter emanating toward me. He slapped his leg before slapping the back of the guy who'd clearly made him laugh. I grinned, memories resurfacing of the same exuberant actions from the guy I'd seen in both North Carolina and Connecticut.

"Yo, Starman!" I called out as I strode over to him.

He turned toward me, and recognition quickly dawned on his face.

"Sharkbait, hoo ha ha!" He rose and greeted me just as I expected, still full of boyish excitement.

"Didn't think I would see you here," I said. The Highland Center was about five miles down the mountain from the official AT, so most thru-hikers didn't plan a stop there on their way through the Whites.

Starman smiled and thumbed toward the windows. "The damn weather made me retreat. May need to change my name to Dogman with this tail tucked between my legs!"

I glanced sideways out of the full-length windows to see the sun beginning its gold-tinted trail down over the clear horizon. Today had been 75 and sunny, and the last time I checked my weather app, tomorrow was looking to be the same.

"You don't like the sun? Too beautiful a day?" I asked him, the corner of my mouth tipping up.

Starman's hearty laugh burst forth again. "It's not today that's the problem. Thursday is looking like hell, and that's the day I'm supposed to be walking those high-up ridgelines between Galehead Hut and Zealand Falls Hut." He scratched at the scruff that covered his face. "When I saw that, I said, 'No, thanks.' So I decided to make a stop here and rest up for a couple of zeros."

Devorah and family were supposed to join me at that same place on Thursday, which was two days from now. I pulled out my phone and opened my weather app. Sure enough, Thursday showed rain and thunderstorms with wind gusts up to 85 miles per hour on the mountains. The kind of conditions that every hiker hears stories about, and those stories never end well.

I thanked Starman for the information and made my way back over to Devorah and Kevin to discuss. It was quickly decided that instead of three continuous days on the exposed ridge, we'd do two big days on either end of a zero at Galehead Hut. That way, we could relax in the safety of the hut during the bad storm and hike out the next day, which was expected to be nice again.

A quick conversation with the reception desk, and our new reservations were set.

We caught a shuttle to the trail the next morning under clear blue skies that showed not a hint of inclement weather. I was psyched to be back on the trail and with a lighter pack that didn't have to accommodate my quilts, hammock, tarp, or much food. Devorah's family would do a shorter five-mile hike up the Gale River side trail from the road, while I got in my 13 official miles over several large peaks.

It didn't take me long to realize that this part of the trail, which I'd read time and again was the most beautiful the AT had to offer, was not going to disappoint. The views at each summit were simply breathtaking, the kind even Dad would have looked at in awe. But the hiking was not easy. It was one of the toughest days I'd tackled since Georgia, rivaled only by Rocksylvania and the recent memory of Mount Moosilauke.

Mount Liberty, Mount Lincoln, and Mount Lafayette were checked off early in the day, with incredible views of the White Mountains staying with me while I made my way along Franconia Ridge. Then I dropped back below the tree line, and my day turned from difficult to obnoxious. The next section over Mount Garfield was extremely steep on both sides, so upright hiking turned into scaling over and maneuvering through giant rock boulders. And as if that wasn't hard enough, when I started to descend, I discovered a creek flowing over the trail of rocks too. Just to add to the fun.

I finally reached Galehead Hut at 6 p.m., having moved at a very slow 1.8 miles per hour pace. When I first booked the huts in my planning stages, I was warned that a hiker who could average 20 to 25 miles a day should expect to hike no more than 15 through the Whites. After my first day, I wholeheartedly agreed. The trail was challenging, and I was beyond exhausted by the end. The college-aged crew (or Croo as they lovingly spelled it) was serving dinner as I arrived, and I was more than grateful to sit down for a family-style meal rather than another ramen soup over my tiny propane stove.

I caught Devorah and her family up on my day's adventures and listened to the boys' excited chatter about their own hike as we ate. Then, dinner complete, the evening began as the next twenty-four hours would continue—with good conversation, competitive board games, and lounging in the beautiful AMC hut with family.

44

THE THUNDER ROLLS

Thursday's storm raged around us, rain pounding the roof and wind rattling the windows. We were happy to be ensconced in the safety and warmth of Galehead Hut, and the day slipped by in a cozy fashion.

Friday morning came, along with hope that the weather would be clear for the day's hike. The plan was for the whole family to walk with me along seven tough ridgeline miles to the next hut, Zealand Falls, where Devorah and the two younger boys would stay the night. Our updated reservations could only secure three beds at Zealand Falls Hut, so Kevin and my oldest nephew would join me in hiking 5.5 more miles back to the Highland Center along a remote side trail.

The hut's Croo advised us at breakfast that the weather would not be as compliant as we'd hoped. Thunderstorms were unfortunately on the horizon again that afternoon. Outside the windows, it was cloudy and dry, but we knew better. It was a race against time.

Gobbling down the remains of our breakfast, we hurried to get everything packed and made it out the door at 8:30 a.m. The first part was a treacherous mile straight up 1,200 feet of elevation to the top of South Twin Mountain. The pace was very slow as tiny boy legs scrambled up rocks and slippery trails through the clouds, making it to the summit in an hour's time. As if the mountains recognized our determined willpower, the sun peeked out just as we reached the top, rewarding us with evaporating clouds and stunning White Mountain landscapes.

We continued along the ridgeline to a couple more small peaks under sunny blue skies, regularly cheering our good luck and fortune. And it looked like that luck was going to continue, but a mile shy of Zealand Falls, the skies quickly turned gray and Devorah suddenly stopped. She scanned the sky above us, then turned and scanned behind.

"Was that flash what I thought it—" Her words were cut off by a cracking sound wave of thunder that bellowed along the ridgeline, jolting the trees and echoing in the hills below us for far longer than felt normal. Her eyes widened for a second before they landed on her boys, who'd all gone into deer-in-headlights mode.

Knowing protective mother mode was about to take over, I gave her a look only siblings can interpret. Her eyes pivoted from fear to reassurance as she tracked with me. We knelt together in front of the boys, painting smiles on our faces that we hoped would be contagious.

"Hey, I have an idea. Let's see if we can count between the flashes and booms as we hike toward the hut," I said playfully. "My guess is there will be ten between each. What do you think?"

They looked at their mom, their dad, then me. The oldest smiled and the others followed suit. With each little boy now refocused on fun over fear, we continued at double-time pace to reach the hut. It quickly became a game, with a trio of young voices belting out the seconds between flash and boom. But each time we counted, the numbers got lower—the storm was quickly inching closer. With half a mile to go, the temperature dropped ten degrees in an instant, and a strong gust of wind rushed through the trees that sent chills down my spine. Knowing what that meant, I dropped my pack and yelled out, "Rain gear, stat!"

Seconds later, the skies dumped a waterfall of rain as thunder crashed around us. Instantly, we were right in the eye of the mountain storm. The boys whimpered, but Devorah now took control, making a new game out of the puddle side-stepping and rock jumping that the deluge forced us into.

With exclamations of, "Guys, look, a flash flood!", "Let's use that fallen tree as a bridge!", and "Wow, is that a fish swimming in the waterfall?!", we made it to Zealand Falls Hut, and the boys cheered as they jumped onto the dry safety of the front porch.

We all breathed a momentary sigh of relief. The seven-mile stretch had taken us 7.5 hours, and it was finally over for half our group. For me, Kevin, and his oldest son, Jonah, we could only rest for a few minutes and have a dry snack before heading out again. The worst of the storm was now passing through, with only light rain remaining. So we hugged Devorah and the two younger boys goodbye and set out for what I assumed was a short trip down a side trail to the AMC Highland Center. But as usual, I was wrong.

The trail was barren and in rough shape, clearly not seeing more than a handful of hikers a year. It had distinct yellow blazes, not the typical blue for a well-maintained AT side trail, reminding me this was far from a common walking path. It was an extremely technical hike over Mount Tom, with countless water crossings, made deeper by the day's rain, and rough bushwhacking through overgrown foliage. I was concerned that Jonah might not be able to handle it, but my incredible nephew stayed stride-for-stride with me the entire way. Of course, it didn't hurt that I'd also packed a bag of gummy worms for energy and emergency motivation.

Finally, at 8:05 p.m., we made it back to the Highland Center. Dinner closed at 8:00, but we begged the Croo to hold off on clearing up for five minutes while we grabbed three plates of hot food. They cheerily obliged, helping us pile up the calories we needed after such an epic adventure. Jonah didn't seem in the least bit fazed by the extra-hard hike, recounting his highlights of the day with gusto to all the Croo.

The tenants of the Highland Center's room 208 slept like wee babes that night. Jonah was out within minutes, and I tried to write my daily blog post but drifted off to sleep mid-typing. The next morning, we got up early and drove to the Zealand Falls trailhead parking area, where we could hike an easy 2.5 miles back to Zealand Hut to meet the other three family members. About halfway up, they bounded down the trail toward us in great spirits. They were too eager to wait and decided to hike down and meet us at the road.

And so another family adventure was over. This time, though, our time on the trail would end for good, as Devorah, Kevin, and the boys had to return to Maryland while I carried on northward through the White Mountains to Katahdin. It would be the last time they drove to join me on the AT, but most certainly not our last hiking trip together. And like with Dad, the stories of their trips on the AT with me would live on for years to come. But, just to make sure, right before they were out of earshot, I yelled out, "Guys, look, a flash flood!" They responded with a resounding, "Rain gear, stat!"

With goodbyes done, I hiked toward the hut intersecting the AT again. Then, turning left, I spotted a white blaze heading north and picked up where I'd left off the day before. And as had become normal for the White Mountains, I was greeted with rough-and-tough terrain. The first eight miles were relatively level, but not easy. The two days of rain had left deep puddles in the trail that I tried to hopscotch around, with limited success.

The trail wound down to Crawford Notch and Highway 302, then climbed steeply over the last three miles, gaining 2,800 feet to the twin summits of Mount Webster and Mount Jackson. I was trying to make it to Mizpah Falls Hut before 4 p.m. so that I could hopefully claim a work-for-stay spot before other hikers did, but with the slow-going terrain, it was looking increasingly unlikely. Finally, I looked up the trail to see the hut above me. It was now 4:30 p.m., so my hopes of securing a spot were low, especially when I saw how packed the hut was. But when I checked with the Croo, it turned out I was the first hiker that day to ask. Fortune was on my side.

In exchange for dinner and a sleeping spot on the dining room floor, I was assigned to do night dishes—the dishes after the guest dishes, when the staff had eaten. We ate about 8 p.m. and got to work with the help of Soulshine and The Kid, two hikers from Canada who'd come in after me to claim the remaining work-for-stay spots. Fifteen minutes later we were finished, and I set up my bed for the night. As I cozied down into my pad and quilt, the rain started back up again, pelting the windows and roof in earnest. My eyes drifted closed to the comforting sound and warmth from the hut floor.

I woke with a jump as a crack of thunder shook the ground and me. My elbow and hip hit the ground hard. Much harder than they should have, considering I was lying on the most comfortable sleeping pad I'd ever bought.

"What the—?" I muttered as lightning lit up the still-dark sky and dining room. It also illuminated the reason for my proximity to the floor... my rarely used sleeping pad was completely deflated. I checked my watch. It was 3 a.m. Not an ideal time to discover a deflated bed. A quick investigation revealed a small hole in one corner.

"Dammit. How did that happen?" I muttered. I didn't want to wake Soulshine and The Kid, who were sleeping next to me, but this was a conundrum too great to process internally.

Another crack of thunder vibrated through the ground around me, and any thought of sleep slipped farther away. The storm was fun to watch from the safety of the dry lodge, so instead of fighting to go back to sleep on the hard ground, I watched it roll through.

One particularly bright shaft of lightning burst through the sky just as a tiny scurrying form ran to the same corner of my sleeping pad that now featured a hole. A mouse had appeared from some dark crevice, and it was now nibbling joyfully at my sleeping pad! I shooed it away, and it scurried off into the shadows. A minute later, it was back. This game of man and mouse went on for several more rounds before I decided that enough was enough. I grabbed a hiking pole and stood up, waiting frozen and silent. It didn't take long for the relentless little rodent to return. I was poised and ready, my hiking pole raised like a spear. I jabbed down, hearing a tiny squeak, and flung the skewered offender into the nearest wall. I approached cautiously and saw it was trying to get back up. A few brush strokes of my pole saw the miscreant out the back door, where it limped off into the stormy night. I liked to think of myself as an animal lover but was content with my actions. This vermin had signed his death warrant the second he chose my expensive bed as his late-night snack.

With that start to my morning, I was ready to leave Mizpah Falls at 6:30 a.m. I entered a very wet and foggy world and was immediately met with an extremely windy climb upward. The next section of the AT traveled around the summits rather than up and over them. But each mountain had an optional blue-blazed trail hikers could take over the top to claim the Presidential peaks. The first was Mount Eisenhower, but with the thick fog, it was clear the views would be nonexistent, so I skipped it. Mount Monroe was next. I'd already decided to skip this one too, but then discovered that the AT path going around it was closed, so the only option was up and over. As I suspected, the views were invisible behind the wall of fog. I quickly descended, and a few miles later, I walked into the Lakes of the Clouds Hut. And I mean literally walked into it. It was the largest hut maintained by the AMC and should be visible a mile away, but the fog was so thick that I couldn't see a foot in front of my face and didn't know it was there until a few feet from its door. It turned out Lakes of the Clouds was a very appropriate name.

I enjoyed a generous breakfast of leftover cold pancakes and lukewarm coffee for two dollars from the Croo before hiking out again. I still had three mountains to traverse before arriving at

Madison Spring Hut, and the iconic Mount Washington was my next challenge. As the highest peak in the White Mountains and the most accessible to day-hikers traveling by car, it was packed. I didn't blame them for how they chose to enjoy this landmark, but I felt very out of place being the only thru-hiker on the summit. I took some quick pictures of the summit sign, grabbed a hot dog from the concessions near the parking lot, and left. And then, finally, the clouds broke.

Over the next few hours, the fog slowly cleared, revealing beautiful blue skies and bright sunshine. By noon, I could see the whole landscape, and it was breathtaking. In front of me lay Mount Jefferson and Mount Adams, the third and second highest peaks in the Presidential Range. And to celebrate my good mood and weather, I took the blue blaze trails over the tops of both summits. The views were worth enduring the craggy rocks and swarms of black flies that greeted me. It was like looking at scenery straight out of *The Princess Bride*, and I may have yelled, "As you wish!" into the surrounding valleys for anyone to hear.

45

FREE FALLIN'

I made it to the Madison Spring Hut at 4:30 p.m., and was fortunate to earn another work-for-stay spot for the night. A few more hikers appeared, and the Croo must have been feeling generous because soon a crowd of five of us were volunteering in exchange for a place to sleep.

We introduced ourselves with our trail names, and when it came to my turn, a guy with pale, freckly skin and a shock of red hair, who had just introduced himself very appropriately as Irish, yelled across the circle, "Sharkbait?!"

"Hoo ha ha?" I replied hesitantly.

"You're the guy putting those stickers in the registry books that link to that awesome blog?!"

I grinned widely. I was still putting the orange "Hello My Name Is" stickers at all the shelters with a snippet that teased people to read more on my blog, so coming across another person who appreciated them was nice.

"Man, me and Beach Bum started a few days after you," Irish continued, indicating a stocky guy next to him. "Your blog has got us out of more than one jam. Been great to see what's ahead. We were hoping to catch up to you. This is almost surreal!"

It was another exciting realization of this thru-hiker community, seeing that we were all on our own personal journey but also walking the same path. The conversation continued as we shared tales and adventures from our collective weeks on the trail. Irish and Beach Bum informed me they were consistently several days behind me, but while I was off-trail for the wedding, they'd caught up. Many of our experiences were similar, having been on the same sections of the trail around the same time. We even knew some of the same people, as they'd hiked a bit with Nubs and Fun Facts in Virginia. It felt like a lifetime ago since our tramily split ways, so it was great to hear they were still on the trail!

The hut got a lot of work out of us. I did the dishes while the others scrubbed the oven, organized the spice rack, stirred the compost pile, and cleaned the dining room. Eventually the work was complete, just in time to watch an incredible sunset together over the ridge. At 9:30, lights were shut off, and we set up our beds in the dining room. I'd learned my lesson from the previous night's rodent-related escapades and decided to sleep on top of a bench. It was hard and uncomfortable without a working sleeping pad to cushion it, but the most important feature was the elevated protection from destructive vermin.

The next morning, Irish and Beach Bum decided to hike out with me, and I was glad for the company because the hike was grueling. It started with the last Presidential summit up Madison, involving a 600-foot climb for half a mile over huge rock boulders. And that wasn't even the real struggle. No, the true challenge came on the descent. It was straight down 3,000 feet to the base in just over three miles. The rocks continued, but after descending through the tree line again, there were also narrow winding corridors to contend with. That stretch from Madison Spring Hut to the base took us three hours.

The next four miles to Pinkham Notch were thankfully over

flatter terrain, which meant we could increase our pace, only stopping to read the dozens of signposts that directed us through the maze of trails in this popular day-hike area. I didn't need to add any more negative miles to my hike, especially because the next challenge to close out the Whites was right ahead—the ruthlessly unforgiving Wildcat Mountains. The peaks were a series of rough climbs with little place to rest, forcing me to ascend 2,000 feet in two miles to a ski gondola. Then, as my reward, I immediately climbed up another 400-foot rocky climb to Wildcat Summit.

It was now 4:30 p.m., and I was exhausted. I stumbled into Carter Notch Hut ready to hang up my pack and claim one of the work-for-stay spots. But no dice. Two southbound thru-hikers had beaten me to it, and I was turned away. Irish and Beach Bum walked in a few minutes later and faced the same fate, so with exchanged looks of weary resignation, we took a quick break and marched on to find stealth spots.

The summit of Carter Dome just beyond the hut held a rare flat clearing with no rocks, so they both peeled off to set up their tents. But the trees were too small and weak to hang from, so I had no choice but to continue onward. I made my way farther down to a pass where the trees were sufficient. My feet were tired and sore, my shoulders were aching, and my legs felt like lead pipes. On the plus side, I was now three miles closer to Gorham and the Rattle River Hostel where I would stay the next night. I was eager to get there as Keg and The Captain were flying in to rejoin me one last time on the AT and hike southern Maine together.

It struck me suddenly that this was the first time I would be sleeping solo on the trail since starting my journey 124 days earlier. I'd never slept alone in the woods before, but I felt more peace with it than anxiety. At some point out here, the woods simply felt like home. So I rigged up my hammock and ate a quick dinner, then went to lie down before the last big push to close out New Hampshire.

The next morning, I stared down at the sheer, wet rock slabs that made up the trail. Blowing out a breath, I took my first step slowly, carefully down, using my hiking poles to stabilize my weight. The rock beneath me was just as slippery as I suspected, so each step felt precariously placed. It took some practice to get into a good stride, but my confidence increased as I remained upright. Then, *wham*, I hit the ground, falling backward onto my pack. It saved me from badly hurting any part of my body, but one of my hiking poles didn't fare so well. I held it up, the end bent and dangling uselessly.

I groaned, easing myself up slowly into a standing position. Without two working poles, the trek down had just gotten significantly more difficult. Twice more, my feet left the ground in hard and painful falls before I made it to the bottom of Mount Moriah. My legs were weary, having been beaten and battered for too many days in a row without a day of rest. Combined with the terrain and the broken pole, it was too many hazards to handle at once.

Eventually, I made it down and out of what I was now calling the 'Mount Moriah Massacre.' The last three miles were thankfully on a well-groomed trail alongside the beautiful Rattle River, but at that point, I was mentally checked out. I needed a shower. Bad. A bed was also a comfort I desperately longed for, but my immediate need was to get rid of the sweat, mud, and grime that had permeated every part of my body over the last three days.

The Rattle River Lodge appeared as a white farmhouse-style mirage at the end of its curving driveway. I soon discovered they were well-accustomed to beaten and battered hikers, as the side door's entryway featured a shower with a sign stating that all hikers must clean up before going farther into the house. And I was more than willing to put in the work.

Somewhat cleaned and much more refreshed, I was shown to the bunk room. Then it was time to get to work fixing my gear. I called LEKI, the manufacturer of my hiking poles, to claim my warranty and get a free replacement part shipped ahead of me on the trail, then soaped up my inflated sleeping pad to find the bubbly sign of holes as air escaped. Once patched up, I spent the rest of the day lounging in the yard waiting for my friends to arrive.

Around 4:30, a rental car pulled up, and Keg and The Captain piled out.

Handshakes, back slaps, and jokes about my diminished weight and thru-hiker chic were exchanged as I showed them the bunk room. We laughed over dinner and beers that night, reminiscing about the earlier part of this adventure and how much different it now felt. I enjoyed the laughter and memories, but I knew it was time to change the conversation toward the upcoming three days together. They were going to be difficult hiking through conditions that were no joke compared to Georgia, and I wanted to make sure they both knew what they were getting into.

I took them through point by point of what to expect—rocky trails, steep heights, steeper descents, stream crossings... and the dreaded Mahoosuc Notch, infamous for being the most difficult one-mile stretch of the AT.

The Captain clapped a hand on my shoulder, his brown eyes sparking with amusement. "We've already done Glacier, Yosemite, and Denali together. We're up for the challenge."

Keg added, "Besides, we've hiked part of the AT. We know what we're up against."

I nodded, smiling back at their enthusiasm, hoping to communicate a quiet confidence in their abilities. But I had a feeling they were grossly overestimating what they could handle in Maine compared to the gentle knolls of Georgia. Only time would tell.

46

FRIENDS IN LOW PLACES

The day began with one of those hazy rings around the sun that meant the heat index was going to rise swiftly. The green tunnel had returned, providing us with rustling shade that meant we could hike in cool air for most of the day over Mount Hayes and Cascade Mountain. At each summit, we were treated to a dazzling display of the White Mountains to the south, beneath a blue sky filled with golden sunlight. The ascents were all part of a typical day for me in this stretch of the AT, but they were tough for my comrades. So we rested often, drank plenty of water, and kept a slow-and-steady pace.

By late afternoon, we reached Gentian Pond Shelter. The campsite around the shelter consisted of elevated wooden platforms, perfect for Keg's small tent, but there was also a side trail to a stealth site I'd read about that was too intriguing to pass up. The Captain and I scrambled up a rocky cliff to a plateau overlook that appeared beautiful for one tent or hammock, but definitely not big enough for the three of us. So we scrambled back down to the official camp area, where Keg set up his tent on a platform near the shelter. After seeing my earlier setup, The Captain had now switched to a hammock, so we set ourselves up in the fir trees surrounding the platform.

Gentian Pond Shelter was situated next to a beautiful lake, high up in the mountains. The view was clear for miles, and as the sky darkened around our dinner conversations, we watched 4th of July fireworks light up the sky over Gorham, now 12 miles behind us.

After watching in silence for a while, Keg asked me, "On a scale of one to ten, how difficult was this section for you? What would you give it?"

I took a swig of whiskey, thoughtfully supplied by The Captain, and pondered the question. After everything I'd just finished in the Presidentials, the trail we walked today had been fantastic in comparison. "Hmm, I'd say a two."

I looked back at their incredulous faces. "Maybe a three?"

Keg snorted and looked back out at the view just as a spectacular red, white, and blue starburst illuminated the skyline.

"How was it for you?" I asked him.

"Honestly?" he asked, turning to grab the whiskey and take a long, drawn-out swallow. "Eleven. This is the hardest hike I've ever done."

I laughed and raised my cup to him in a toast. "That's the AT for you."

The main obstacle for the next day was to summit Mount Success, a 3,500-foot climb with pretty steep sections. We reached the top around noon, which meant our pace had been half that of the day before. I was so used to these intense climbs that I couldn't tell anymore whether the trail was significantly worse or if my friends were just worn out from yesterday's harsh hike. The summit wasn't even halfway to our day's stopping point, so after a quick lunch at the top, I pushed everyone to their feet, wanting to make it to Carlo Col Shelter before nightfall.

A sign at the bottom of Mount Success caused me to pause in my onward push.

"Look!" I called out.

"Maine?" Keg asked, reading the sign.

A huge grin spread across my face. Crossing this imaginary line would put me in my fourteenth and final state—the one that contained Katahdin's glory and the end of my thru-hike. There weren't words to describe the feelings swirling in my mind, but elated, victorious, and exuberant came close.

We reached the Carlo Col Shelter around 2:30. I was still on a high from crossing into Maine, but seeing the fatigue on my friends' faces brought me back to reality. There was still plenty of time to hike the 4.5 miles to Full Goose Shelter, the next campground on the trail, but Keg and The Captain looked exhausted, and the weather wasn't heading in the right direction. The day was hot again, and the fast change in temperatures meant we could also see thunderstorms brewing along the horizon. With three more climbs up Goose Eye West, Goose Eye East, and Fulling Mill Mountain still to come, it felt like the odds were stacking up against us.

However, I wasn't only considering the rest of the day. Tomorrow's plan was to do ten miles, and these were supposed to start with Mahoosuc Notch. The Notch would require maneuvering under, over, and through giant boulders at a snail's pace. From what I'd read, hikers typically had to constantly throw their gear through narrow rock gaps before squeezing their bodies through. The 0.8-mile section usually took thru-hikers an hour to complete, in good conditions.

Following that would be the climb of Mahoosuc Mountain, known as the Arm. There, the trail would rise 1,500 feet in one mile, earning the Arm's reputation as one of the steepest climbs of the entire AT. I'd read countless stories of hikers breaking bones, getting lost, and even dying in this section in bad conditions. It was known for having no phone service, and there was no easy exit to civilization if something went seriously wrong. Doing this section in the rain created an even greater threat—a water slide of life-threatening proportions. The chance of rain and thunderstorms currently forecasted from 5 a.m. to 2 p.m. the next day was 90 percent.

With all that before us, I decided it was time to voice everyone's feelings on our situation. Emotions were split between wanting to hike on and not wanting to widow their wives, so I cast the deciding vote for us to go off-trail the next day and spend the rest of our time together back at the Rattle River Lodge in Gorham. From Next Time's medivac a few weeks earlier, I knew there had to be a side trail down the mountain. And sure enough, I spotted a blue blaze following a creek and scouted it to learn it could lead us to a road and shuttle service off the mountain tomorrow.

It was a wise decision, but it turned out to be an enjoyable one as well. With a whole afternoon free of hiking, we got time to hang out, catch up on each other's lives, and go swimming in the creek. We stayed up late storytelling and laughing (with the aid of the remaining whiskey), and I spent the final moments before bed lying in front of the shelter staring up at the stars. It had unexpectedly turned out to be a great nero day.

The next morning, we woke to the anticipated rain and thunder, but it began clearing around 10 a.m. We arranged for the shuttle to pick us up at noon and began our hike out. The side trail we'd scouted had been next to a gently flowing creek, but now it was overtaken by a much faster flowing river over the trail. This meant we faced multiple calf-deep water crossings. It really was incredible how high water levels could rise from a day of rain, and how treacherous a previously tranquil creek could quickly become.

We made it, thankfully without incident, off the mountain, and the shuttle picked us up for a rough pot-hole-dodging ride along a gravel track back to the main road. Backtracking to Gorham meant my friends wouldn't experience as much of the trail with me as we'd intended, but we would get to enjoy a day of small-town shenanigans. I was pretty sure they preferred the trade.

The morning after our full day of relaxed fun, Keg and The Captain headed back to their regular lives, and I got back to the business of thru-hiking. It was a perfect weather day, with highs in the sixties and bright sunshine. I hiked back up the blue-blaze side trail and marveled again at how much lower the creek was now compared to yesterday. Not even one river crossing to be found.

The real fun came when I got back to the white blazes of the AT. I'd gone into the day knowing there would be a ton of steep climbs, and that was before I reached Mahoosuc Notch. It wasn't long before I was faced with my first, complete with metal rungs of rebar drilled into the rock to form a ladder. It was slow going, but eventually, I scaled Mount Carlo, Fulling Mill Mountain, and the Goose Eye peaks. And with those behind me, all that was left was Mahoosuc.

I climbed down into the valley where a giant boulder field greeted me. The dreaded Notch. I spotted the first hole I had to maneuver through and took my bag off my shoulders. I slid it along one wall of the rock, tossed my poles through, and then crawled in after on hands and knees, pushing my bag and poles and then inching my way after them. A few feet later, I was out on the other side. I stood up and surveyed the hole that was now behind me. The first obstacle was complete... and it had been quite fun!

After that, my confidence instantly boosted, and I continued to navigate the boulder field with care and ease. I stopped to drink from waterfalls that poured down so cold it made my teeth ache, and hiked past patches of snow on the ground in areas that clearly never got to see the light of day. It was much cooler in the valley, being so protected from the elements.

Mahoosuc Arm was my last challenge of the day, and while the Notch had boosted my confidence, the Arm was a different matter.

Instead of traversing boulders, I was now climbing straight up an incredibly steep and sheer rock slab. I could see immediately why those who'd traversed it cautioned against doing this portion when wet. It was so steep and smooth that it would be all too easy to slip and seriously damage something while tumbling aimlessly down the mountain... or worse. For the unconditioned, it would be serious danger, and I was grateful the vote with my friends had gone the way of a zero day in Gorham.

I reached the summit and celebrated with a trail mix snack as I looked out over the majestic Maine views. A group of thru-hikers were already at the top enjoying their own snacks, and I gathered from their excited conversation that they were hiking south. I filled them in on my experience of the Arm and Notch, which got them even more pumped up. After a few more words of encouragement, I was ready for the final few miles of my day.

As I took a slow and steady walk to Grafton Notch, I thought about the southbound hikers and their journey. They were just beginning their thru-hike, while the end was in sight for mine. I felt a strange mix of excited anticipation for the completion of my lifelong dream and a strong urge to turn around at Katahdin and hike back to Georgia with them. This adventure I'd dreamed of for so many years was almost over, and I wasn't quite sure how I felt about that yet.

The Baldpate Lean-to was my stopping point for the night. The lean-to name Maine had chosen for their shelters made them sound more rustic than the shelters along earlier portions of the trail, but the setup was the same—three walls, a roof, and hardwood floors. Although any shelter now felt more rustic after the beautiful accommodations of those AMC huts in the White Mountains.

As I boiled my water for dinner, I looked ahead to the final stretch. I'd made up some miles from the ones I had to forgo because of my friends, but I was still eight miles behind schedule. Looking ahead at the terrain, it seemed like those would be easy to make up. Also, in my planning, I'd allowed a generous amount of time in the upcoming 100-mile wilderness, a stretch of trail lacking towns or amenities to support hikers crusading through. I figured I could hike more miles at this point, and could likely get to Baxter State Park surrounding Katahdin at least a day earlier than planned. That was my preference because it would give me a couple of shots at good weather for the final climb. It also meant that in a little over two weeks, my trek to the AT's northern terminus would be complete.

47

INSANE IN THE BRAIN

The next day began in a leisurely fashion. I knew it would be shorter getting to the next town of Andover, the road access being only an eight-mile hike away. I could have altered my original plan to go farther, but a resupply box was waiting for me at the Pine Ellis Hostel, so I had to stop.

When I eventually got hiking, the day continued to progress slowly. Maine was determined to show off its treacherous climbs and steep summits. Today, I felt like I was climbing up the largest rock in America. Baldpate Mountain's west and east peaks were one giant 3,800-foot-high solid slab with sides that were smoother than a glassy lake at dawn. Needless to say, after my recent falls coming down to Gorham on very similar terrain, these were navigated with great care.

While snacking and taking in the incredible view at the summit, a young woman hiked up. With her hair in two braids and the easy smile she threw my way, I instantly thought of Fun Facts. Besides the comment from Irish a few days earlier, I hadn't thought of her in weeks, and I made a mental note to check in later.

The young woman introduced herself as Bethy, a day-hiker

who'd driven from Andover to walk the AT for a few miles on a whim. Upon hearing my plans for the day, she graciously offered to give me a ride into town, which I willingly accepted.

The rock-climbing portion of the day ended, and the trail began to follow a stream down toward Dunn Notch, creating some excellent waterfalls and creeks as it forged its path through the mountains. I knew I still had a couple of hours before meeting Bethy at the parking lot, so I decided today was the day to take a blue blaze side trip to stop at one of the many swimming holes rather than do my usual stroll past.

A spur trail to Upper Dunn Falls promised a hidden gem—a swim spot where the creek collected just below the falls. My mind formed visions of standing at the edge of an idyllic pool of water hidden just beyond the trees, like in Brooke Shields's 1980 film, *The Blue Lagoon*. I hadn't seen many people on the trail other than Bethy, so I was hopeful for a private dip in the cool water. The trail soon curved around toward the falls, but before I could see the rushing water, I heard a raucous chorus of screams and giggles instead. The falls came into view, and my heart sank. At least fifteen teenagers were splashing and swimming in the creek below. So much for a private dip. I made an immediate U-turn back to the AT's familiar white blazes and followed the creek a mile farther up the road. Just before the parking lot would come into view, I came across another swimming hole as picturesque as the first, and this time completely empty. The waterfall cascaded over twenty feet of rock, forming a perfect sunlit pool. I peeled off my hiking garb down to just my briefs and eased my way in, letting the pain of the day's climbs wash away with a serene smile on my face. For the next twenty minutes, the only sounds or movements were those of water pouring off the rocks and birds singing through the trees. It was perfect.

After drying off, I continued down to the parking lot to meet Bethy, and it wasn't long before she appeared. She took me to downtown Andover, dropping me at the Red Hen for lunch. I waved goodbye, thinking how awesome it was that a young woman had so much confidence to hike in the woods alone. She couldn't have been more than 2 or 3 years younger than me and had no issue picking up a random stranger for a ride to town.

The rest of the day passed in the usual way of town stops... doing laundry, organizing my resupply box, consuming anything greasy or fermented, and chatting with other hikers doing the same.

I headed to bed early that night, wanting to get an early start tomorrow for a 20-mile day. It was time to start making up some miles if I was going to stay on track for Katahdin before August.

"Gah! Why did you step there if you knew it was a loose stone?!" I berated myself aloud the next day as I massaged my ankle from yet another painful misstep. I hadn't seriously injured either ankle yet, but it wasn't the first time I'd come close, including falling once again on slick rock earlier that morning.

Another half-mile along a series of pointless ups and downs, I now started lovingly referring to as PUDs, and I rolled my other ankle, this time on an exposed tree root.

"Goddamnit! Who maintains the trail up here?" No answer was forthcoming because no one was near me. Although if they had been, I doubt they would have answered the frustrated rantings of an exasperated thru-hiker.

Talking to myself had become all too common lately. It seemed that since Vermont, the desire to verbalize every inner thought and observation had only grown stronger. It had started with yelling at myself for doing something dumb, like taking a bad step or wrong turn, but it was now more diversified. If I spotted something particularly nice, I'd say, "Well, would you look at that," or "Hey, look at that yellow flower over there. I wonder what its name is?" Sometimes I'd even rope nearby animals into the conversation. A swell of birdsong in the trees might draw a "Hey, bird, I like your song." A skittish squirrel might get a "Sorry, bud. Didn't mean to scare you!"

Most of the time, I didn't even realize I'd spoken out loud until after it was verbalized to the world, which then meant I issued myself a chastisement for being a madman. In thinking it over, as I pulled myself up a series of sixty-degree embankments using trees for climbing holds, I concluded that I wasn't going crazy... it was just part of the magical transformation my mind went through after hiking mainly alone for months.

Lately, I was mostly happy in my own company, and making these observations to myself seemed to satisfy the need for social interaction. And then, as if on cue, such an occasion presented itself as I approached the summit of Bemis Mountain. I rounded a corner to see a giant bull moose munching grass on the side of the trail. He froze, staring at me with half-chewed grass hanging out of his mouth. Two seconds of eye contact was enough for him though, and he bounded away up the ridge before hearing my, "Hey, Moose, how's the mountain treating ya?"

Seeing that moose was a milestone on the AT, but without photo evidence or another living soul to document the experience, it felt like my brief bear encounter at the farmstand in Vermont. Did it really even happen?

I plowed on until I came to a big stealth campsite on the other side of Bemis Stream. I'd heard this was a river that required fording, but luck was on my side that day. The water level was low enough to reveal rocks I could use as stepping stones. This was a real perk because I was not in the mood to end my long day with wet feet.

Several more hikers turned up, including a couple named Honey and Moon I'd seen off and on the last couple weeks. Their trail names were creatively given because they started their thru-hike right after getting married, and we chatted over dinner before heading to our respective beds. Sleeping next to the river with its soothing sounds of rushing water was an extra treat, and I was asleep in no time.

The next morning, I had a quick, cold breakfast and headed out for the day. I only needed to go 14 miles to the town of Rangeley, so it wasn't going to be as tough a day. Soft, wide trails that wove around various lakes would ensure it. Really, the only tough part about it was the bugs. Mosquitoes and horseflies attempted to make me their breakfast (and lunch and dinner), and any bug spray I applied soon slid off my sweat-soaked skin. I donned my head net and kept full-length sleeves on my arms, determined to wear them even in the heat. With all the stagnant lakes and creeks in the back half of Maine, it felt like this may become my daily wardrobe.

I arrived at the highway to Rangeley at 2:30, but instead of hitchhiking the twenty or so miles to town, I continued a short few hundred yards to a place called The Hiker Hut I'd found in my pre-trip planning. This hostel described itself as a "restful sanctuary with flower gardens, hummingbirds, and pet chipmunks." I knew I had to see it, and when I approached, I saw that it was that and more. In fact, the layout felt more like a hippy commune than a hiker hostel. The beautifully landscaped property consisted of three modest buildings: a small bunkhouse, a one-room cabin, and a tiny one-room kitchen between the two. Surrounding them were flowers roughly contained by stacked rock walls, whimsical decorations, and a random assortment of outdoor seating. It looked like a life-sized fairy garden.

The owners, Steve and Cathy, lived on-site in the tiny cabin and were among the most relaxed, welcoming hosts I'd yet experienced. They lived without modern plumbing, electricity, or cell service, and their casual contentment was contagious. After a trip into Rangeley for dinner with the group staying that night, we all relaxed around the campfire Steve skillfully got going. Cathy appeared out of their cabin with a guitar.

"Anyone play?" she asked, holding it out to the group.

I looked around and, seeing no one else raise their hand, offered mine. "I do."

I don't usually play for a crowd, but this setup reminded me too much of my nights as a camp counselor decades earlier, where I'd play calm tunes to quiet the kids for bed. Cathy smiled serenely and handed the guitar over. "Play whatever you want. I'm sure someone will know it."

So I did, and she was right. Everyone, at one point or another, joined in singing the soft classic rock songs I'd learned growing up with Dad. Soon melodies of Simon and Garfunkel, The Eagles, and Leonard Cohen floated around the crackling fire. It was a perfect evening with a great group of people. As I headed to bed, Cathy thanked me for playing, joking, "Nights like this? Our little Hiker Hut always reminds me more of an adult summer camp."

I laughed before adding, "I couldn't agree more."

I got up the next morning refreshed and recharged. I'd heard the next four days of hiking would be tough with some steep 4,000-foot peaks. I was on a tight schedule if I was going to make it to Katahdin in time, though, which meant no more nero or zero days.

Early on, I knew the day would be a special one. The trails were beautifully maintained and the views on the summits were stunning, including a mile of ridge-walk in the sun that felt like I was literally hiking across the top of the world. Before lunch, I'd already scaled Saddleback Mountain, The Horn, and Junior Saddleback. I'd also encountered the oddest privy to date at the Piazza Rock Lean-to—two toilet seats, side by side. And if sharing a bathroom break with a friend wasn't enough, one could also enjoy a game of cribbage together as a board was built into the wooden planks between the seats.

My day didn't afford the luxury of waiting on an awkward crib partner, so after a quick stop, I kept making progress toward Spaulding Mountain Lean-to for the night. A couple hours later, I strode down the blue blaze trail, ready for another night of peaceful rest. But when I got there, I stopped dead in my tracks. A group of loud middle-school girls on some summer excursion had taken over every part of the campground area, and I was not in the mood to ruin my beautiful day with a restless night.

Instead, I headed to the back of the shelter and hiked another fifty yards until I found a secluded place away from the giggles and chatter. I strung up my hammock and then went to get water. Returning with my filled bottles, I found a family of three setting up camp uncomfortably close to my hammock. A huff of breath left me as I surveyed the situation. There were at least a dozen other tent sites between me and the shelter. Why had they decided to set theirs up literally three feet from the end of my bed?

The only male of the group turned to me and cheerily called out, "We hope you don't mind. Couldn't find another place!"

My frustrated mind produced an answer that begged to come out of my mouth. *I would be happy to find you another place for your tent... in the creek, with you inside it.* But the words that actually came out were decidedly different. "Oh, no worries. I'll be heading to bed soon anyway."

The guy waved at me in thanks and turned back to prepping dinner outside their tent. I ate my own cold dinner of raw ramen noodles and granola bars, opting for speed over taste, and hoping that by disappearing into my hammock, they would understand the need for quiet. But those hopes were quickly dashed as the family decided to enthusiastically eat their dinner on a log between their tent and my hammock. Which meant they were literally now one foot from my face. They finally got into their tent for bed, which actually meant giggling, bickering, and making loud movements on their air mattresses for the next two hours.

It was about this time that my frustrated mind got loud again. *They're so close I could piss on them. Hmm, actually, that's not a bad idea. Maybe a little late-night revenge pee?* It was crude, but would be decidedly better than the other homicidal thoughts also running through my mind. So much for avoiding a restless night.

48

INTO THE GREAT WIDE OPEN

A round 10 p.m., my camping neighbors finally quieted down for the night, and so did the distant giggles of teenage girls. With peace restored, any further ideas of bathroom-related payback disappeared, and I fell into a deep sleep.

I wanted to put in 18 miles and make it to the Horns Pond Lean-tos. The name was plural because the campsite was huge, containing three shelter structures, two brand-new privies, and a half-dozen tent areas all clustered around a picturesque pond.

But before I got there, I needed to hike up and down Crocker's south and north peaks. It was also a big day because of another major milestone. During the morning, I came across my last significant mile marker before the grand finale: 2,000 miles hiked from Springer Mountain. Like most signposts on the AT, it was tacked to the trunk of a tree, and it was about 15 miles off the actual 2,000-mile mark according to this year's Guthook data. Regardless, it was a huge moment of celebration that I embraced with selfies for the blog and an extra candy bar.

Even after four and a half months of walking, the magnitude of these milestones was just as epic. I sent one of the photos to The

Captain with a text saying, *"I've now walked the equivalent of my LA apartment to your front door in Chicago."* The three dots signaling he was typing a response immediately appeared, and when his reply appeared, my sudden burst of laughter sent a nearby foraging squirrel skittering up a tree. *"Would you give that difficulty a two or a three?"*

Then I got back to what I was out here for... hiking, hiking, and some more hiking. The trails were well groomed, and the mosquitoes were now (mostly) well-behaved, so I made good progress to the Horns Pond Lean-tos.

The accommodations were even more impressive than I was expecting. A caretaker resided onsite during the hiking season, and he'd done a wonderful job maintaining the area. Everything was clean, the privies were spotless and surprisingly smelled halfway pleasant, and there were even large plastic buckets with secure lids at each tent site to store one's food.

Setup for the night was quick and easy, leaving me with ample time to swim in the still water of the pond and give myself a much-needed bath. I climbed out onto the sun-warmed rocks to dry off and spent a few quiet moments before dinner just watching the breeze ripple along the water, distorting the image of trees and clouds mirrored along its crystal surface.

The next day's hike took me up and down Mount Bigelow and Avery Peak, about one mile apart and each over 4,000 feet in height. Both were bittersweet moments. Standing on the summit of Mount Bigelow, I saw the AT's northern terminus for the first time in the distant horizon. Katahdin's pointed peak stood out on the ridgeline of mountains to the north. Standing at the top of Avery Peak, I could see both my end goal beckoning me forward and the miles I'd come as just a memory behind me. This was my last big climb. After descending Avery Peak, I wouldn't rise much above 3,000 feet again until Katahdin.

And as if the lofty peaks wanted to give me a parting gift, I tripped and fell. Twice. The first was on the descent of Avery Peak and involved only a scratch on my palm and a round of yelling at my clumsiness. The second was on Little Bigelow, where I was walking down a small rocky area and took a bad step. One of those ankle-breaking steps I'd been avoiding for over 2,000 miles. Somehow, instinct took over, and instead of letting it snap my ankle to smithereens, I leaned into the roll instead. It may have saved my ankle, but unfortunately didn't stop the inevitable hard nose-dive onto pointy rocks.

Breathing hard, I picked myself up to see long scratches down my legs already blossoming with beads of red.

"Come on!" I yelled, throwing my poles ten feet in front of me as all my frustration blew out in one spectacular tantrum.

I didn't understand why I was suddenly falling so much more on the trail. The hike wasn't that much harder, and my legs were significantly stronger, but maybe my ankles had loosened or I was too much in my head about it all. Maybe I just needed to accept that falling was a part of my journey now.

I brushed myself off, muttering, "I can take it. I won't let you beat me... not this close to the end." Retrieving my poles, I set off again for a, thankfully, fall-free rest of the day.

I arrived at West Carry Pond Lean-to at 5:30, having completed 18 miles for the day. But I quickly realized I'd made a mistake in my planning. I would now be 14 miles from the Kennebec River, and that could only be crossed by ferry... which was a fancy name for a canoe paddled across the river by a volunteer oarsman.

However rudimentary, though, this ferry was necessary. Attempting to ford the river without it was an extremely dangerous undertaking. It was basically a real-life version of *The Oregon Trail*, the computer game from my childhood, where life-altering events could befall those daring to cross. The water was too deep to stand in the middle, and an upstream dam could release rushing water quickly and without warning.

But the ferry and its captain only ran until 2 p.m. each day. Relying on my ability to hike 14 miles before then, even in good conditions, was taking a big risk. Missing the ferry meant I would have to wait until the following day, and I didn't have a day to spare. So, after some pep talking and girding of the loins, I decided to hike on. If I did an extra 3.7 miles, I could end up at East Carry Pond and set up at a well-established stealth spot near a sandy beach.

Flat trails let me complete those miles in under ninety minutes, and I soon found the campsite. And what a campsite it was! The pond was actually a vast lake with private cabins and boats lining its shores, and the beach sat less than ten feet from the campsite. It wasn't large, but with clean white sand at a low-grade entry, so I ate dinner and then dove in for an evening swim. The sky darkened the horizon as the sun set behind me, and I knew I would be waking up early the next morning to watch it rise over the pond's far shore.

The sunrise was entirely worth the early morning. It even seemed to make my nine billionth instant coffee and oatmeal taste better.

Feeling completely restored emotionally after the previous day's tough falls, I set off for the Kennebec River. The trail was soft on my feet with piles of fir needles to walk upon. It was such a contrast to the impossibly steep mountains I'd climbed just days before that I couldn't decide if I loved the AT or hated it. It was more often the former, but some days it was just too close to call.

But the flat path that circumnavigated Maine's plentiful lakes and ponds was so well groomed that I could actually look up from my feet and enjoy the forest around me. With a 3.5-mile pace, I arrived early to the Kennebec River, finding a line of people waiting for the ferry. I could easily see why the river gained its reputation. It was huge, at least 500 feet wide, and the rushing sound of water told me all I needed to know about the current.

When my turn came to board the canoe, the captain handed me a waiver to sign. My written agreement not to sue completed, I was allowed to step onto his vessel with one other hiker and our gear. It wasn't the most efficient way to travel, but as it was part of the official miles of the AT, complete with its own white blaze painted on the base of the hull. I didn't mind sitting back and letting my legs get a break, and when our captain told us a hiker had died earlier that season attempting to ford the river without his canoe, it only reinforced the necessity of such a system.

After disembarking on the far shore and thanking our oarsman, all that was left for the day was a nice leisurely walk up a short hill to "town." Caratunk loosely defined that word because it consisted of a hostel, B&B, and a couple of white-water rafting agencies.

Upon discovering the hostel was full, I hiked over to the Sterling Inn B&B, which turned out to be roughly the same price and much nicer accommodations. After the past week, Caratunk was a welcome day of rest and relaxation. My ankles and knees needed a break, and my soul needed some hot food and cold beer.

By 8 a.m. the next day, I was antsy to get going again. The Sterling Inn was a great resting place, and it was tempting to stay, but with the end of July approaching, I knew there could be no delay. And the weather forecast only reaffirmed that decision, predicting thunderstorms later. In fact, I could already see rain clouds gathering in the distance.

By 9 a.m., I realized the distant storm was in fact not so distant after all. Rain hit in a heavy and constant flow, saturating all my rain gear instantly. But I pushed onward, determined to get to Pleasant Pond Shelter to dry off and eat a snack. I arrived at 10 a.m., soaked but happy. And as I tossed another handful of trail mix in my mouth, I realized it hadn't been so bad hiking in the morning showers. The trail was well maintained, and the overwhelming stench of fir trees was temporarily muted by the rain, which was a nice reprieve.

The rain started to lighten, so I decided to wait out its end in the shelter. As soon as the air mostly cleared, I got back out on the trail, ready to climb Pleasant Pond Mountain, the first of my two peaks for the day. It was a friendly hill, with only a 1,500-foot elevation change over five miles. At the summit, the sun shone in a blaze of glory, so I laid out my rain gear to dry on the rocks. That's when I spotted a glorious sight... blueberry bushes. Lining the peak in all directions and filled with fresh, sweet, and welcoming berries for the taking. I gathered a few handfuls of the ripest in my cook pot and sat next to my drying rain gear to enjoy my fresh treat. I'd eaten a lot of dehydrated fruit over the last few months, but ripe berries? That was a rarity. How aptly named Pleasant Pond Mountain now seemed, I decided, as I devoured my fresh feast.

Making a mental note to commit some words to Pleasant Pond's finer qualities on my blog later, I descended its northern slope, stopping for lunch at the next lean-to before my final day's climb. This would take me 20 miles to the Moxie Bald Mountain Lean-to for the night, and it looked like it was going to be the nicest 20-mile day in weeks.

Feeling great, I threw on my backpack, ready to head out. But an ominous sound made me pause. Thunder. The sun, hearing the same sound, made a quick retreat behind very gray clouds.

I hesitated, one foot on either side of the shelter's threshold. It would be much wiser to wait out the impending storm inside the shelter or just call it a night and set up a bed right there. But the good luck of the day sent my thoughts in a different direction. *It's only four miles up and over to the lean-to on the other side. I can do that in an hour and a half and be safe and dry long before whatever this is hits.*

A little too confident in my decision, I stepped over the threshold and set off. It was just two miles up and two miles down. Easy peasy. Besides, I was already soaking wet. What else could go wrong?

49

THE MOUNTAINS WIN AGAIN

The answer to my naïve question didn't take long. About halfway up Moxie Bald, rain started plinking off my backpack's rain cover, landing in my exposed hair. It was still light, but thunder rumbled off in the distance. I increased my pace, committed to making it over Moxie Bald to the shelter as soon as possible. I reached the very exposed 2,800-foot summit as the thunder became less of a rumble and more of an ear-deafening boom. The view from the mountaintop was spectacular, affording an all-too-clear view of what was speeding across the valley toward me.

As I studied the dark clouds, trying to gauge their distance and speed, a piercing flash of lightning ripped through the sky. I switched tactics, resurrecting the game meant to keep my nephews calm in the White Mountains.

"One Mississippi, two Mississippi, three Mississippi..." Eight Mississippis later, and I heard the thunderclap around me. "Okay. Eight miles away. No worries," I announced to no one. Even so, seeing that brilliant flash compelled my feet to move a little faster. I was beginning to understand the level of danger I'd put myself in because, while the storm still appeared far enough away, Moxie Bald featured a rare one-mile stretch of fully exposed summit. Under normal circumstances, the ridgeline walk would've been beautiful, but now it was more than a bit risky. To be on a mountain summit, above the tree line, watching a storm approach, with aluminum poles in each hand? All of a sudden, I felt I was dancing with death.

I increased my pace, but either my Mississippis estimate was way off, or the storm moved in extremely fast. Five minutes later, still on the exposed ridge, the rain tripled its force, sending a deluge of water at me from every direction. Pea-sized hail joined the torrential downpour, hammering my arms and head with the rapid-fire sting of an Uzi loaded with BB pellets. I stopped to throw on my raincoat but looked up just as a bolt of lightning crashed through the trees, striking the bald less than a hundred feet away. Thunder clapped at the same instant and the ground shook below me. *Screw the jacket!* My mind screamed at me to run, as I realized instantly I was now in serious danger. I had to get off this exposed mountaintop, and I had to do it fast.

Raincoat still grasped in hand, I began running full speed down the ridge of smooth granite slabs, desperate to get below the tree line and out of the line of fire. I had no concern for slipping on wet rock, and even when I fell twice, I bounced back up and sprinted on, adrenaline overpowering any pain. I ran past rock cairns marking the path, through puddles of collected hailstones, and amid countless booms of deafening thunder and cracks of lightning. After ten minutes of sprinting, the heavy curtains of rain finally gave way to lighter plinking, and I felt safe enough to slow to a light jog. Heaving in deep lungfuls of air, I tried to regain my breath as I briskly continued down the mountainside. A mile later, I walked into Moxie Bald Lean-to, soaking wet and ecstatic to see the dry shelter still had space to accommodate another hiker.

Several others were already there, and as I appeared from underneath my rain gear, one yelled out, "Sharkbait, hoo ha ha!"

I peered into the deeper dark of the shelter's corner to see

Starman grinning back at me. Next to him, with equally wide grins, sat Tarzan and Happy Feet cuddled in sleeping bags.

"You guys all found each other?!" I asked as I shed my wet layers. "Starman mentioned losing you guys back in Connecticut." Even when we crossed paths again in the Whites, I recalled he was still solo.

Tarzan smiled sheepishly from under the baseball cap I had rarely seen him without. "Pennsylvania whipped my ass, man."

We all nodded our agreement, fully aware of the ass-whipping Pennsylvania gave all thru-hikers.

"Honestly, I almost quit," he continued, "but then I reached Delaware Water Gap and just decided I was going to make it. And not just that... I was going to find these guys. Been putting in big days with only quick town stops and finally caught up a few days ago."

"That's amazing," I replied, fully meaning it. I thought I was covering some ground, but Tarzan must've been consistently putting in 25 to 30 miles a day. And if not for my delays out of and back to Gorham with Keg and The Captain, I probably would've caught up days ago too.

"We only just got ahead of you, though," Happy Feet added as she straightened her sleeping bag. "We'd been seeing your stickers in the logbooks until a couple days ago so knew you were close by."

"We kept asking, 'Is today the day we see Sharkbait?'" Starman turned to Tarzan and Happy Feet, extending his hand. "I won that bet, by the way."

Happy Feet rolled her blue eyes but dutifully rummaged in her backpack and slapped a Baby Ruth into Starman's hand. His enthusiastic laugh rebounded off the walls and I grinned, happy to be back in their exuberant company.

As I hung my clothes to dry from the shelter awning, I retold the day's adventures to my captive audience, who all agreed it was an incredibly courageous but incredibly stupid decision to hike up a mountain toward thunder. They'd all made it to the shelter long before the storm started, making the wise decision not to venture farther.

I ate dinner and cozied into my quilt, but even after agreeing my risky decision was reckless and unnecessary, I couldn't help thinking it had actually been a pretty nice day.

Over breakfast the next day, we talked through our strategies for the final stretch to Katahdin. They had similar plans to mine, so we decided to hike the upcoming 100-mile wilderness together. We all needed to stop in Monson for a last resupply, and wanted to summit Katahdin within a week, depending on the weather. By 7 a.m. we were up and on the trail, headed to our final AT trail town. The terrain was easygoing, following a river slowly into town. It was also beautifully sunny.

Monson itself was a small but heavily supported hiker town. It consisted of a few hostels, a general store, a gas station, and a couple of restaurants, both of which were closed when we arrived. We booked a stay at Shaw's Hostel, which could host a couple dozen hikers indoors and more in an overflow tenting area in the yard.

I was extra grateful I'd landed a spot inside when Tarzan pulled up the weather report that evening over dinner. Thunderstorms overshadowed the next twenty-four hours. I quickly agreed with the others that adding an unplanned zero day was necessary. No way was I repeating my mistake of hiking into sky-fire again.

We spent the remainder of dinner planning our last 115 miles, realizing we could easily arrive at Katahdin's base in Baxter State Park by July 22nd. If the weather wasn't ideal that day, we could even zero again and summit on the 23rd.

I was looking forward to finishing with a group. It was how the journey started all those months ago in Georgia, and it felt right to end it that way too. Even if the members changed, the idea of hiking as a tramily brought comfort and camaraderie that I wanted at the end.

The next day was a typical town zero, except for one difference. Everyone was keenly aware it was our last stop before finishing our thru-hikes. When we came down Katahdin's other side, the adventure would be over, and we'd go back to being normal people again. No longer thru-hikers, no longer vagabonds of the AT. That weighed heavily on all of us, and our conversations centered around what was next. The hostel was full of hikers booking plane tickets, scheduling job interviews, coordinating family meetups, and other transitional life activities. It brought home to me that the real world was quite literally waiting for us on the other side of the 100-mile wilderness.

Probably due to that creeping feeling of impending reality, none of us were eager to get back on the trail the next day. We had a lazy breakfast and an even lazier stroll out of town, but eventually the desire to triumphantly cross that finish line overtook the urge to drag it out.

I'd spent the better part of eighteen years planning, outfitting, and preparing for this thru-hike. As Dana had reminded me almost a year earlier, it was the only thing on my bucket list for as long as I remembered having one. Over the years, I'd read countless books, online journals, and testimonials about the Appalachian Trail. I'd watched movies, documentaries, and YouTube channels chronicling past hikers. I pre-planned every day with meticulous detail, and now I was 95 percent of the way to fulfilling that dream.

I stood back on the edge of the trail with Starman, Tarzan, and Happy Feet the next day, and I knew I was ready to finish my hike. The sky was blue, the sun was shining, and I was full of hearty blueberry pancakes. It was time to meet Katahdin. Only the 100-mile wilderness stood in our way.

"You know," I remarked as Happy Feet and I hiked alongside each other a couple hours later, with Starman and Tarzan somewhere ahead, "considering there's no public access to the trail here, I figured the path would be overgrown and unruly. But it's actually great."

"I know, right?" Happy Feet replied, her ponytail flicking across her shoulder as she turned to look up at me. "Just more of the same Appalachian Trail. Mountains, lakes, trees—"

"With no way out but through," I interrupted. She smiled quietly and we both returned to pleasantly hiking together in silence.

Over the next few days, it would just be us thru-hikers and the woods. It felt like the perfect way to end the adventure.

The weather was good to us as we crossed three different rivers, each about twenty feet wide, then climbed Barren Mountain. I fell twice more on slick, slate rocks, but shook each fall off. At this point it was becoming all too common, but thankfully both had mostly just hurt my pride. The rest area at the top of Barren offered a spectacular view over a large lake. *It would be a dream to live out here*, I thought to myself. *Maybe when we retire, we could buy a spot on the shore and build a small cabin off the grid.* A musician Dad loved from Montana wrote an album about doing something like that once, and I never understood the desire until that moment.

It was a couple miles down to a stealth campsite at the base of the mountain. The others wanted to set up camp early, but I was happy sunning myself on the cliff in front of the staggering view for a while longer. They hiked on, leaving me alone with my thoughts as I watched birds of prey circling over the lake below.

Camp that night was peaceful. There were no other hikers aside from our group, and no roads or creeks nearby to disturb the silence. Sleep came easily, setting us up well for the following day, which we'd been warned was a tough climb up and down the four peaks of the Chairback Mountains and followed by the four peaks of White Cap Mountain.

The Chairback peaks were rocky in sections, bringing to mind painful memories of New Hampshire, but they were smaller and easier to manage than the behemoth Presidentials. Our group split up as we each found our own strategy for managing the climbs, and by mid-morning I was alone again.

By lunch, my feet and back were beat up, so when I reached Carl E. Newhall Lean-to, I dropped my bag and lay down, exhausted. A quick ten-minute nap, followed by a big intake of calories got me moving again around 3 p.m. The quadruple peaks of White Cap Mountain loomed ahead, and not to be outdone by the Chairback Range, they too offered impressively steep ascents and descents. Thankfully, this time the Maine ATC club helped out, carving rock steps into the more difficult climbing areas.

At the final summit of White Cap, I was greeted with a momentous view—an up-close and clear sight of Mount Katahdin. She was both beautiful and monstrous, towering over the Appalachian Mountains surrounding her. It was also now the only challenge ahead of me. The rest of the trail to her base would be reasonably flat and manageable, like gliding a plane in for landing. And what a landing it would be.

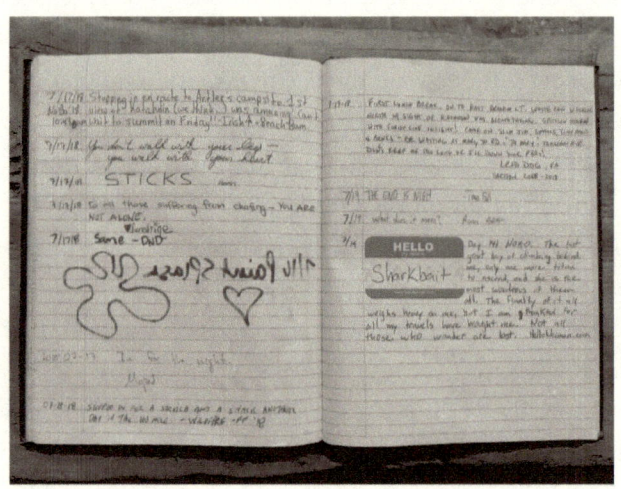

Journal entry in the 100-Mile Wilderness on Day 141.

50

THE CLIMB

The plan the next day called for 23 miles to Potaywadjo Spring Lean-to, and the weather showed temperatures rising fast. It was cool under the green tunnel, but any time we exited to traverse the edges of the many navigated lakes, the temperature instantly felt 15 degrees warmer. I wasn't complaining and hoped the sunny weather would last through the end of the hike. But it didn't look likely, as the forecast called for more rain and thunderstorms again by Sunday... the day before we were due to summit Katahdin.

To combat the heat, our group took many water breaks. At each stop, I also nibbled on snacks, attempting to satiate the hunger pangs gnawing at my stomach. I thought I'd packed enough food for the 100-mile wilderness, but that infamous hiker hunger had finally found me, and my carefully rationed portions simply weren't cutting it. I was constantly dipping into another day's provisions, and if I didn't start conserving, I'd run out before we made it through to Baxter State Park.

Instead of breaking into our natural hiking rhythms that typically dispersed us along miles of trail, we chose to stay together at the same sedate pace. Even so, by the time we passed the 21-mile mark, we were all soaked through with sweat.

"I could really use a bath," Starman announced, lifting his shirt collar to get a closer look and immediately recoiling in disgust.

"There's another lake coming up," I replied, scanning Guthook on my phone. "Looks to be a decent size."

Starman's face lit up. "If it is, I'm stripping naked and sprinting straight in." We all chuckled as Starman yelled out, "I'm not kidding!"

A few hundred feet later, the opportunity presented itself. Jo Mary Lake was a large expanse of water that featured a gradual entry along a sandy beach. Starman, as promised, dropped his pack and clothes mid-stride as he ran down to the water's edge. The awkward hopping while he attempted to remove his shoes wasn't working, so he gave up and made a spectacular, mostly nude run into the water before diving and vanishing into its depths.

Not to be left behind, we all followed quickly, swimming in lazy semi-clothed circles in the cool water. It was hard to leave, and we stayed at the lake for close to an hour. We knew we still had a couple miles to hike before dark but couldn't bear to leave the refreshing cool for the oppressive heat.

The next day, the trail was tougher with rocks, roots, and mud as we meandered for miles around Nahmakanta Lake, Rainbow Lake, and the streams connecting the two. But that didn't mean the miles weren't enjoyed. Knowing I was nearing the end of my hike made the usual terrain more amenable, and I fully embraced the precarious footwork.

The only ascent was a small hike up Nesuntabunt Mountain, and I couldn't help thinking how Dad would've welcomed the 500-foot climb instead of the strenuous trail and elevation changes our hike together had forced upon him back in New York. And when I reached the top, I couldn't help making a quick video call to share my appreciation of the view with him. A sparkling lake greeted me, leading straight to Katahdin's towering peak. It was the type of clandestine view every Appalachian Trail guidebook showcased on its cover, urging you to come find for yourself.

I swung my phone around to give Dad the full panoramic view. His deafening silence overtook my narration of the scenery, and I flipped it back to make sure he was still there.

"Now that's a view! I'd be happy to hike that any day," he finally said. "Why the hell did I join you in New York?!"

"Because you were jealous of all the fun I was having in Rocksylvania," I replied with a grin.

A slow shake of Dad's head was the only response I got.

We reached our stealth campsite on the far side of Rainbow Lake, and after 25 miles of walking, Starman, Tarzan, and Happy Feet disappeared into their tents almost immediately. But I wasn't ready to call it a night. The next day would be my last full one on the trail, and it would be an easy hike with campground accommodations at the end. That meant this would be my last true night on the trail in the privacy of the woods. Emotions flooded through me at the thought. After everything I'd seen and accomplished the last 143 days, I simply didn't have the words to describe how important this last night in the woods felt. It was tough to accept that my thru-hike was essentially over.

I sat on a boulder on the water's edge, savored the moment for as long as I could, watching the sun paint the horizon red and purple as stars pricked out against the darkening sky. I finally crawled into my hammock and allowed the whispering sounds of fish jumping and loons calling to serenade me to sleep. It was peaceful and perfect.

The next day's hike to Abol Bridge was an easy eight miles. We'd made it through the 100-mile wilderness in just four days. My food rations were down to the bare minimum, but they'd lasted. Now, our biggest and final challenge to summiting Katahdin was the weather.

While we tried to relax into a nero day at Abol Bridge Campground, we checked the weather over and over, watching the hourly forecast like children keeping a vigil for Santa Claus on Christmas Eve. The rain looked like it would stay away until mid-afternoon the following day, so we allowed ourselves to hope a summit was possible before anything hit. We needed to hike ten miles tomorrow, through Baxter State Park and up to the mountain's base, then it would just be a 4.5-mile ascent straight up Katahdin's 5,200-foot summit.

Sleep that night was fitful as my mind and body stayed on alert for the final miles ahead. And it turned out I wasn't the only one. We were all packed and ready while the sun was still low in the sky the next morning. I ate the rest of the food in my bag, saving one granola bar for emergency needs.

By this time of year, the Baxter State Park rangers required that all thru-hikers summiting Katahdin arrive before 12 p.m., and for good reason. The hike up Katahdin's slope is strenuous and time-consuming, even for a thru-hiker who just walked nearly 2,200 miles to get there. We needed time to get up and back down before dark set in.

The ten miles through the state park were over easy terrain and on legs pumping full of adrenaline for what was finally before us. The short trail took us along the Penobscot River, up a creek, and past Daicey Pond. All were beautiful, but with our minds set on Katahdin, we didn't linger.

And then we were there. The base of Katahdin. A final check of the weather showed we should have several hours of clear skies before any rain hit in earnest. It was time. We were going up. We filed into the Ranger Station to complete our final check-in of the thru-hike. I received a permit card stating I was northbound hiker #151 to arrive. Then we were ready to go.

Katahdin featured several trails up, but the white blazes of the official AT required thru-hikers to take the Hunt Trail. And the Hunt Trail was a beast. An incredibly steep incline was only made more so by the severely tall steps over monstrous, house-sized boulders. And that was before scaling two miles up a sheer rock cliff called The Gateway. All this time, the desire to not hike in the rain was to ensure we got some great views at the summit, but now I realized that the Hunt Trail truly would've been deadly when wet.

After two hours of scrambling, we reached the base of the final summit and stopped for a much-needed rest. While my hiking companions were just as exhausted as I was, we all grinned at each other in anticipation of our final climb.

The last mile of the Appalachian Trail was all that remained, and suddenly, I didn't want to climb it with anyone but myself. I packed up my water and trash, hopped up quickly, and set out quietly while the others rested. With a quickened pace in my gait, I started walking, letting silence spread my emotions across the canvas of the panoramic mountain landscape before me. Each step was like a thundering drumbeat in my heart, parading me through this dream-like place I'd envisioned for so long. Everything I'd experienced over the past five months rushed through me in waves of memories as I watched the famous brown sign on the summit get closer and closer. Theme songs echoed between my ears like a documentary of my life being filmed before my eyes. Other thru-hikers were ahead and behind me, but I was fully wrapped in a bubble of personal solitude. I walked alone, but I wasn't lonely.

Suddenly, I was there. The giant brown sign stood affixed to a large wooden step-stool-shaped frame with the mountain's name etched across the top—Katahdin. It beckoned me to it, looking immeasurably more real than the thousands of photos I'd seen before. I walked up and pressed my hand to its rough wooden surface. Setting my forehead upon it, I exhaled a deep, long-held breath... and I smiled. I didn't cry like I'd read about. I didn't scream like I'd heard from others moments earlier. I just closed my eyes and smiled. As the weight of fifteen years of daydreams rushed over me in a single moment, I felt entirely fulfilled.

A day-hiker approached from my left, breaking the moment's spell as he held out his phone. "Hey, man. Can you take a photo of me?"

I thought for a few seconds. I didn't want to be rude, but this was my moment. "I've just finished walking the entire length of the Appalachian Trail to stand at the foot of this sign. I'll take a picture of you, but only after you take thirty-seven of me first."

He frowned at my exaggerated response but reluctantly agreed. I posed in every way possible with that sign and against the backdrop of vast Appalachian Mountain views before taking his phone and finally snapping one of him.

I took in as much of the experience as I could before Starman, Tarzan, Happy Feet, and a dozen or so other hikers reached the summit to do the same thing.

And then, just like that, it was over. All that was left was the hike back down the other side of Katahdin on the much gentler Saddle Trail. We took one last group photo, then made our way down to the base as rain started to lightly cover us in a fine mist. Our climactic climb had been completed in perfect timing.

As we walked back toward the ranger station, we heard clapping and cheering. Peering ahead, we saw a tall man with short black hair waving at us from the side of a Honda Odyssey minivan.

"Oh," Starman said, a red blush rising up his cheeks. "That's my dad."

Edie had been keeping tabs on our location from the blog and driven all the way from Boston to meet him at the end of his thru-hike. Starman, clearly embarrassed, gave a small wave back, but Tarzan, never one to miss a celebration, returned the cheers with equal enthusiasm.

I went over to introduce myself to Edie and was immediately lifted in the air with a massive bear hug as if he'd known me all my life. It was one of those moments I later thought must be how radio show hosts feel. They spend every day talking to millions of people over the air, never actually conversing with a single one. But to the listener, that one-sided relationship may be one of the closest they have.

Besides the gasp of breath I eventually had to gulp in, I didn't really mind the hug. Edie had been an avid reader, commenting often and even encouraging me to stop in Boston on my way home to share a drink and a few more stories. I guess I wasn't like a radio host, our interactions were two-way and it felt like I knew him too.

After a round of celebratory sandwiches and sodas supplied by Edie, we all hopped in the van and drove to Millinocket for our final hostel. The AT Lodge was owned by the same family as Shaw's Hostel in Monson, and while it was very basic in its accommodations, the real draw was their other business in town: the AT Café. I was ready to satiate my very insistent hiker hunger, and the café's menu of carbs on top of more carbs did not disappoint.

Stomachs overly full, we crawled back across the street to the AT Lodge, and I said goodnight to my hiking companions. I was physically and emotionally drained, but as I lay in bed writing my last blog post from the trail, I was still glowing with pride.

The next day, I would catch a bus to Bangor and a flight to Los Angeles, where Dana and Pippa would be waiting for me and the trip would be officially, officially over. No more living the wanderer's life. No more worrying about nothing more than food, water, and where to rest my head. And no more eating without consequence, knowing I'd burn 5,000 calories a day on my feet. It was time to get back to real life. There'd be plenty to look forward to, but still, I was having a hard time saying goodbye to my Appalachian Trail adventure.

The next morning, I packed my belongings into my backpack for the last time. While I waited somewhat forlornly in the hostel's lobby for the shuttle to appear, I opened up the blog post from last night. Dad's name appeared in the first comment, and I scrolled down to read his thoughts.

I'm happy for you, that you accomplished your life's goal. Your success reflects your thoughtful planning, preparation, and execution, and a keen appreciation for the day-to-day experience rather than simply being locked into completion mode. We're all so proud of you. Not just of what you did, but the much greater importance of how you did it. You faced a myriad of challenges on this experience: snow, rain, heat and cold, aches and scrapes, boulders, scree fields, mud... lots of mud, not to mention one extremely ravenous mouse. You did it with a flair for capturing the daily appreciation of this experience for others through thoughtful reflection and an occasional breakthrough of humor. Well done, Pride.

Tears welled in my eyes even as laughter bubbled up. Somehow, Dad had managed to capture the moment perfectly. The reality of it being behind me was now all too real. I'd hiked the Great Smoky Mountains, the Blue Ridge Mountains, the Green Mountains, and the Whites. I traversed the Roan Highlands, the triple crown of Virginia, Rocksylvania, and the 100-mile wilderness. I walked down the main streets of Hot Springs, Damascus, Harpers Ferry, Boiling Springs, Delaware Water Gap, Dalton, and Dartmouth College. I crossed the Shenandoah, Potomac, Delaware, Hudson, Connecticut, and Kennebec Rivers. I walked for over 2,000 miles through fourteen states. I did all that and so much more.

And now I was done.

Standing at the northern terminus on July 22, 2018.

EPILOGUE

I pulled on my backpack with a huff. It was a little tighter around my waist than I remembered it being in July. I had lost thirty-six pounds by the end of my thru-hike, but it hadn't taken long to start putting some of those back on. Which wasn't necessarily a bad thing either.

I knew I would lose weight hiking the Appalachian Trail and tried to stuff extra calories into my meal plan to mitigate it, but after arriving home, I realized just how much of a physical transformation I'd gone through. I had lost almost 20 percent of my body weight, looked ten years younger, and none of my clothes fit. This had made interviewing for jobs tricky, as putting on my suits to impress corporate recruiters looked more like I'd been playing dress-up in Dad's closet.

I had finished my thru-hike two months earlier, and since then, things had gone more or less back to normal. After returning to Los Angeles, Dana and I packed up our belongings and drove east again with Pippa. We settled into a new home outside Washington, D.C., found new jobs that excited us, and reconnected with friends and family as a married couple again. The next chapter of our life was starting, and the thru-hiker part of mine was beginning to fade away. But not completely.

Even though my official AT hike ended at the summit of Katahdin, and I felt both completely and emotionally fulfilled, I knew I had to go back to complete the miles I'd missed to meet Dad in New York on time. My summit had come with an asterisk, and if I didn't come back, I would feel like a fraud every time I mentioned completing a thru-hike of the AT.

So here I was in October, once again, standing at a trailhead to the AT. I'd driven to and left my car at the Delaware Water Gap parking lot, ready to stamp a footnote on my thru-hike's completion stats.

The idea was to complete the 97 missed miles to Harriman State Park in five days. After consistently hiking 20-plus miles a day months earlier, I felt confident this would be easy before starting my new job on Monday. Secretly, I was even betting myself I could complete it in four.

The first day would be a shorter one, having driven four hours from D.C. to the trailhead that morning. It was meant to be a reasonably easy slope of trail from Delaware Water Gap to the Mohican Outdoor Center where I would stay the night. But the rocks in New Jersey picked up where the rocks in Pennsylvania left off, and the trail was lined with wet boulders intent on tripping up my progress. With the aid of my trusty hiking poles, I managed to stay on my feet all day, crossing into New Jersey, passing Kittatinny Point Visitor Center, Sunfish Pond, and even getting a decent view from a break in the cloud cover atop Kittatinny Mountain. But the clear summit also showed me an all-too-familiar sight from my AT adventure all those months ago... storm clouds rolling in from all sides.

When I checked the weather for this part of the U.S. just two days earlier, it showed sunny or partly cloudy skies for six days straight. I thought I was going to be blessed with dry weather, but it seemed that Mother Nature had her usual plans to welcome me back. I was hiking the AT, and it was once again going to rain. What else was new?

It was getting late in the day, so I called the Mohican Outdoor Center to let them know of my arrival time.

"Oh," responded the twenty-something staff member. "Uh, we close at 5 p.m."

There was no way I would make it by then. It was already 4:30. Scowling at my late start, I quickly made my way down a bit farther to a clearing where I could set up camp for the night.

With the rapidly darkening sky, aided by the approach of what was now clearly rain, I worked double time to get my dinner cooked and my hammock set up. I barely achieved both before the rain started, and I dove into my hammock just as it began to hit hard. Really hard.

It didn't take long before the wind rushed in, then thunder crashed into the party, and lightning quickly made the show complete. It was a symphony of lights and sounds, and my hammock tent was swaying frantically in the middle of it. It was not my idea of fun to be camping under the sky in the middle of a thunderstorm. Any time it looked like rain or storms on the trail previously, I was typically in the safety of a shelter. But this felt like anything but safe, so I got out of the hammock and decided to crouch fully clothed under my tarp instead, poised to sprint down the mountain if disaster struck... figuratively or literally.

What was very likely my worst storm on the AT lasted until 11 p.m., and I eventually got back into bed and fell asleep. I woke around 7 a.m. to a calm and mostly dry hilltop. I checked the weather for the day ahead, only to discover on the app's screen that there had been a tornado watch issued for Stroudsburg, a town just a few miles away from my sleeping spot. I could hear Dad's voice in the back of my mind, lecturing me on how foolish it was to toy with mountain weather. And the voice was right, of course, as I felt lucky to have survived.

But the moment passed, I was still alive, and the AT beckoned me forward. So I packed up and hit the trail, quickly making it to the Mohican Outdoor Center. The facility was operated by the same AMC that ran the huts in New Hampshire, hosting a restaurant, store, cabins, showers, and more.

"It would have been great to make it here last night," I muttered to myself as I looked around for a sunny spot to eat my snack. Spotting a picnic bench with only one occupant, I made my way over to it. As I got closer, the occupant looked up. I froze for a moment, taking in the familiar face that I hadn't seen in months.

"Huevos?!" I called out, just as Huevos yelled, "Sharkbait!"

We clasped each other in a bear hug that communicated the depth of a brotherly bond, bringing back a flood of emotions from our tramily hikes together so long ago.

"I can't believe it. You're still on the trail!" I confirmed more than asked.

"Sure am. When did we talk last?" he asked. "You were in Massachusetts, right?"

I nodded, recalling the video call before I hit Dalton, Huevos's hometown.

"Well," he continued. "After Harpers Ferry, I just kept hiking the trail at my own pace, you know? Slow and steady." He paused, scratching at the beard that had gone from patchy when I had last seen him on that video call to now thick and full. It made him look older, more mature. "Wait a minute, what are you doing back down here again? Shouldn't your hike be well over by now?"

"It is," I responded quickly before stopping and rephrasing. "I mean, I made it to Katahdin, and I've been off the trail for a couple months, but I skipped some miles, so came back to complete them. I read somewhere that if you don't do all the miles within twelve months, it's not an official thru-hike. I couldn't let there be a caveat on my thru-hiker status, you know?"

Huevos hummed his understanding. Then his eyes lit up. "I'm about to head out for the day. What do you say we hike together? Like the good old days."

"Sure!" I readily agreed, smiling big. It would be great to catch up with Huevos and relive the early days of our hike together. "Did you stay here last night?"

"Yeah, and I'm glad I did. That was some wild storm last night."

"I know. I was in the thick of it about a mile from here."

"What?" His eyes got big. "You couldn't make the extra push?"

"I would have, but I called and they said they were closing at five. There was just no way I could make it down in time."

Huevos frowned his confusion. "Closing at five? Maybe the main office, but they told me that building over there always remains open in case of an emergency."

Huevos pointed toward a rustic-looking lodge, and I grunted my frustration, adding a curse word under my breath. It would have been nice to be informed about that option on my call yesterday. I think if anything constituted an emergency, it would be sleeping exposed on top of a mountain during a tornado.

I tried to swallow the frustration, not wanting yesterday's experience to color the rest of the day. I ate my snack, and then Huevos and I headed north. The next eight hours of hiking were much more pleasant with his company and the exceptional views atop Catfish Fire Tower, Blue Mountain, and Rattlesnake Mountain. My feet were starting to get tired though. Not used to covering 20 miles of distance anymore, they started screaming in protest several miles before the end. Huevos chatted merrily along, so I knew he wasn't hurting, and not wanting to admit defeat, I didn't complain.

By the 21st mile, I could tell I was beginning to hobble. I had avoided serious injuries for the entirety of the thru-hike, and I was proud of that. One of the keys to that success, I was sure, was listening to my body and allowing it to strengthen gradually over time. But the familiar feeling of drunk feet got me worrying about the plan I had set for the days ahead. I didn't have much leeway in my schedule for these last miles before needing to get home, but if I wanted to avoid injury, I could always shorten the daily miles and come back another time. I definitely wanted to get this wrapped up, but I reminded myself that it was still an option. I had nothing left to prove.

We crossed Culvers Gap and stopped to watch the sunset at the Culver Fire Tower. I took my boots and socks off, and it felt so divine that I told Huevos to hike on while I gave my toes some much-needed air. My confidence to hike three more days at this pace was taking its first hit.

With some more cursing, this time not under my breath, I forced my feet back into my boots and slowly crawled down the hill to Gren Anderson Shelter. Huevos had already set his tent up and was getting a fire going. He grinned knowingly at my hobbled gait. "Fresh legs again, huh?"

We woke the next morning to reports of afternoon rain. I had no desire to be out in that again, so even though it took Huevos and me a bit to get going, we agreed to push our pace to get 18 miles in before the rain hopefully found its way to us. Our destination was a place called the Secret Shelter, so named because it wasn't in any printed guidebook, although it was marked on the Guthook app. A thru-hiker from the '80s had bought the land and built a small cabin as a refuge for hikers along our current section of New Jersey, which didn't allow stealth camping. I was excited to see it, and even more excited to stay dry and away from the rain.

We started slow, as my feet and legs grew accustomed to the hiking life again, but they weren't as beaten up as I had feared, and we sped up as the day wore on. Not enough, however, to beat the rain. At 2 p.m., an hour earlier than forecasted, it hit us in a straight downpour and continued until we made it, drenched, to the Secret Shelter two hours later.

This week was supposed to be my swan song, but I could not catch a break with the weather, and it did nothing to help my mood, which was turning increasingly sour. The trail was waterlogged, I had already soaked through two pairs of socks, and even my waterproof socks could not hold up to the deluge from above and below.

Huevos and I discussed our plans for the next day. He wanted to slow down again, not needing to push against a deadline like me. I needed to do either 18 miles to a shelter or 26 to a town. Preferably the latter. Even though I kept telling myself that coming back would be fine, I was concerned that I might never finish if I didn't do it all now.

I crawled into my quilt that night, pondering the choices before me and trying not to let the circumstances outside my control get to me. The frustration bubbled in my gut though, letting me know that I wasn't winning that battle. Even in this short return to the AT, the rough terrain and wet weather simply continued to overpower my best laid plans.

The next morning dawned bright, and as I stepped out onto the trail again, rays of golden sunshine pierced through the branches of nearby trees. They bathed the trail in a soft aura of yellow light, almost as if someone was illuminating an encouraging path forward. I looked up to where the rays touched the sky, and my breath caught in my chest as I saw the sun piercing through the canopy in a perfectly heart-shaped halo. Not sure if it was real or a rain-induced mirage, I stopped to snap a photo and marvel, knowing no one would believe me if I didn't have proof that captured the moment. Even with the nonstop onslaught of rain across 2,000 miles of roots and rocks out to trip me, I still loved this trail—and fate, it seemed, felt the need to remind me in glorious fashion.

It was right then and there that I decided to have an amazing day. Attitude was always a choice, and I had been choosing the wrong one since I had stepped onto the trail again. I had spent my entire adult life dreaming of walking this path. And although my journey was over, these catch-up days were the last moments of my white blaze adventure. The weight of that realization cleared my mind like the heart-shaped sun cleared the morning fog. I decided to once again reframe whatever the trail threw at me in a positive way and enjoy the next few days for all they were worth.

And it worked. I had an incredible day as I walked along the majesty of the AT once again. Huevos and I had started hiking together, but he soon decided to slow down again. We said our goodbyes, promising to keep in touch once everyday life claimed us again.

I quickened my pace, helped by the fact that the trail was much less rocky now. It also didn't hurt that I was hiking through magnificent scenery, including the Wallkill River National Wildlife Refuge, a gorgeous wetland of marshes and bird sanctuary. As I walked along the path circling the marshy refuge, I watched geese, cranes, ducks, swans, and countless other birds bask lazily in the sun. I threw some soft John Denver tunes in my ears to maximize the beauty's effect, singing along quietly as I walked. By lunchtime, I had reached the 18-mile mark and shelter, but it was early, and I was in great spirits. I knew my body had more to give, so I hiked on.

I was now heading for the town of Greenwood Lake ten miles away, where Guthook informed me of a new trail angel hosting hikers coming off the mountains. His name was Carl, and when I called him to inquire about a bed for the night, he offered to pick me up at the trailhead and bring me back to his home, which was being converted into a hiker hostel. The basement was still under construction, but he said the bunkroom was done. At ten bucks for the night, it sounded perfect.

After I got home from Maine, I spent some time totaling how much I had actually spent on the thru-hike versus how much I had initially budgeted. Back in my obsessive planning phase, I had worked out a meticulous budget of $6,066 to cover food, lodging, town stops, gear upgrades, and other miscellaneous expenses. But, after all was said and done, the actual cost was closer to $7,000. I could have spent more nights camping in the snow, I could have skipped restaurants for ramen, and I could have forced my gear to last with MacGyver-like duct tape and sewing skills... but that would have made the whole thing much less enjoyable. So, indulging in an inexpensive, comfortable night's stay felt like a platinum experience worth splurging on.

The trail wasn't too bad for the next ten miles, but there was a significant shift in terrain at the exact moment I hit the state line for New York. I made the most of the situation, brushing off the less-than-ideal hiking conditions as I had told myself I would, and enjoyed the fact that it was sunny and dry.

Carl was waiting for me as promised, and his place was as good as he claimed. He offered me a beer and lit up a bonfire in the backyard, eager to hear stories of my life on the trail. I was tired but stayed up to share adventures of my journey with him—the Smoky Mountain blizzard, Grayson Highland wild ponies, McAfee Knob at sunset, Happy's spiritual awakening, my Massachusetts "Climb of Insanity," the best (Woods Hole) and worst (Mountain Garden) hostels, and the countless trail angels like him that always seemed to show up when I needed them most.

As the fire died down, the big push I'd made that day started to take its toll and I retreated to bed, exhausted. Tomorrow would be my final day on the AT, and although it felt good to relax and reminisce, the mountains were calling one last time.

I got up the next day, ready to make the final push to the end. The weather, determined to leave a final impression on me, decided to end my AT adventure just like it had started. Where the forecast showed dry and cloudy, the reality was mist and rain the entire way. I thought about how waking up to those conditions a few months ago would have typically rattled my mood, but instead, I thanked the rain for not being hail and the fog for not being snow. I made the most of it, remembering why I was out there, and wandered along the day's trail in peace.

I stopped for a brief snack at Fitzgerald Falls and looked out at a foggy but quietly beautiful view atop Mombasha High Point. I scaled Buchanan Mountain and Arden Mountain, forded a creek, walked through a very well-maintained Harriman State Park, and sucked in my gut to fit through the infamous Lemon Squeezer, which was an aptly-named crevice the AT traversed between two enormous boulders. And then I was done. Again. I walked the last few steps to the Harriman State Park ranger station, quietly released my backpack from my shoulders, and called an Uber to take me to the train station where I could make my way back to my car.

It felt anticlimactic after the rush of Katahdin, but that was also true of real life. Sometimes our most momentous accomplishments are the vividly loud, mountain-top pinnacles, and sometimes, they're the quiet release of heavy burdens. The most important lesson from it all was to hike your own hike, and I had done just that. Now, real life was calling me again, and with my Appalachian Trail adventure finally over, I felt like I might be ready to answer it.

A heart-shaped sun poking through the trees in New York.

ACKNOWLEDGMENTS

Writing this memoir as narrative fiction has been a thru-hike in its own way, complete with unexpected wrong turns, moments of pain and doubt, and more trail magic than I thought possible. They say we all have one book in us, and I am deeply grateful to everyone who helped turn this five-month adventure into the story you hold in your hands.

Above all else, thank you to my family for their support of this adventure. Hiking is in our blood, and you are all in my heart for encouraging me to follow my dream and helping make it possible. Especially to Dana, Dad, Mom, Mirra, and Devorah... without the support you each gave to this idea, I would never have reached Amicalola Falls, let alone Katahdin. You made trail magic mean more than just food from strangers, bringing support and encouragement critical to my ability to put one foot in front of the other.

To everyone else who followed my journey, your presence, both online and on the trail, reminded me I was never walking alone. And that the miles of pointless ups and downs were worth it. To Rob, Craig, Mikey, Max, Aaron, Adam, Devorah, Kevin, Jonah, Caleb, Zachary, and Dad, thank you especially for lacing up your boots and allowing me to share the trail with you in person.

To my fellow thru-hikers, trail angels, hostel owners, shuttle drivers, and the entire Appalachian Trail community... this book belongs to you as much as it does to me. There is not enough room to list you all, but I hope you find yourself mentioned or referenced in the stories on these pages. You inspired the moments of my hike, whether through a shared roof or a spontaneous meal, and you all left lasting footprints on my journey.

This book would not exist without the thousands of readers who followed along on my blog each day, even when my fingers were too cold to type and my mind too tired to edit. Your comments and encouragement reminded me that the story was worth telling—then and now.

Finally, my gratitude to those who helped transform a trail journal into a memoir worth sharing. Thank you to Becky, whose expertise and coaching kept me focused when the story felt too big or lost in inner monologue. To Emily, who created the beautiful book jacket and map illustrations I never could. And to Malory and Walter, whose editorial eyes helped polish the chapters to perfection.

And to you, the reader. Thank you for walking this path with me and giving me a reason to relive it a second time. May these pages give you a glimpse of the magic that lives between Georgia and Maine, and maybe even inspire you to chase a white blaze or two of your own.

ABOUT THE AUTHOR

Michael Neiman, trail name Sharkbait, is a lifelong backpacker and outdoor enthusiast who first learned of the Appalachian Trail in his twenties. Almost two decades later, he set out to complete a continuous thru-hike from Georgia to Maine, chronicling each day of his five-month journey on a personal online blog. His journal drew a dedicated following of friends, fellow hikers, and strangers, and later inspired his co-authored guidebook, *Platinum Blazing the Appalachian Trail: How to Thru-hike in 3-Star Luxury* (2019, available on Amazon). This memoir brings those daily reflections to life and weaves them together with the people, places, and challenges that defined his adventure.

When not on the trail, Michael lives in Ridgefield, Connecticut, with his wife and family. He can often be found exploring local trails or introducing others to the magic of the AT, whether in person or through his writing. Readers can connect with him at HelloNeiman.com or on most social media as @HelloNeiman.